Modern Dating

by Tiff Baira

for dummies
A Wiley Brand

Modern Dating For Dummies®

Published by: **John Wiley & Sons, Inc.**, 111 River Street, Hoboken, NJ 07030-5774, www.wiley.com

Copyright © 2025 by John Wiley & Sons, Inc. All rights reserved, including rights for text and data mining and training of artificial technologies or similar technologies.

Media and software compilation copyright © 2025 by John Wiley & Sons, Inc. All rights reserved, including rights for text and data mining and training of artificial technologies or similar technologies.

Published simultaneously in Canada

No part of this publication may be reproduced, stored in a retrieval system or transmitted in any form or by any means, electronic, mechanical, photocopying, recording, scanning or otherwise, except as permitted under Sections 107 or 108 of the 1976 United States Copyright Act, without the prior written permission of the Publisher or authorization through payment of the appropriate per-copy fee to the Copyright Clearance Center, Inc., 222 Rosewood Drive, Danvers, MA 01923, (978) 750-8400, fax (978) 750-4470, or on the web at www.copyright.com. Requests to the Publisher for permission should be addressed to the Permissions Department, John Wiley & Sons, Inc., 111 River Street, Hoboken, NJ 07030, (201) 748-6011, fax (201) 748-6008, or online at http://www.wiley.com/go/permissions.

The manufacturer's authorized representative according to the EU General Product Safety Regulation is Wiley-VCH GmbH, Boschstr. 12, 69469 Weinheim, Germany, e-mail: Product_Safety@wiley.com.

Trademarks: Wiley, For Dummies, the Dummies Man logo, Dummies.com, Making Everything Easier, and related trade dress are trademarks or registered trademarks of John Wiley & Sons, Inc. and may not be used without written permission. All other trademarks are the property of their respective owners. John Wiley & Sons, Inc. is not associated with any product or vendor mentioned in this book.

LIMIT OF LIABILITY/DISCLAIMER OF WARRANTY: THE PUBLISHER AND THE AUTHOR MAKE NO REPRESENTATIONS OR WARRANTIES WITH RESPECT TO THE ACCURACY OR COMPLETENESS OF THE CONTENTS OF THIS WORK AND SPECIFICALLY DISCLAIM ALL WARRANTIES, INCLUDING WITHOUT LIMITATION WARRANTIES OF FITNESS FOR A PARTICULAR PURPOSE. NO WARRANTY MAY BE CREATED OR EXTENDED BY SALES OR PROMOTIONAL MATERIALS. THE ADVICE AND STRATEGIES CONTAINED HEREIN MAY NOT BE SUITABLE FOR EVERY SITUATION. THIS WORK IS SOLD WITH THE UNDERSTANDING THAT THE PUBLISHER IS NOT ENGAGED IN RENDERING LEGAL, ACCOUNTING, OR OTHER PROFESSIONAL SERVICES. IF PROFESSIONAL ASSISTANCE IS REQUIRED, THE SERVICES OF A COMPETENT PROFESSIONAL PERSON SHOULD BE SOUGHT. NEITHER THE PUBLISHER NOR THE AUTHOR SHALL BE LIABLE FOR DAMAGES ARISING HEREFROM. THE FACT THAT AN ORGANIZATION OR WEBSITE IS REFERRED TO IN THIS WORK AS A CITATION AND/OR A POTENTIAL SOURCE OF FURTHER INFORMATION DOES NOT MEAN THAT THE AUTHOR OR THE PUBLISHER ENDORSES THE INFORMATION THE ORGANIZATION OR WEBSITE MAY PROVIDE OR RECOMMENDATIONS IT MAY MAKE. FURTHER, READERS SHOULD BE AWARE THAT INTERNET WEBSITES LISTED IN THIS WORK MAY HAVE CHANGED OR DISAPPEARED BETWEEN WHEN THIS WORK WAS WRITTEN AND WHEN IT IS READ.

For general information on our other products and services, please contact our Customer Care Department within the U.S. at 877-762-2974, outside the U.S. at 317-572-3993, or fax 317-572-4002. For technical support, please visit https://hub.wiley.com/community/support/dummies.

Wiley publishes in a variety of print and electronic formats and by print-on-demand. Some material included with standard print versions of this book may not be included in e-books or in print-on-demand. If this book refers to media that is not included in the version you purchased, you may download this material at http://booksupport.wiley.com. For more information about Wiley products, visit www.wiley.com.

Library of Congress Control Number: 2025940264

ISBN 978-1-394-31579-6 (pbk); ISBN 978-1-394-31581-9 (ebk); ISBN 978-1-394-31580-2 (ebk)

Printed and bound by CPI Group (UK) Ltd, Croydon, CR0 4YY

C9781394315796_070725

Contents at a Glance

Introduction 1

Part 1: Getting into the Modern Dating Game 5
CHAPTER 1: Modern Dating: Has Romance Turned into Horror? 7
CHAPTER 2: Tinder, Hinge, Bumble, Oh My! Navigating the Dating Apps 17
CHAPTER 3: Finding Love While Loving Yourself 29
CHAPTER 4: Deciding to Date — Setting Standards and Having
a Solid Dating Blueprint 39
CHAPTER 5: Resetting Your Dating Mind: Breaking the Rules
and Building Your Own 47

Part 2: Meeting Someone and Setting Up a Date 51
CHAPTER 6: Flirting 101: The Flirtation Formula to Get 'Em Hooked 53
CHAPTER 7: No Wi-Fi Needed: Where and How to Meet People in Person 69
CHAPTER 8: How to Ask for or Reject a Date Invitation 77
CHAPTER 9: Right Place, Right Vibe: Nailing the Perfect Date Location 97
CHAPTER 10: Plan with Caution: Spotting and Avoiding Red Flags
When Setting Up a Date 105
CHAPTER 11: Who's Got the Bill? Navigating the Check Etiquette 111

Part 3: Swipe Right to Date Night: The
Ultimate GRWM Playbook for Your First Date 127
CHAPTER 12: From Outfit to Attitude: Making a Great First Impression 129
CHAPTER 13: Bye-Bye Butterflies: How to Crush First Date Nerves
and Boost Your Confidence 139
CHAPTER 14: Big Date Energy: Starting and Keeping the Date Fun
and Flirty 151

Part 4: Date or Fade? What Happens after
the First Date 169
CHAPTER 15: Making the Most of Date Number Two and Beyond 171
CHAPTER 16: Ghosts, Goodbyes, and Getting Over It: Surviving
the Heartbreak 185
CHAPTER 17: Beyond Small Talk: Asking the Questions That Really Matter 203

Part 5: Romance, Rewritten: Loving and Dating on Your Own Terms 221

CHAPTER 18: No Pressure, Just Pleasure: Navigating Sex in the City 223
CHAPTER 19: Second Chances: Thriving in the Dating World Post-Divorce 233
CHAPTER 20: Out and About: Navigating the LGBTQIA+ Dating Scene 243

Part 6: The Part of Tens 259

CHAPTER 21: Ten Things to Tell Yourself Before and After a Date 261
CHAPTER 22: Ten Red Flags to Avoid at All Costs 265

Index 273

Table of Contents

INTRODUCTION 1
    About This Book 1
    Foolish Assumptions 2
    Icons Used in This Book 2
    Beyond the Book 3
    Where to Go from Here 3

PART 1: GETTING INTO THE MODERN DATING GAME 5

CHAPTER 1: Modern Dating: Has Romance Turned into Horror? 7
    Navigating the Modern Dating Mess 8
        Situationships versus relationships: Is anyone even committing anymore? 9
        "What are we?" has now become "Will we ever?" 9
        Rosters: Unlimited options end up limiting connection? 9
        Casual sex and casual feelings? 10
        Catfishing: The dangers of deception 10
        Post-pandemic dating anxiety 11
        Heartless romantics: Dating for entertainment instead of love 11
        Profile reviews, TikTok Storytimes, and endless swiping: The commodification of love 12
    Dating Advice Overload — What to Listen to and What to Ignore 12
        Social media gurus: Are they helping or just talking? 13
        The dating "rules" that do more harm than good 13
    Texting, Flirting, and the Great Divide between Online and IRL 14
    How to Navigate the Madness and Actually Enjoy Dating 15

CHAPTER 2: Tinder, Hinge, Bumble, Oh My! Navigating the Dating Apps 17
    Seeing How Dating Apps Have Changed the Dating World 18
    Using Dating Apps to Crush Your Relationship Goals 19
        Choosing an app based on what you're looking for 20
        Communicating if you want a hookup, situationship, or serious commitment 20

> Guarding Your Heart (and Health): Prioritizing
> Sexual Wellness 21
> Swipe Smarter, Not Harder: The Ultimate Setup Guide 22
>> Photos: Because first impressions matter..................................... 23
>> Bio bootcamp: Turning boring into boo worthy 24
> Taking It Offline: How to Transition from App to Reality............... 27
>> What to do if you are not getting any matches........................... 27
>> Match secured! How to take it further 27

CHAPTER 3: Finding Love While Loving Yourself............................ 29

> Looking for Love in All the Wrong Places (and Finally
> Getting It Right)... 30
>> Stop dating the wrong people just because they're there........ 30
>> Creating standards that you deserve 30
>> Dating yourself first 31
>> Changing your relationship with relationships 31
>> Dating from desire, not desperation... 31
> Knowing Your Dating Value: Stop Settling and Start Thriving........ 32
>> Acting like you're expensive — because you are 32
>> Never settling for the bare minimum.. 33
>> Stopping dating out of loneliness or boredom 33
>> Practicing and projecting confidence 33
>> Focusing on attracting, not chasing.. 33
>> Remembering that you set the standard..................................... 34
> Rejection Is Redirection: Stop Doubting Yourself............................. 34
>> Stop comparing yourself — it's a losing game 35
>> Owning your unique perfection... 35
>> Knowing you're already complete — no one else
>> can "fix" you 36
>> Realizing no one is judging you like you think they are 36
>> Not everyone has taste, so stop taking every opinion
>> to heart... 36
>> Seeing rejection as a blessing in disguise 37

CHAPTER 4: Deciding to Date — Setting Standards and Having a Solid Dating Blueprint.......................... 39

> Is This Your Perfect Person or Are You Just Their
> One-Person Entertainment Act?... 40
> Drawing Up Your Dating Blueprint — Because Love
> Shouldn't Be a DIY Disaster 42
>> The blueprint for love: Crafting your ideal partner
>> checklist... 42

　　　　Zero tolerance: Defining the dealbreakers you
　　　　won't compromise on 43
　　　　Toxic bingo: Uncover just how messy your dating
　　　　patterns are 43
　　　　Butterflies or red flags? Learning to tell the difference 44
　　　　Your ex is a lesson, not a standard: Learning and
　　　　moving on 44
　　　　Saying no to mediocrity: Holding out for the right choice 45
　　　　The dating checklist for what really matters 45
　　　　Mastering the discipline of your standards 45
　　　　To hook up or hold off: Finding your sexual comfort zone 46
　　　　Ditching the need for outside opinions 46

**CHAPTER 5: Resetting Your Dating Mind: Breaking
the Rules and Building Your Own** 47
　　　　The Old Rules That Need to Go 48
　　　　Building Your Own Dating Rules 49

PART 2: MEETING SOMEONE AND SETTING UP A DATE 51

**CHAPTER 6: Flirting 101: The Flirtation Formula
to Get 'Em Hooked** 53
　　　　Flirting with Rejection 54
　　　　The Texting Playbook: Tips for Flirty and Fun Chats 55
　　　　　　Knowing the rules of flirting via text 55
　　　　　　Kicking things off with a good opener 56
　　　　　　Keeping it fun with flirty techniques 56
　　　　　　Handling social media flirting 57
　　　　　　Avoiding texting pitfalls 57
　　　　　　Knowing when to transition to real life 58
　　　　Tailored Texting That Matches Your Vibe 58
　　　　In-Person Flirting: Turning a Smile into a Date 60
　　　　　　Flirting in the wild: Fun and playful examples
　　　　　　for in-person encounters 61
　　　　　　Keeping the vibes going 63
　　　　　　Dipping out gracefully and securing the date 65

**CHAPTER 7: No Wi-Fi Needed: Where and How
to Meet People in Person** 69
　　　　Finding the Best Places to Be Single and Mingle 70
　　　　Choosing the Best Professional Cupids 72

Finding your match(maker) 72
Speed dating: Rapid-fire romance? 73
Blind dates and asking your friends to set you up 74
Passport to Connection: Finding Love in New Places 75
Mastering the Art of the Solo Date... 76

CHAPTER 8: How to Ask for or Reject a Date Invitation........... 77

Should You Make the First Move? 78
Navigating who should ask who out first.................................... 78
When's too long to ask someone out? 79
Nerves and Courage: How to Be Nervous and Do It Anyway 80
How to Smoothly Ask Someone Out on a Date in Person 81
How to Ask Out a Friend or Colleague Without Making It
Awkward... 83
How to Ask Someone Out Digitally 85
When should you take your digital relationship into
the real world?.. 86
From screen to reality: Ensuring a safe first offline date 89
Proceed with Caution: Should You Ask This Person Out? 91
Emotional baggage check: Are they really ready?..................... 92
Baggage check: Are lingering issues going to derail you?........ 92
Goal alignment: Do your futures even match? 92
Single status: Are they really unattached?................................. 93
Cubicle Cupids: The risks of dating in shared spaces............... 93
How to Delicately Decline a Date Invitation 94
Be honest, but don't go full brutal 94
Blame it on timing, not on them 95
Don't become Caspar the Unfriendly Ghost............................... 95

**CHAPTER 9: Right Place, Right Vibe: Nailing the
Perfect Date Location** 97

Love's Launchpad: Finding the Perfect Place for
Your First Date 97
Choosing a Date Night Spot That Fits Your Budget........................ 99
Happy hours lead to happy dating 100
Free museum or park show days 100
Reinventing the coffee date... 101
BYOB restaurants and cafés.. 101
The picnic is the ultimate pick 101
Steering Clear of Date Spots That Can Lead to
Awkward Moments 102

CHAPTER 10: Plan with Caution: Spotting and Avoiding Red Flags When Setting Up a Date 105

    Setting Clear Expectations 106
    Netflix and Not Chill: Dates Should Be Public First, Private Later 107
    Time-Wasters 101: How to Spot the People Who'll Never Commit to a First Date 109
    Love Bombers and Text Overload: When Enthusiasm Becomes a Red Flag 110

CHAPTER 11: Who's Got the Bill? Navigating the Check Etiquette 111

    Knowing Your Standards on Payment Before the Date 112
    Breaking Down Payment Options and Debates on a Date 114
        The great debate: Who should pay the bill? 114
        Paying the bill in LGBTQIA+ dating: Communication over assumptions 116
    Red Flags When Splitting the Bill 118
    When the Bill Doesn't Go as Planned: A Survival Guide 120
        Scenario 1: The "Oh, I forgot my wallet" move 120
        Scenario 2: The surprise split request 120
        Scenario 3: The silent bill stare-off 121
        Scenario 4: They assume you're paying 121
        Scenario 5: The cultural or personal expectation 122
        Scenario 6: The overly generous offer 122
    Champagne Taste on a Beer Budget: Dating Across Income Brackets 122
        Weighing the positives and challenges 123
        How to make it work without losing your mind (or savings) 125
    Dating Without Breaking the Bank 126

PART 3: SWIPE RIGHT TO DATE NIGHT: THE ULTIMATE GRWM PLAYBOOK FOR YOUR FIRST DATE 127

CHAPTER 12: From Outfit to Attitude: Making a Great First Impression 129

    Looking Your Best for a First Date 130
        The glow-up recipe: Turning insecurities into confidence 131
        How to have the dream outfit for the dream date 132

Fresh and Flawless: Your Pre-Date Hygiene Checklist 134
Presenting Yourself Authentically from the Jump 135
The Right Scent, Right Time.. 136
Sit Up, Smile, and Slay: Posture Power for Your Date 138

CHAPTER 13: **Bye-Bye Butterflies: How to Crush First Date Nerves and Boost Your Confidence**............ 139
Why Do We Get Nervous Before a Date? 140
Swapping the "What Ifs" for "What Could Be" 141
How to Turn Nerves into Excitement.. 142
The SOS Call: Why Friends Always Have the Best
(or Worst) Advice 144
Tricks to Get Out of Your Head and Stay Present 145
Every "No" Is Just a Detour to Your Eventual "Yes"...................... 146
To Sip or Not to Sip: The Pre-Date Drink Debate 147
The Confidence Check-in: Affirmations to Combat
Date Nerves.. 148

CHAPTER 14: **Big Date Energy: Starting and Keeping the Date Fun and Flirty** 151
Salutations: Greeting with Style.. 152
Relaxing and Engaging with Your Date 154
Topics and Actions to Avoid on the Date...................................... 155
    Avoiding trauma dumping 156
    Avoiding talking about your exes....................................... 156
    Love bombing — When "too good to be true"
    is exactly that.. 157
    Saving the spicy talk for later 158
    Keeping your hands to yourself (until it feels right) 158
    Keep the first date light — Save the existential crises
    for later.. 159
The Graceful Exit: How to Leave a Bad Date without Drama 161
    The emergency call: Your classic get-out-of-jail-free card 161
    Being honest: When the vibes are off, just say it 161
    Skip the "Irish exit" — unless they deserve it 162
    Your comfort comes first — always...................................... 162
Date Night Finish Line: How to End on a High Note 162
    First date kiss: Hit or miss? 162
    Sex on the first date: A gamble, a game changer,
    or a trip to Situationshipville?... 163

"Can't wait to see you again"; When to drop that line 165
Text timing: When to hit send after the date 165
Post-Date Check-in: Questions to Ask Yourself Afterward 166
How to Lock in That Second Date 166

PART 4: DATE OR FADE? WHAT HAPPENS AFTER THE FIRST DATE 169

CHAPTER 15: Making the Most of Date Number Two and Beyond 171

The Second Date: Where Compatibility Gets Real (or Reality Sets In) 172
    Making the date an activity, not just dinner and drinks 173
    Asking questions that actually matter 173
    Focusing the conversation on key topics 174
    Do they have a "roster," or are they actually looking for something? 174
    Are you getting comfortable or losing interest? 175
    Gauging their effort: Are they actually trying? 175
When Is It Time to Meet the Friends? 175
    Consider the intent: Why are you introducing them? 176
    The "too soon" zone: When to hold off on friend introductions 176
    The right time: When it makes sense to introduce them 177
    How to make the introduction feel natural 177
    What if it goes . . . horribly? 178
When to Have Sex: The Ultimate Timing Debate 178
    The right time to have sex? Whenever YOU feel comfortable 179
    Will they lose interest if you sleep with them? 179
    The third date rule: Still a thing or just dating mythology? 180
    What if you're not sexually or mentally compatible? 180
    How to make sure you won't regret it 180
When to Commit: Decoding the "What Are We?" Phase 181
    Building a roster: How many people can you date at once? 181
    Knowing when it's getting serious 182
    How to tell if they're still seeing other people 182
    Sharing phone passwords and managing Instagram love 183
    When to delete the dating apps for someone 183

Table of Contents   xi

CHAPTER 16: Ghosts, Goodbyes, and Getting Over It: Surviving the Heartbreak 185

    Ditching the Wait: Stop Gluing Your Eyes to Your Phone 186
    Healing from a "Situationship": Getting Over Someone You Never Really Had 187
        What are situationships? 187
        Getting over a situationship that didn't go as planned 188
    Rejection to Redirection: How to Grow Through the No 190
        Accepting that rejection is a normal part of dating 190
        Knowing that compatibility isn't about your worth 190
        Stop trying to make the wrong person like you 191
        Redirecting your energy into something better 191
        Remembering that the right person won't reject you 192
    Surviving the Dating Chaos 192
        Avoiding dating burnout 193
        Disaster date? Here's your next move 194
        They're just not that into you: How to spot the signs early 194
    Dodging the Dating Villains: Cheaters and Manipulators 196
        Spotting early signs of disrespect 196
        Setting boundaries and staying safe 198
        Recognizing shady behavior before it escalates 198
        Spotting manipulative and toxic traits 199
        Self-respect first: Knowing when to walk away 200
    Turning Pain into Power: Finding Confidence After a Breakup 201

CHAPTER 17: Beyond Small Talk: Asking the Questions That Really Matter 203

    Money Moves: Navigating Finances While Dating 204
    Balancing Lifestyles and Focusing on Shared Values 206
    Navigating Religion in Modern Dating 207
    When Dating Gets Political 209
        What if you find out you're politically opposed? 211
        Aligning your ethics before you hear wedding bells 211
    Dating Within or Outside Your Culture 212
        The "but my family will lose it" dilemma 212
        How to talk about culture on early dates 213
        When family just won't get on board 213
    Aligning Sexual Values Without the Awkwardness 214

Waiting until marriage versus waiting until Thursday.........214
So how do you even bring this up?...................................215
Tackling Other Big Topics: Family, Your Future, and More 216
    Handling different family goals when you're not aligned.......217
    Successfully prioritizing your social life, work, and dating schedule...217
    What to do when their family isn't a fan of you 218
    Winning over the friends: How to make a good impression 219
    How to share mental health struggles with your partner 219

PART 5: ROMANCE, REWRITTEN: LOVING AND DATING ON YOUR OWN TERMS 221

CHAPTER 18: No Pressure, Just Pleasure: Navigating Sex in the City 223

Staying True to Your Boundaries Without Feeling Pressured 224
The Truth about Sex: It Won't Make Someone Love You More 226
Owning Your Choices Without the Guilt Trip 227
    Casual sex without the emotional hangover.........................227
    Virginity and embracing your journey....................................228
Reclaiming Your Confidence in Sex..229
Knowing How to Tell Your Partner Your Specific Needs 230

CHAPTER 19: Second Chances: Thriving in the Dating World Post-Divorce 233

How to Move on Without Bringing the Past to Dinner 234
Dating for Fun After Losing "the One": Deciding What You Want 236
    Deciding whether you even want to get married again.........236
    Letting go of thinking you need to have it all figured out now 237
    Taking a crack at dating without an end goal.........................237
    Avoiding letting your past relationship define your future 237
    Remembering that love doesn't have to be the same every time...238
How to Fully Let Go of Your Ex 238
How to Reenter the Scene Without Looking Like a Lost Tourist 240

CHAPTER 20: Out and About: Navigating the LGBTQIA+ Dating Scene 243
    Figuring Out Your Identity: Embrace Self-Discovery and Be Proud of Who You Are 244
    Putting Yourself Out There When You're Still Figuring It Out 245
    Queer Dating Cheat Sheet: How to Navigate Love in Every Category 246
        Gay men dating (man x man) 247
        Lesbian dating (woman x woman) 247
        Bisexual or pansexual dating (men and women and/or all genders) 248
        Trans dating (trans and nonbinary love) 248
    Using LGBTQIA+ Dating Apps Like a Pro 249
        The Grindr grind: The Wild West of dating apps 249
        Field: The playground for exploration 250
        Hinge, Tinder, and the more mainstream apps: Where the bios matter 251
        Archer: A New Era of LGBTQIA+ Dating 251
        The IG DM slide: A classic that still works 252
    Flirting and Putting Yourself Out There in LGBTQIA+ Spaces 253
        Eye contact: The ultimate queer love language 253
        The art of the compliment 254
        Flirt like you're already friends 254
        Body language: Open, relaxed, and facing them 254
        Make the first move without overthinking it 255
        The power of walking away at the right moment ... 255
        Confidence is key — even if you have to fake it 255
    Where to Go and Meet People: Your Queer Social Playground 256

PART 6: THE PART OF TENS 259

CHAPTER 21: Ten Things to Tell Yourself Before and After a Date 261
    Confidence Boosters: Being Your Own Hype Squad 262
        "I am the prize." 262
        "I look amazing, and if they don't notice, they are blind." 262
        "The goal is to have fun, not to find 'the one.'" 262
        "I will not let my overthinking ruin this." 262
        "My ex is not a reference point." 262

Reality Checks: Managing Your Expectations 263
"If it's bad, I can leave." 263
"I do not owe them anything, no matter how nice they are." 263
"I will not take it personally if they don't like me." 263
Post-Date Pep Talk: No Matter What Happens, You Win 263
"I survived, and that's a win." 264
"I will not spiral if they don't text first." 264

CHAPTER 22: Ten Red Flags to Avoid at All Costs 265

The Love Bomber 265
The "You Up" 4 a.m. Texter 266
The Jealous Type 267
The Gaslighter 268
The Freeloader in Disguise 268
The Zero Boundaries Person 269
The Secret Keeper 270
A Little Too Close to Their Ex 271
The "Joke" Insulter 271
The Control Freak 272

INDEX 273

Introduction

Welcome to *Modern Dating For Dummies*, aka So You Drunk Texted Your Ex Again. It's okay. You're safe here.

You probably picked up this book and thought, "Do I really need this? How did I get here?" First off — yes, you do. Second — probably something to do with that 2 a.m. text that said, "U up?" to someone who should definitely be blocked.

But I'll let you in on a secret: No one actually knows what they're doing when it comes to dating. Whether you've been out here since the prehistoric era — pre-iPhones, pre-dating apps, back when you actually had to make eye contact — or this is your first time putting yourself out there after a long hiatus (or a long situationship), this book is your new BFF.

About This Book

Hi, I'm Tiff Baira. I'm 28, live in New York City, and I'm a dating coach and matchmaker. I've helped hundreds of singles stop spiraling and start dating with confidence — both through coaching and my show *Streethearts*. And yes, I've also had my fair share of "what are we?" texts and romantic chaos. I've been through and seen everything from Prince Charming without the charm, to the person perfect on paper and a nightmare to talk to, and don't even get me started on the toxic musicians who try to play you like a key. I've put in the work to build true confidence and say no to the actions that don't align (no matter how hot they are) to build my dream dating life.

Dating is wild. It makes you feel vulnerable. It's a little terrifying. But I'm not here to change you — I'm here to elevate the dream version of you, and help you find a partner (or partners, or situationship, or hot fling — you do you, boo).

There's no one-size-fits-all anymore. Gone are the days of meeting at a grocery store, dating for a year, and settling in the suburbs. Now we've got ghosting, breadcrumbing, dating apps, catfishes, and your one persistent crush who lives in your head rent-free.

In this book, I help you replace anxiety with confidence. I show you how to flirt without spiraling, how to know your worth (and stop begging), how to determine who pays on the first date, how to dress like your hottest self, and more.

By following the tips and advice in this book, you'll know your core values, your dating intentions and boundaries, and maybe even feel excited to get out there again. Rejection? Just redirection. You? Always deserving of love.

Foolish Assumptions

Maybe your friends threatened to stage an intervention if you sent *one more* voice note crying about your ex. Maybe your mom passive-aggressively gifted you this book because she wants someone at the holiday table whose name isn't Blaze and who doesn't have a septum piercing. Whatever got you here, know that you are not broken. You're not undatable. You just need a little push (and maybe a cocktail).

You're single and looking — not just to collect situationships or rack up ghost stories, but to make real connections. Whether you're new to dating, diving back in, or just trying to upgrade your game, this book is for you.

While I'm in my 20s and speak from that perspective, this is an ageless guide. The tips and tools in here apply to all genders, sexualities, and stages of life. Whether you're 21 or 61, dating is confusing — and you're not alone. Let's figure it out together.

Icons Used in This Book

TIP Dating can be hard enough. Make things easier on yourself by following the tips and tricks marked with this icon.

REMEMBER These icons mark the information that's especially important to know. To cut to the chase and grab the most important information in each chapter, just skim through these icons.

WARNING: This icon alerts you to red-flag behaviors and potentially dangerous situations to avoid.

TIFF SAYS: This icon points out personal stories and wisdom I've gained over my time as a dating coach and going on dates myself that you may find interesting or helpful.

Beyond the Book

In addition to the abundance of information and guidance related to modern dating that I provide in this book, you get access to even more help and information online at Dummies.com. Check out this book's online Cheat Sheet. Just go to www.dummies.com and search for **Modern Dating For Dummies Cheat Sheet.** Here you'll be able to bring all the tips you read here on the go, the ultimate bestie for any date.

Where to Go from Here

The great thing about Dummies books is that you can start anywhere, and you can dip in and out to get the info that's most relevant and important to you. If you're new to the dating scene or back after a long time off the market, consider starting with Part 1, where I describe the modern dating landscape, help you navigate various dating apps, and start you on your way to a healthy dating life. If you struggle with meeting people, check out the advice in Part 2. And if you've had a few good dates with someone and are wondering what comes next, head to Part 4.

Whether you're in college, post-divorce, or the last of your friends not married and wondering what the hell is going on — it's time. There's love waiting for you. Grab a martini (or a strong sparkling water if we're being responsible) and get back in the game.

Oh — and if this book gets you married, promise me now: I'm officiating the wedding. Deal?

1
Getting into the Modern Dating Game

IN THIS PART . . .

Get a handle on what it means to date in the modern age.

Explore dating apps and how best to use them.

Focus on loving yourself and boosting your confidence before putting yourself out there.

Determine who and what you're looking for and when.

Feel empowered to take the wheel and make your own dating rules.

IN THIS CHAPTER

» Feeling your way through the modern dating landscape

» Knowing which rules and advice to follow and which ones to avoid

» Figuring out how to date in the modern age and actually enjoy it

Chapter 1
Modern Dating: Has Romance Turned into Horror?

From ancient times, finding love has never been a straight path — more like a chaotic obstacle course with questionable detours. People went to war for love, wrote tragic poetry, and we got stuck with *Romeo and Juliet* as the ultimate romantic standard (even though, let's be real, they knew each other for three days and it ended in a double suicide). Fast forward, and here we are — post-pandemic, chronically online, and swiping like our thumbs are training for a marathon.

At this point, many of us have a stronger relationship with dating apps than with the people on them. Ghosting is a national pastime, "talking stages" last longer than some marriages, and somehow, despite having more ways to connect than ever, we're in a loneliness epidemic. What happened to the clarity of old-school dating? Courtship, love, marriage — it used to be a simple formula. Now, we're out here navigating rosters, *what are we* talks, and situationships so vague they could be the subject of a philosophy class.

But here's the deal: The old rules no longer apply, so it's up to us to create new ones that actually work. It's time to stop clinging to outdated timelines, stop trying to fit love into a perfect mold, and start figuring out what we actually want. Whether it's redefining commitment, dating for fun, or just trying to survive yet another Hinge voice memo introduction, let's dive into the madness that is modern love — chaos included.

Navigating the Modern Dating Mess

If you've ever felt like dating today is a social experiment designed to test your patience, your self-worth, and your ability to decode mixed signals — congratulations, you are not alone. Dating used to be about finding someone you connected with. Now, it's about *not getting played*. Red flags? We spot them from a mile away but sometimes still ignore them because they have great hair. Some common modern dating traps include

- **Breadcrumbing:** Someone texts you just enough to keep you interested but never actually makes plans. (You're not a pigeon — stop accepting crumbs.)
- **Ghosting:** They disappear with no explanation. (Honestly, the only ghosts we should be dealing with are in horror movies. See Chapter 16 for more on ghosting and goodbyes.)
- **Situationships:** The relationship that's not a relationship, but it *feels* like one, except there's no commitment. (If you have to ask, "What are we?" more than once, you already know the answer.)
- **Rosters:** Having multiple people in rotation but committing to none. (Having options is great, but at some point, you have to pick a main character. Chapter 15 gives you the lowdown on rosters.)

The key to surviving? Recognize the games early, set your standards, and don't waste time on people who bring more confusion than connection. The following sections break down the absolute chaos that is the modern dating scene and explain how we can make it work without completely losing your sanity.

Situationships versus relationships: Is anyone even committing anymore?

Situationships are basically the modern version of purgatory. You like each other, you spend time together, you might even meet their dog — but there's *zero* commitment. It's fun until you realize you've been in one for two years and you're still "just seeing where things go."

TIP: The difference between a relationship and a situationship? Consistency, clarity, and actual plans for the future. If you're stuck in something vague and they "don't like labels," ask yourself: Are you okay with that, or are you just afraid to leave because you don't want to start over?

"What are we?" has now become "Will we ever?"

Gone are the days when defining a relationship was a normal milestone. Now, we're out here trying to make "exclusivity" happen like it's some rare unicorn. The longer you avoid "The Talk," the messier it gets. If you're confused about where you stand with someone, ask yourself:

- Are they making future plans with me, or am I just a placeholder?
- Do they match my effort, or am I doing all the work?
- Am I actually happy with this arrangement, or am I just afraid of scaring them off?

REMEMBER: You deserve clarity, and the right person won't leave you hanging in uncertainty.

Rosters: Unlimited options end up limiting connection?

Having a "roster" is the modern version of keeping your options open. But at what point do options turn into distractions? Dating multiple people at once can be fun, but if you're constantly cycling through people without forming real bonds, you might just be using dating as entertainment rather than actually looking for a connection.

Signs it's time to trim the roster:

>> You don't actually like any of them that much, but you keep them around for validation.
>> You forget who you told what story to.
>> You're exhausted trying to keep up with multiple conversations.

If your roster feels more like a chore than a love life, it's time to narrow it down and focus on quality over quantity.

Casual sex and casual feelings?

Casual sex can be amazing. It can also feel like an emotional roller coaster designed by someone who really enjoys watching people suffer. One minute you're both on the same page — "just fun, no feelings" — and the next, one of you is staring at your phone, trying to decode why they left your last message on read for *exactly* 8 hours and 14 minutes.

The truth? Sex is not casual if you're catching feelings but pretending not to. If you know you can separate emotions from intimacy, great! But if you're secretly hoping that *one more hookup* will change their mind and make them see you as "relationship material," please save yourself the heartbreak. You deserve someone who wants to be with you because they actually like you — not because they occasionally want company at 1 a.m. (Chapter 18 covers all you need to know about sex and modern dating.)

Catfishing: The dangers of deception

Dating apps should come with a disclaimer: "Warning: Some people here are not who they claim to be." You match with someone who looks like a Greek god in their photos, and then — boom! — you meet up, and they suddenly look like the "before" picture in a skincare commercial.

And it's not just about looks. Some people catfish with personality. You think you're talking to someone fun and interesting, but then you meet them in person, and they have the charisma of a tax return. If their energy over text is giving "romantic comedy lead" but in real life they're drier than an unsalted cracker, you've just been personality catfished.

TIP Lesson here? Video calls before the first date can save you from unexpected jump scares. Also, if they only have one blurry group photo and won't send a selfie? Run.

Post-pandemic dating anxiety

Remember when we all collectively forgot how to socialize for two years? Yeah, dating post-pandemic still feels like that. Half of us reentered the dating world with the energy of a puppy finally let outside, while the other half still flinch when someone reaches for a handshake.

Common symptoms of post-pandemic dating anxiety include

- Overthinking *every* interaction because you forgot how to flirt in person
- Wondering if the bar is too crowded and if it's socially acceptable to wear a hazmat suit on a date
- Forgetting how to make eye contact and choosing instead to stare intently at their forehead

The good news? Everyone else is feeling just as weird. Dating is awkward. You'll get through it. Worst case? Blame any social awkwardness on the pandemic and order another drink.

Heartless romantics: Dating for entertainment instead of love

Some people treat dating like it's a reality show — except instead of competing for love, they're just collecting players and seeing who keeps their attention the longest. You know the type:

- They flirt like a pro but have no actual interest in commitment.
- They treat dates like entertainment, not emotional connection.
- They don't want love — they want an audience.

If you've ever felt like you were on an episode of *The Bachelor* but with none of the roses, you've probably been played by a heartless romantic. The key to avoiding these people? Look at their actions, not just their words. If someone is stringing you along for fun, they're not your person. Move on before you become just another episode in their highlight reel.

Profile reviews, TikTok Storytimes, and endless swiping: The commodification of love

Dating has gone full *Black Mirror*. Love is now a marketplace where people analyze profiles like they're making a major investment decision. We sit in group chats reviewing our friends' dating app matches, breaking down their "vibe" like FBI agents studying surveillance footage.

Meanwhile, TikTok has turned dating into content. Someone ghosts you? Storytime. Someone says something cringe on a date? Screenshot it, post it, and let the internet roast them. While hilarious, this has also turned dating into a weird, competitive sport where we're constantly chasing the next best option.

At some point, we have to remember that we're not shopping for a new phone — we're looking for a person. The best way to get out of this cycle? Delete the apps for a bit, go on a few real-life dates, and remember that love isn't something you order with next-day delivery. (See Chapter 7 for more on how to get out and meet people in real life.)

Dating Advice Overload — What to Listen to and What to Ignore

At this point, dating advice is everywhere — your favorite influencer is giving it, your best friend is contradicting it, and your mom is still trying to set you up with the "nice neighbor's son who just got a job" (who, for the record, is absolutely not your type).

With social media gurus, countless dating rules, and text message game-playing, it's easy to feel like dating is an impossible puzzle where everyone else has the answer but you. But here's the truth: There's no one-size-fits-all approach to love, so let's break down what advice to actually take and when to ignore the noise.

TIFF SAYS

At the end of the day, the only dating rules that matter are the ones that work for you. Some people meet their soulmate after sending a double text. Others marry the person they hooked up with on a first date. Some take things slow, while others dive in fast. Your love life doesn't need to follow someone else's playbook. Make your own rules, date with intention, and don't let TikTok tell you who to be. The best dating advice? Trust yourself, and go after what you really want.

Social media gurus: Are they helping or just talking?

Ever scrolled through TikTok and suddenly found yourself questioning your entire approach to dating? One video tells you to act uninterested to be more attractive, while another tells you to be upfront and authentic. Meanwhile, someone else is yelling that if they "really liked you," they'd be obsessed in three seconds. Which is it?

Here's how to know when advice is worth listening to:

- ❯❯ Does it align with your values? If it feels like manipulation, it probably is.
- ❯❯ Is it based on confidence, not games? Good advice encourages self-worth, not mind games.
- ❯❯ Would you give this advice to a friend? If it sounds ridiculous when flipped, toss it.

And when in doubt? If a 20-year-old finance bro wearing sunglasses indoors is telling you how to find love, keep scrolling.

The dating "rules" that do more harm than good

We've all heard them:

- ❯❯ Wait three days before texting back.
- ❯❯ Don't be too available.
- ❯❯ Never double text.

> ### "DATING IS TRASH, BUT CAN WE RECYCLE?"
>
> Modern dating often feels like a landfill of bad conversations, ghosting, and half-baked connections, but let's not lose hope just yet. Instead of throwing the whole thing away, let's recycle our approach and make it better.
>
> - Instead of endlessly swiping, try meeting people in real life. Your next great match might be in a coffee shop, not just on an app.
> - Instead of obsessing over "what are we?" too soon, focus on how they treat you in the moment. The label matters, but so do actions.
> - Instead of playing games, be real. If they don't appreciate directness, they're not the one.
>
> The key? Dating isn't trash — it's just about sorting through the waste to find the real gems.

These so-called rules were written by people who think love is a chess match instead of a connection. The reality? If you like someone, text them. If they like you, they'll respond. If they don't, it's not because you broke some mythical dating law — it's because they're not your person.

Some dating rules are helpful, like not ignoring red flags (see Chapter 10) and respecting your own boundaries. But most of the others? Throw them out like last season's trends. (Chapter 5 is all about breaking the rules and making your own instead.)

Texting, Flirting, and the Great Divide between Online and IRL

The modern romance struggle: Why is someone so bold in the DMs but a nervous wreck in person? We've all seen it — the flirty, confident texter who turns into a human version of the buffering symbol at dinner.

>> Online flirting works best when you treat it like a preview of your actual personality. Don't be the person who's charming over text but awkward in real life.

>> IRL chemistry matters more than emoji-filled texts. If you're texting for weeks with no real-life plans, that's a problem.

>> Match the energy. If they're writing paragraphs, don't just hit them with "lol, nice." If they're dry, don't carry the whole conversation yourself.

Flirting isn't about being perfect — it's about being playful, showing confidence, and creating connection. Whether it's online or in person, be yourself, and let the right people gravitate toward you.

TIP: Need a refresher in Flirting 101? Head to Chapter 6.

How to Navigate the Madness and Actually Enjoy Dating

Now that we've established that dating today can feel like an episode of *Survivor* — full of mind games, unpredictable eliminations, and an occasional immunity idol (aka a decent date) — how do we actually thrive in this chaos?

>> **Date with intention — not just for distraction.** If you're going on dates because you're bored, lonely, or just need someone to text "Good morning" to, you're setting yourself up for frustration. Instead of swiping endlessly just to have something to do, get clear on what you actually want. Casual? Cool. Serious? Great. Just be honest with yourself and whoever you're dating.

>> **Ask the right questions early.** Instead of waiting six months to realize you've accidentally entered a situationship, start asking questions early:

- "What are you looking for right now?" (*Yes, it's scary, but so is wasting time.*)

- "How do you feel about commitment?" (*If they start twitching, take that as your answer.*)

- "Are you actively dating other people?" (*Better to know upfront than find out via Instagram story.*)

- **» Stop chasing confusion — if they want you, you'll know.** The person who actually wants to be with you will not have you decoding their mixed signals like you're in a *National Treasure* movie. If you're constantly overanalyzing their texts or wondering if they're actually into you, that's your answer. Move on and save yourself the emotional energy.

- **» Quality over quantity — trim the roster if it's not serving you.** If you've been seeing multiple people but none of them make you feel valued, it might be time to Marie Kondo your dating life. If they don't spark joy (or at least text back in a timely manner), thank them for their time and move on.

- **» Stay optimistic (without being delusional).** Yes, dating today can feel like a mess, but love still exists — you just have to be patient. Stay hopeful, keep putting yourself out there, and remember that every bad date, ghosting, or confusion-filled situationship is just leading you one step closer to someone who actually deserves you.

TIFF SAYS

Go in with an open heart, and keep your standards high, your expectations realistic, and your sense of humor fully intact. Because one day, you'll be looking back at all these wild stories, laughing with your person, and thanking the dating gods that you never settled for anything less than what you truly wanted.

IN THIS CHAPTER

» How to use dating apps effectively for your goals

» Creating the ultimate dating profile

» Mastering the art of online flirting

» Taking it offline and finding your IRL match

Chapter 2
Tinder, Hinge, Bumble, Oh My! Navigating the Dating Apps

Let's be real: If your longest relationship has been with your dating apps, you're not alone. Welcome to the modern dating cycle! It goes something like this: You delete all your apps, swearing you're "over online dating" and ready to meet someone "in the wild." You imagine yourself bumping into your perfect match at a coffee shop, only to realize the only person who notices you is the barista — and he's already taken. So what do you do? You re-download the apps, convinced that true love is just one swipe away.

Sound familiar? You're not alone. The dating app space has changed a lot since the days when eHarmony made you feel like you needed a personality makeover just to get a date. Fast forward to today, and we're living in a world where over 300 million people are swiping, matching, and hoping to find their soulmate (or at least someone who won't ghost them) on their phones. Your options? Endless. Your chances of finding someone who doesn't immediately disappear after one text? Still a work in progress.

In this chapter, you find out how to pick the right app for you, how to craft a profile that gets noticed (Hint: A photo with your ridiculously cute puppy helps), and how to take your digital connection from swipe to real-life date.

REMEMBER

You're not looking for a pen pal. You're looking for a partner. And after reading this chapter, you'll be equipped with the real strategies you need to stop getting stuck in dating app purgatory, to avoid endless app conversations that go nowhere, and to start enjoying the process of swiping — with purpose. Whether that's making a Tinder Sleepover where you and your friends connect the app to the TV and swipe together, or having a dating accountability partner who makes sure you're actually going on those dates and not just leaving matches on read, you'll learn how to turn the endless swiping into actual dating fun. It's time replace love at first sight with love at first swipe!

Seeing How Dating Apps Have Changed the Dating World

To all my fellow '90s babies, we're officially old enough to start using phrases like "back in my day." Back then, your options for meeting singles were pretty limited: Your best friend set you up with their co-worker's cousin, you hit up the local church or community event for a "singles night," or you relied on Steve, your neighborhood bartender, to be your unofficial matchmaker. Sure, there were a few dating apps like eHarmony, and Facebook messages from old flings were a thing, but the idea of having *thousands* of eligible singles at your fingertips? Unimaginable.

Fast forward to 2025, and dating has turned into something resembling a Black Friday sale — except instead of flat-screen TVs, you're shopping for love. And those premium app fees? They might as well be the coupons to get a discounted soulmate. Now we have access to *everyone* (okay, not everyone, but it feels that way) from all over the world, each looking for something slightly different. A whirlwind of possibilities lies in the palm of our hands, but all this choice can lead to one big problem: dating paralysis. How do you pick "the one" when it feels like you're endlessly swiping through the clearance rack of humanity?

Dating apps have revolutionized how we meet people, no doubt about it. According to a 2023 study, nearly 50 percent of couples now report meeting through dating apps, making it the most popular way to find love. And while it's great to have this level of access, it's also a double-edged sword. Swiping fatigue is real, people. There's something overwhelming about having *too many* options, and let's be honest — most of us are guilty of collecting matches like Pokémon cards, only to never message them back.

REMEMBER Here's the kicker: Dating apps aren't the problem. The problem is how we use them. They're meant to be a tool, not a crutch. Just like GPS on your phone, apps are here to guide you, not drive the car for you. Swiping doesn't replace the work of putting yourself out there in real life. You might feel like you're making an effort because you matched with three people while bingeing Netflix, but if you never follow up or actually meet them, are you really trying? (Spoiler: You're not.)

We're in an exciting era where the best of both worlds can coexist. Dating apps give you access to people you might never meet otherwise, but they shouldn't be your *only* strategy. Think of it this way: Apps are the plane to your destination of love, but the in-person stuff — flirting at a coffee shop, making conversation at a party — is what makes the trip worthwhile.

TIP The secret isn't choosing between apps and IRL connections. It's using both. Treat dating apps as a supplement to your love life, not the entire buffet. Swipe, match, and message with intention — but don't forget to close your phone, go outside, and let the magic happen in real life.

Using Dating Apps to Crush Your Relationship Goals

Dating apps are like the bread aisle at the grocery store — there are endless options, and everyone has a slightly different way they like their slice. They can help you find anything from a casual fling to a lifelong partner (or at least someone who won't ghost you after you tell them you only sleep on the left side of the bed). The trick is knowing what kind of "bread" you're looking for and using the app to your advantage. If you're after a serious relationship, be intentional and make that clear on your profile. And please, for the love of all carbs, skip swiping right on the ripped shirtless photos, and gentlemen — don't post them if you're looking for a wife. No matter how good you look! Add prompts that reflect your goals, like "Looking for someone to share Sunday brunches and random road trips with." For casual dating? Keep it playful and light, maybe something like "Professional third-wheel eliminator — apply within." And if you're somewhere in the middle (like most people), don't overthink it — just be clear about wanting connection, whether it's for a season or the long haul.

Choosing an app based on what you're looking for

It's helpful to know your intention, because that will guide you to the apps that best match your interests. For example, Tinder could be your focaccia — it's versatile, globally loved, and has the largest network of singles, making it perfect for travelers dreaming of meeting their Italian love interest.

Bumble, on the other hand, is like brioche — soft, approachable, and great for anyone who loves to take the lead (especially women, who make the first move here).

If you're into curated, thoughtful connections, Hinge is your sourdough: classic, reliable, and made to be savored — it even markets itself as "the app designed to be deleted."

And then there's the League, which is basically the gluten-free artisan loaf of dating apps — exclusive, niche, and definitely not for everyone, but some swear by it if you're looking for elite networking vibes alongside potential love.

Communicating if you want a hookup, situationship, or serious commitment

Honestly, there are probably more dating apps than singles in the world, so you're bound to find one that matches your vibe. And remember, whether you're searching for a soulmate or just someone to share the last fries with, there's no wrong way to use these apps — just don't let the loaf go stale before you meet up!

When it comes to dating, communicating your intentions doesn't have to feel like a visit to your therapist or a thesis on your emotional availability. Whether you're looking for something casual or a long-term romance, the key is honesty wrapped in a little charm. Instead of dropping a heavy "So, are you here for forever or just for fun?" mid-conversation, try keeping it natural. If you're into something serious, you can say, "I'm really enjoying getting to know you. I'm at a point where I'm looking for something meaningful. How about you?" Or if it's a casual vibe you're after, go with something light like "I'm here for good times and great company — let's see where this goes!"

> **REMEMBER**
>
> The goal is to make it clear without making it awkward — kind of like ordering at a restaurant. If you don't tell the waiter how you like your steak, you might end up with something you didn't want. Dating's the same. Speak up, but make it easy, because nobody likes a confusing menu that has situationship written all over it.

Guarding Your Heart (and Health): Prioritizing Sexual Wellness

Dating apps have become a playground for all kinds of connections, including the — *ahem* — very casual ones. And while there's nothing inherently wrong with using apps to find a one-night stand (you're an adult, after all), it's important to keep both your heart and your health in check. Think of it like eating sushi — it's fun, spicy, and spontaneous, but you also want to make sure the place has a health rating higher than your ex's maturity level.

First, let's talk about health. Whether it's a casual hookup or a potential partner, protection is nonnegotiable. Pack those condoms like you pack your phone charger — always. And yes, if you're sexually active, regular STI testing isn't just responsible, it's downright essential. Apps like Tinder and Bumble won't send you a push notification about this, but trust me, your future self will thank you. Oh, and if they say, "Don't worry, I'm clean," smile politely and still wrap it up. Nothing kills the mood like a trust fall with someone else's hygiene routine.

> **WARNING**
>
> During a casual hookup, someone might try to persuade you with lines like "Condoms are such a turn-off," or the classic "I just don't enjoy it with them on." Spoiler alert: This isn't just a red flag — it's a burning building, and you should be sprinting in the opposite direction. Respect for boundaries is the bare minimum anyone you're intimate with should offer. If they're pressuring

you to forgo protection or dismissing your comfort and safety, they've shown you exactly who they are. And trust me, they're not worth your time.

The reality is, only *you* will be sitting in that waiting room, anxiously waiting for test results, after deciding that the one-night stand who seemed cute enough to ditch your condom standards for was worth the risk. Spoiler: They weren't. Nobody wants to feel the agonizing uncertainty of wondering if their health hangs on one decision made after a few drinks. Protect yourself — always. Just like you'd say a hard *no* to eating questionable sushi from a gas station, condoms should always be your hard line. No exceptions. Confidence is sexy, safety is essential, and putting your health first is never up for debate.

Now for your heart. One-night stands can be fun, liberating, and exactly what you're looking for — as long as you're honest with yourself about your intentions. Apps make it easy to swipe into bed with someone, but if you're secretly hoping for breakfast dates and matching sweaters, make sure you're on the same page before things get . . . cozy. Communication is sexy, and so is knowing when to say, "Hey, this is fun, but I'm looking for something more."

REMEMBER

Humor aside, prioritizing your sexual wellness isn't about being boring or killing the vibe. It's about enjoying yourself responsibly, whether that means finding sparks in a fling or pursuing something long-term. Because at the end of the day, the best connection — physical or emotional — is one that leaves you feeling good about yourself. And maybe ready to swipe again — this time with even more confidence.

Swipe Smarter, Not Harder: The Ultimate Setup Guide

You don't need a marketing degree to date, but you do need to market yourself correctly on dating apps if you want high-quality matches. Think of your dating profile as a business card or a 30-second commercial that makes people want to get in line to date you. The key? Be your true self — but the best version of it. And no, that doesn't mean slapping on heavy filters or using a picture from high school 20 years ago and pretending you've just "had a lot of Botox."

REMEMBER

The goal is to meet in person, so it's crucial to stay true to who you are — both physically and personality-wise. Seriously, who wouldn't want to date you? That being said, this section covers some tips to make your profile stand out (in a good way).

Photos: Because first impressions matter

I get it — putting pictures of yourself out there can be terrifying. You've asked everyone, from your mom to the deli guy, for their "expert" opinion on your photos. (Spoiler: The deli guy isn't an expert, and your mom loves you no matter what.) The truth is, no one knows your best angles like you do, so pick photos *you* feel good about. I know when it comes to my profile I like to make it as tastefully curated as the Louvre.

Here are some tips to make your photo game strong:

- **Lighting is everything:** Make sure your photos have good lighting and actually show what you look like. Natural light works wonders.
- **No filter overload:** Avoid heavy filters and ancient photos — people are swiping for *you*, not a vintage version of you.
- **Keep it current:** Gained or lost weight? That's life. Post pictures that reflect who you are now.
- **Three's company:** Never post just one photo. Aim for three to five pics that show off different sides of your personality.
- **Story starters:** Each photo should spark a conversation — travel shots, concert pics, hobbies, or anything that screams "this is my vibe."
- **Keep it classy:** Skip the shirtless gym selfies and overly explicit shots, even if you're just looking for a hookup. Trust me, classy gets clicks.
- **No guessing games:** Avoid group photos where no one can figure out which one is you. (Hint: They'll assume you're the least attractive one.)
- **Selfie rules:** Take selfies from good angles that highlight your best side. No one likes the dreaded "up-the-nose" shot.

- **Ditch the flashy flex:** Even if you've got a yacht, keep the bragging subtle. You want them to like *you*, not your bank account.
- **Keep it balanced:** A mix of close-up, full-body, and candid shots works best. Variety keeps your profile interesting.
- **Pets are a plus:** Got a dog, cat, or even a pet iguana? Include them! People love a cute animal pic.
- **Dress to impress:** Your clothes say a lot about you. Pick outfits that make you feel confident and reflect your personal style.
- **Skip the sunglasses:** Avoid photos where your face is completely covered by sunglasses or hats. People want to see your eyes!
- **No exes allowed:** Don't crop your ex out of a photo and leave a mysterious arm lingering. It's weird. Just take a new picture.
- **Background check:** Pay attention to what's behind you — no messy rooms. Show you put effort into this profile!

Bio bootcamp: Turning boring into boo worthy

In the world of modern dating, your bio is your chance to show you're more than just a pretty face — so don't make people want to swipe left faster than they can say "Bye-oh!" A good bio strikes the perfect balance between being honest, intentional, and a little fun. Here's how to do it:

- **Keep it short and sweet.** Nobody's looking for your autobiography on a dating app. A concise, clever few sentences are all you need. Think of it as a mini-commercial that sparks curiosity. If your bio reads like a PhD dissertation, you're doing it wrong.
- **Stay positive and lighthearted.** This isn't LinkedIn — keep it fun! Your bio should feel approachable, not like a life manifesto. Humor goes a long way, but avoid being overly sarcastic or negative.
- **Add conversation starters.** Include relatable tidbits or quirky details that invite matches to message you. Some ideas:
  - Favorite pizza toppings? Pineapple or pepperoni wars, anyone?

- Go to binge shows? (*The Office* and *Friends* are always solid talking points.)
- Karaoke dreams? Who's your go-to pop star? (Cue "Dancing Queen" in the background.)

» Be clear about your intentions. Apps like Tinder and Hinge let you state your goals (marriage, a "situationship," or even the new "nano-ship"). Use your bio to reinforce what you're looking for! Be upfront but polite:
- "Looking for a long-term partner."
- "Down for drinks and short-term fun — no judgment!"
- "It's cuffing season, and I'm ready for the one."
- "If you smoke, please swipe left — dealbreaker alert."
- "Dog lovers only, please. My furry roommate has standards."

» Show, don't tell. Instead of saying, "I'm funny," let your bio *be* funny. For example: "Once got kicked out of trivia night for knowing too much about '90s boy bands. No regrets."

Let your personality shine through actions, quirks, or funny anecdotes.

» Don't be generic. Vague bios are forgettable. Instead of saying, "I like music," go with something more specific:
- "Big fan of Chappell Roan heartbreak era and Kendrick's energy — don't judge my playlists."
- "I won my high school spelling bee and I'm still not done talking about it."

» Balance confidence with humility. Confidence is attractive, but overdoing it can seem arrogant. Show self-assurance while staying relatable: "I know my way around the kitchen, but I'll never say no to ordering takeout."

» Showcase your passions. Highlight what excites you — it gives people something to connect with:
- "Weekend warrior: cycling, trying new recipes, and searching for the best tacos in town."
- "If I'm not at work, you'll find me on a hiking trail or experimenting with latte art."

» Drop a fun fact. Random but intriguing facts make great conversation starters:
- "Once won a watermelon-eating contest and will talk about it forever."

- "Can fold a fitted sheet like a pro. It's my only superpower."

>> **Don't be afraid to be quirky.** Quirky bios stand out. Embrace your weirdness!

- "I judge people based on their ranking of Pixar movies — choose wisely."
- "Ask me about the time I accidentally adopted a goat."

>> **Don't overshare or be negative.** Keep the bio upbeat and avoid TMI. For example, skip things like, "Fresh out of a toxic relationship, looking for someone better." Instead, say, "Excited for a fresh start and some great conversations."

>> **Include a call to action.** Give people an easy way to message you:

- "Tell me your dream vacation spot."
- "If you love dogs, we'll get along — what's your favorite breed?"

WARNING

Be cautious of profiles with overly edited photos, because they might not be real. Pay attention if someone insists on only communicating through the app and avoids moving the conversation elsewhere. Messages that seem unnatural or robotic can be a sign of an AI bot. Another major red flag is if they ask for any sort of money transfer, which should always be avoided. If you're ever unsure about someone's identity, consider verifying them through a FaceTime or video call.

SAMPLE BIOS THAT WORK

"Fluent in sarcasm, love languages, and Netflix recommendations. If you can quote [insert show you've rewatched 200 times], we're already off to a good start."

"Professional brunch enthusiast, amateur plant mom. Looking for someone to split fries with and pretend to like my dog's Instagram."

"80% coffee, 20% bad jokes. If you laugh, it's meant to be."

Taking It Offline: How to Transition from App to Reality

The only thing harder than swiping is taking it from small talk to a big first date. This section offers advice and tips to navigate the app to turn dream matches into real first dates.

What to do if you are not getting any matches

If you're hearing crickets on dating apps, don't spiral into "Nobody likes me" or "I'll be cuddling my phone forever." Sometimes, it's not you — it's the app! There are countless dating apps, and finding the right one is half the battle. While the big three — Tinder, Hinge, and Bumble — are popular, there are niche apps tailored to specific cultures, interests, or even tax brackets (*cough*, Raya).

REMEMBER

Love isn't a numbers game. It's about finding the one match that counts, not a hundred meaningless ones. If you're looking for more than a hookup, it might take time, but patience pays off. And hey, if waiting isn't your thing, apps offer upgrades like unlimited swipes and sneak peeks at who already likes you (instant confidence boost, anyone?). So keep swiping — you can't lose if you don't quit! Additionally, don't be afraid to keep tweaking your profile — change the photos and bios and find what works best! Throw everything at the digital wall and see what sticks to your matches!

Match secured! How to take it further

Once you match, the nerve-racking question pops up: Who messages first? The answer: you! You miss every shot you don't take, so why not go for it? They swiped on you too, which means there's already interest. Skip the endless app refreshing and confidently send a message — you've got nothing to lose and everything to gain.

When starting a convo, think compliments (but keep it classy). Instead of going for clichés or anything overly flirty, focus on the story behind their photos or bio. For example, if they have a beach photo, try: "You look great in that beach pic! Where was it taken? I'm planning a trip soon and could use some ideas." It's personal, engaging, and keeps the conversation flowing naturally. Compliments on their outfit or hobbies also work wonders — bonus points for humor! The worst thing you can do is rely on your friends or AI to text for you. Only you will be on that in-person date, so start showing your sparkly personality in your messages.

TIP: Keep the chatting fun but efficient. If the vibe is good, move things along after 24–48 hours. Suggest a call or, better yet, an in-person date. Staying in the app too long is like leaving leftovers in the fridge — they get forgotten. To transition naturally, ask for their favorite restaurants or music spots and say something like "That sounds amazing! Let's go check it out together." Boom — date secured!

Once you've locked in a date, the next big question is this: What do you want from it? Are you looking for a hookup, a casual fling, or the first step toward forever? There is a false stigma that dating apps are just for hookups when that couldn't be further from the case. I have multiple clients with a Tinderella story and just as many Grinder Grooms! There's no shame in any of those answers, but it's good to have a loose idea beforehand. Life can surprise you, though — like that time I was solo traveling in London and hopped on Tinder to meet a local. What started as a casual date turned into such an amazing connection that I extended my trip for two weeks. No, he's not my husband now (and we're not even still in touch), but I'll always think of that whirlwind British romance as simply smashing.

REMEMBER: Dating apps can lead to all kinds of unexpected adventures, but it doesn't hurt to keep your goals in mind. You've already done the hard work — swiping, crafting the perfect profile, and putting yourself out there. Now it's time to sit back, relax, and enjoy the dates. Trust that your swiping skills will pay off, and whether it's love, fun, or something in between, you've got this!

WARNING: When meeting someone off the app, make sure never to go to their house, or get picked up from yours. Meet in a safe, secure public location and share your location with friends!

IN THIS CHAPTER

» Looking for love in all the wrong places

» Knowing your dating value

» Seeing why you feel insecure and figuring out how to fix it

Chapter **3**
Finding Love While Loving Yourself

D o you remember the first time you were taught not to like yourself? That moment when the world, in all its unsolicited wisdom, told you that you weren't enough? I do. It was middle school. I was flipping through *Vogue*, staring at impossibly thin models, and for the first time in my 11-year-old life, I thought, "Well, guess I'm ugly. Nobody will ever like me unless I look like that."

Unfortunately, that mentality didn't just vanish after a snack and a nap — it followed me into my 20s, lurking like a toxic ex who just *won't* move on. The comparison game. The habit of putting myself down before anyone else could. The mindset of rejecting myself before I even gave someone the chance to do it. And let me tell you, that is the biggest dating sabotage of all time.

If you want a thriving love life, you need to love yourself first — the way you want your future partner to love you. One of my favorite quotes from *The Perks of Being a Wallflower* says, "We accept the love we think we deserve." And if you're treating yourself like a beat-up Honda Civic instead of a Ferrari, guess what? That's the kind of treatment you'll learn to accept. In this chapter, you find out how to stop playing small, own your value, and walk into every room (and every date) like you're the prize — because *you are*.

Looking for Love in All the Wrong Places (and Finally Getting It Right)

We've all been there — dating the wrong people, making excuses for bad behavior, and convincing ourselves that "this time it'll be different" while rereading texts that barely qualify as words. The truth is, finding love isn't just about swiping right or sending the perfect flirty DM. It starts with knowing what you want and what you deserve, and refusing to settle for less than that.

Stop dating the wrong people just because they're there

Listen, I get it. Sometimes it feels like the dating pool is more like a kiddie pool — shallow and full of... well, let's call it "questionable water quality." But just because someone is available doesn't mean they're right for you. If your dating history looks like a list of people who "weren't that bad" or "had potential," it's time for a glow-up in your standards.

Ask yourself: Am I dating this person because I genuinely like them, or just because I don't want to be alone? If the answer is the latter, then congratulations! You just unlocked level one of self-awareness.

Creating standards that you deserve

Having standards doesn't mean being "too picky." It means having self-respect. It's not about wanting someone who looks like they walked off a Calvin Klein ad (though, if that happens, go off, queen), it's about wanting someone who treats you with kindness, consistency, and respect.

If someone is texting you only after 11 p.m. or responding with "wyd" instead of making actual plans, that's disrespectful behavior. A good standard to have? If they can make time to order Door-Dash, they can make time to ask you on a proper date.

Set your nonnegotiables and stick to them. Think of your time like VIP bottle service — not everyone gets access.

Dating yourself first

Before you worry about whether someone else likes you, ask yourself: Do I like me? If the answer is "eh, sometimes," then it's time to start romanticizing your own life. Take yourself on solo dates. Buy yourself flowers. Wear the outfit that makes you feel hottest, just because.

Here's the thing: When you treat yourself the way you wish someone else would treat you, two things happen — your standards rise, and people start seeing you as the confident, self-loving powerhouse you are. Confidence isn't just attractive, it's magnetic. And it's a lot harder to be played when you know your own worth.

Changing your relationship with relationships

Not every person you date needs to be The One™. Maybe they're The One Who Introduces You to Sushi, The One Who Makes You Laugh Until You Cry, or The One Who Teaches You Exactly What You Don't Want. Relationships — whether they last a week or a decade — should add to your life, not subtract from it.

Instead of seeing dating as a job interview where you're desperately hoping to be hired, start seeing it as an experience that should be enjoyable. You are also assessing them. If someone isn't making you happy, why keep them around? You wouldn't keep wearing shoes that give you blisters, so why keep dating someone who makes you feel like you're not enough?

Dating from desire, not desperation

Desperate dating energy is like a neon "open" sign for the wrong people. If you're dating just to fill a void, you'll end up with someone who thrives on that — someone who breadcrumb texts, plays games, or makes you feel like you have to earn their attention. You don't.

When you're secure in yourself, you date because you want to, not because you need to. The difference? People who truly want to be with you will make an effort. And if they don't? You won't waste your time chasing someone who isn't running toward you.

TIFF SAYS

You set the tone for how people treat you. At the end of the day, your dating life is in your hands. If you keep allowing people to show up half-heartedly, they will. If you keep making excuses for bad behavior, it will continue. The good news? You can change the narrative. Love yourself so fully that anyone who enters your life has no choice but to level up or leave. And when you stop settling, you start attracting the kind of love you actually deserve. Now, go forth and date like the high-value, self-respecting icon you are.

Knowing Your Dating Value: Stop Settling and Start Thriving

Let's get one thing straight: You are not a clearance item. You are not some last-minute airport snack someone picks up because they're desperate and hungry. You are a top-shelf, limited-edition, highly coveted kind of person. But if you don't see yourself that way, how can you expect anyone else to?

Most people don't struggle with being "not good enough" in dating. They struggle with believing they're not good enough, which is a completely different thing. The good news? That's fixable. The bad news? If you keep accepting half-hearted efforts and situationships where you're nothing more than a late-night "wyd?" text, you're actively training yourself to accept less than you deserve. It's time to rewire your brain, boost your standards, and start attracting what you actually want.

Acting like you're expensive — because you are

You set the standard for how people treat you. If someone wants to be in your life, they need to show up for you. No "we should hang out sometime" nonsense — make a plan, or don't waste my time.

Stop giving VIP access to people who only deserve general admission. If they're texting you at midnight asking, "u up?" and haven't made an actual plan to see you, consider it disrespectful. You are not a vending machine for validation.

Never settling for the bare minimum

We've all been guilty of seeing the red flags, but deciding they look festive instead of toxic. But let's get one thing clear: The bare minimum is *not* romantic.

If someone is texting you back after two days like nothing happened, that's not effort — that's laziness. If they only make plans that involve *their* convenience, that's not compatibility — that's selfishness. If you're constantly justifying why you're putting in more effort than them, you already know the answer.

REMEMBER: Your standards should make people level up, not make you lower yourself just to keep someone around.

Stopping dating out of loneliness or boredom

If you're only dating because you "need" someone to text, congrats, you're setting yourself up for disappointment. If you don't actually *like* them but enjoy the attention, you're using them as an emotional fidget spinner. If you feel pressure to date because "everyone else is," remember: A lot of people are in *terrible* relationships. Your singleness is not a disease.

TIP: Fill your own cup first. If you're fulfilled in your own life, you won't feel like you need someone to give you purpose.

Practicing and projecting confidence

Confidence isn't about being the loudest person in the room. It's about carrying yourself like you know your worth.

Walk into every date like you belong there, because you do. If they don't text back, it's not a personal attack — it's a blessing in disguise.

REMEMBER: If you wouldn't let your best friend put themselves down, stop doing it to yourself.

Focusing on attracting, not chasing

Your energy is valuable. Don't waste it on people who don't match your effort. If they're inconsistent, they're showing you they don't care — believe them.

CHAPTER 3 Finding Love While Loving Yourself

If someone is making you question your worth, walk away. The right person won't have you doubting yourself.

REMEMBER The more you respect yourself, the more you'll attract people who respect you too.

Remembering that you set the standard

If you've been settling for less, this is your wake-up call. You are not an option, a backup plan, or a placeholder. You are the main event. Start treating yourself accordingly:

- Don't settle for texts that only come because someone's bored.
- Don't accept dates that feel like last-minute thoughts.
- Don't put your self-worth in the hands of someone who barely deserves a handshake.

When you know your dating value, you stop accepting nonsense and start attracting the kind of people who treat you the way you deserve.

TIP Even if it's not natural at first, embody the most beautiful person you know and ask yourself how they would handle a situation. How would they talk to themselves? Embrace that energy until it becomes your norm.

Rejection Is Redirection: Stop Doubting Yourself

Most of us didn't just wake up one day and think, *Wow, I feel amazing about myself all the time!* No, we've been conditioned to doubt ourselves since childhood. Maybe it was a mean girl in middle school, a bad haircut in high school, or that one time you sent a risky text and got left on read. Regardless, self-doubt is sneaky, and it creeps into dating faster than a "wyd?" text at 2 a.m.

But here's the truth: Your insecurities are lying to you. You don't need to be perfect, you don't need to be someone else, and you definitely don't need validation from people who don't even know how to use a calendar properly to schedule a real date.

The following sections give you advice on to how to stop spiraling and start thriving.

Stop comparing yourself — it's a losing game

To compare is to despair, and let's be honest, half the people you're comparing yourself to online don't even look like that in real life.

That influencer posting "casual" selfies at golden hour? She took 200 shots, Face-tuned her pores into oblivion, and added three filters.

That couple looking sickeningly in love? They probably just fought about where to eat five minutes before posting that picture.

That ex who seems like they upgraded? They didn't. You're just romanticizing the past because rejection messes with your brain chemistry.

Moral of the story? The only person you should be competing with is *yourself*. Aim to be a little better than you were yesterday, and leave the Photoshop Olympics to the professionals.

Owning your unique perfection

If everyone looked the same, acted the same, and had the same quirks, the world would be so boring. Your so-called flaws are what make you memorable.

That laugh you think is too loud? Someone out there is going to love it. Your weird hobbies? That's what makes you interesting. The way you overanalyze texts? Okay, maybe we should work on that one.

But seriously, you are enough exactly as you are. The right person isn't going to wish you were different — they're going to love you for being unapologetically yourself.

Knowing you're already complete — no one else can "fix" you

We've all been sold the "you complete me" lie. But let's get something straight: You are not half of a person walking around waiting for your missing puzzle piece. A relationship should add to your life, not define it.

You don't need someone to "choose" you to be valuable — you choose yourself. If you don't enjoy your own company, why would someone else?

REMEMBER Work on being whole on your own, so when the right person comes along, they're a bonus, not a necessity.

Realizing no one is judging you like you think they are

You ever go out, trip over nothing, and then spend the next two hours convinced that *everyone* saw it? Spoiler: They didn't.

People are too busy worrying about their own lives to dissect every little thing you do. That awkward joke you made? They probably forgot about it five minutes later. That one "embarrassing" moment from a date? If they're worth your time, they won't care. And if they *do* care? You're dodging a bullet.

Bottom line: People are not analyzing your every move, so stop overanalyzing yourself.

Not everyone has taste, so stop taking every opinion to heart

Everyone is going to have an opinion on how you should date, who you should date, and how you should live your life. But just because someone has an opinion *does not* mean it's valid.

Your great-aunt thinks you should be married by now? Cute. Does she even know how to send a text without caps lock? Your friends think your type is *too specific*? Cool, but are they happily in love? Exactly.

That one person didn't like you? So what? Not everyone likes chocolate, and chocolate is still amazing.

> **REMEMBER** At the end of the day, the only opinion that truly matters is yours. Everyone else is just background noise.

Seeing rejection as a blessing in disguise

Yes, getting ghosted or rejected stings. But you know what's worse? Wasting your time on someone who was never meant for you.

If someone doesn't want you, let them go — why are we fighting to sit at tables that don't even have chairs for us?

> **REMEMBER** Rejection is redirection. It's the universe's way of saying, *Not this one, babe. Keep it moving.* Every "no" gets you closer to the right "yes." The next time you feel rejected, remind yourself that it's just clearing the path for someone who will actually appreciate you.

> **TIFF SAYS** You deserve the kind of love that makes you feel safe, excited, and valued — not like you're constantly waiting for them to "decide" if they want you. You are not an option. You are the prize. If someone is making you question your worth, they don't deserve you.

IN THIS CHAPTER

» Raising your standards: Stop settling in love

» Drawing up your dating blueprint: Setting standards, spotting red flags, avoiding toxic patterns

Chapter 4
Deciding to Date — Setting Standards and Having a Solid Dating Blueprint

Choosing the right partner is about discipline, not just feelings. Love is great. But you know what's even better? Love that's actually healthy, fulfilling, and doesn't leave you emotionally drained. You need to have the discipline to walk away from what *looks good* but *feels wrong*. Think of this as a dating diet, a way to no longer eat something that has made you sick in the past. To not waste time trying to convince yourself that *maybe* this is love when, deep down, you know you deserve more.

In this chapter, you ask yourself some important questions to help ensure you aren't just settling for whoever is in front of you. You then work on setting some new standards and avoiding red flag behaviors and toxic patterns.

Is This Your Perfect Person or Are You Just Their One-Person Entertainment Act?

In today's dating world, it can feel like you're standing in the bread aisle — so many options, yet somehow you still don't know what you're in the mood for. Do you go with the classic whole wheat (reliable but boring)? The trendy gluten-free one that looks good but crumbles under pressure? Or do you just grab the cheapest loaf because, well, *it's there*?

The dating pool is no different. There are so many choices, and yet it's even harder when you've spent your whole life fantasizing about your "perfect person." You've put together a Pinterest board of your future wedding, decided on their job title, their height, their favorite indie band — and then, reality hits. They don't exist.

But you know who does exist? Chad. Yes, *Chad*. And before you judge me, just know that on paper, Chad was *the* dream guy. Tall, successful, *great suit*. But in reality? I was in a one-woman performance, and he was just my reluctant audience. I carried every conversation, cracked every joke, and at the end of each date, I left feeling like I had just performed a one-hour stand-up special for a guy who barely clapped at the end.

That's when I learned a crucial lesson: *If someone is perfect on paper but a disaster in real life — RUN.*

But how do you know when you've found the right person versus when you're just filling a role in someone else's bad TV pilot? Let's break it down:

> **Are you dating a person or a résumé?** Do you actually *like* them, or do they just check off all the boxes on your imaginary "ideal partner" list?
> - Good job? Great, but are they interesting?
> - Nice apartment? Cool, but do they actually make you laugh?
> - Your mom likes them? Fantastic, but does *your soul* like them?

A relationship is not a business deal. You don't need someone with a corner office, a six pack, and an Ivy League degree — you need someone who makes your life better by just being in it.

> **Are you comfortable, or are you constantly performing?** The right person should feel like a deep exhale, not an ongoing audition. If you're always wondering if they like you, if you're saying the right things, if you need to *act* a certain way to keep them interested — that's not a relationship, it's an unpaid acting gig.

How to test this:

- If you have to constantly make them laugh but they barely entertain *you*, it's a red flag.
- If you feel drained instead of energized after seeing them, that's your body saying *abort mission*.
- If you can't be your true, unfiltered self, then guess what? You're dating an audience, not a partner.

> **Are you in love with the potential or the reality?** Be honest — are you dating the *actual* person, or the *fantasy* of what they *could* be?

A person's *potential* is not a promise. You can't date someone's LinkedIn goals — you have to date them for *who they are today*. If you're waiting for them to "grow" into a better communicator, "change" their bad habits, or "finally" be ready for a real relationship — congrats, you're in a long-term commitment with your own delusions. The right person is not someone you need to fix — they're someone you can build with.

> **Do they fit into your future, or are you trying to fit into theirs?** The right person should want to build something together — not expect you to completely adapt to their life. If they're making all the plans, setting all the rules, and you feel like a supporting character in their main storyline, it's time to rewrite the script.

Relationships should feel like a partnership, not a "keep up or get left behind" situation.

> **Do you feel safe and seen, or are you just "lucky to be here"?** If you constantly feel like you have to prove your worth to someone — that's not love, that's a hostage situation. If they make you feel like you should be *grateful*

CHAPTER 4 Deciding to Date — Setting Standards and Having a Solid Dating Blueprint   41

> they're dating you, they're not the one. If they downplay your accomplishments, your interests, or your personality — why are you even considering them? If you're losing yourself trying to impress them, you already lost. The right person will never make you question your value.

So next time you're asking, "Is this my perfect person or am I just entertaining myself?" — check in with yourself. Are you thriving, or are you just surviving? If it's the latter, pack up the circus, because the show is over.

Drawing Up Your Dating Blueprint — Because Love Shouldn't Be a DIY Disaster

If you've ever tried to follow a vague recipe with missing ingredients and zero instructions, then you already know what dating without a plan feels like — frustrating, confusing, and leaving you questioning your life choices. That's why you need a **dating blueprint** — a set of guidelines, standards, and nonnegotiables that stop you from falling into the same chaotic, toxic patterns and finally get you on the right track.

This isn't about making a list of superficial must-haves like *tall, rich, and good at texting back within 30 seconds.* This is about **real standards,** the ones that determine whether your relationship is built to last or if it's a crumbling foundation held together with emotional duct tape.

TIFF SAYS

If you want love to last, build it right. No matter how much fun a relationship is, it needs to have good infrastructure. If you keep letting in mediocrity, don't be shocked when you keep getting mediocre results. Set your standards. Stick to them. Don't let loneliness trick you into accepting less. Because when you hold out for what's right? You don't just end up with love — you end up with the love you actually deserve.

The blueprint for love: Crafting your ideal partner checklist

Think of this as designing a home — your future relationship should feel like a well-built, comfortable space where you can relax, not a run-down apartment with a leaking ceiling and a landlord who ignores your calls (also known as your toxic ex).

Your checklist should include:

TIP

- >> **Emotional maturity:** Can they handle a disagreement without storming off like a teenager?
- >> **Consistent effort:** If they wanted to, they would.
- >> **Respect for your boundaries:** No means no, even when it's about your Friday night alone time.
- >> **Shared values:** If you're planning a future together, at the very least you should be working toward the same kind of life.

This is not just about "vibes." Chemistry is great, but it won't pay your therapy bills if they treat you like an afterthought.

Zero tolerance: Defining the dealbreakers you won't compromise on

A dealbreaker is not being "too picky." It's knowing where to draw the line before you end up justifying nonsense:

- >> **Mixed signals:** If their texts look like a riddle, you don't need to solve them.
- >> **Lack of communication:** If they "don't like labels," they probably don't like accountability either.
- >> **Emotional unavailability:** You are not their personal therapist. If they can't show up fully, let them go.

REMEMBER

A dealbreaker isn't a preference — it's a **requirement** for your emotional well-being.

Toxic bingo: Uncover just how messy your dating patterns are

Do you keep dating the same emotionally unavailable person in a slightly different outfit? If so, congrats, you've been playing **Toxic Bingo** — and winning every round.

CHAPTER 4 Deciding to Date — Setting Standards and Having a Solid Dating Blueprint

Signs you might be stuck in a toxic loop:

- You think, "But they have potential," more than you think, "I actually feel happy in this relationship."
- You're always the one putting in the effort (*relationship or unpaid internship?*)
- You ignore major red flags because *this time will be different* (Spoiler: It won't).

TIP How to break the pattern? Date with your standards, not your trauma.

Butterflies or red flags? Learning to tell the difference

Excitement is great, but if your heart is racing because they're inconsistent, hot and cold, and keeping you guessing, that's not chemistry. That's stress. Breaking down the difference:

Butterflies: You're excited to see them because they make you feel safe and valued.

Red flags: You're excited to see them because you don't know if today they'll act like they care or disappear.

REMEMBER Stop romanticizing chaos. Love should make you feel secure, not like you're solving a mystery.

Your ex is a lesson, not a standard: Learning and moving on

Your ex is *not* a blueprint. They are a lesson plan for what you should never repeat:

- If your ex was emotionally unavailable, you don't date another emotionally unavailable person just because you're used to it.
- If your ex never planned dates, you don't tolerate bare-minimum effort in the next one.
- If your ex treated you like an option, you don't let anyone put you on the bench again.

Learn the lesson so you don't have to retake the class.

Saying no to mediocrity: Holding out for the right choice

Settling is like buying a discount mattress — seems fine at first, but over time you wake up sore and wondering why you didn't just invest in something better.

You don't deserve:

- Texts that come in at midnight but never during the day
- Situationships that leave you confused more than happy
- "Almost relationships" with people who don't claim you but also don't want you to move on

You *do* deserve clarity, commitment, and consistency — not confusion.

The dating checklist for what really matters

Instead of focusing on looks, job title, and height, shift your focus to things that actually matter long-term:

- Do they make you feel emotionally safe?
- Do they respect your boundaries?
- Do they show up for you when it counts?
- Do you actually have fun with them, or are you just keeping them around out of habit?

Attraction fades, but emotional security is forever.

REMEMBER

Mastering the discipline of your standards

It's easy to set standards — it's harder to stick to them when loneliness kicks in. Here's what not to do:

- Don't respond to the "hey stranger" texts from people who don't deserve your energy.
- Don't lower your standards just because you're tired of waiting.

» Don't entertain the bare minimum — you're not a clearance sale.

REMEMBER: Love isn't a reward for lowering your standards — it's what happens when you refuse to.

To hook up or hold off: Finding your sexual comfort zone

Your body, your rules. End of story.

If you want to wait, wait. If you want to have fun, have fun. Just make sure you're doing it for you — not because you feel pressured, not because you're scared of losing someone, and not because society tells you what's "normal."

REMEMBER: Your sex life is your business — no explanation needed.

Ditching the need for outside opinions

If you're constantly asking friends, "Should I break up with them?" you already know the answer. Stop outsourcing your dating life. Only you know what feels right for you. Keep the following in mind:

» Friends can give advice, but they're not the ones in the relationship.

» Your family might have opinions, but they're not the ones dating them.

» Social media might tell you what's "right," but your needs matter more than viral dating "rules."

TIP: Your gut is the best relationship coach you'll ever have — trust it.

PART 1 Getting into the Modern Dating Game

> **IN THIS CHAPTER**
>
> » Your dating life, your rules. How to own your choices
>
> » Dismantling dating myths: The false rules that need to go
>
> » How to rewrite dating rules that work for you

Chapter 5
Resetting Your Dating Mind: Breaking the Rules and Building Your Own

Once upon a time, I picked up *The Rules,* the book that basically told women to act like rare, mythical unicorns who never text first, never show too much interest, and never, under any circumstances, let a man know they liked him. I thought, *Okay, fine. I'll play along.* I followed every rule: I didn't call first, I pretended to be busy when I wasn't, and I let men chase me like I was the last Chanel bag on the planet.

Guess what? I got a few dates. But eventually, the real me came out — because you can only pretend to be a mysterious, unbothered, cool girl for so long before your actual personality shows up. And when it did? Let's just say none of those guys were *The One.* Moral of the story? Playing by someone else's dating handbook is a waste of time.

So let's burn the outdated dating rules and start making rules that work for you. Because dating is *not* one-size-fits-all, and the idea that following a checklist will get you love is about as accurate as your horoscope telling you that Mercury in retrograde is the reason your ex texted you at 2 a.m.

The Old Rules That Need to Go

Let's be honest—those outdated dating rules about when to call or when to sleep over? They're dead. In today's dating world, *you* get to decide who you are and how you want to date. There's no one-size-fits-all formula, and no one knows your love life better than you. So instead of trying to fit into someone else's playbook, it's time to create your own. Here are some tips to help you build a dating blueprint that leaves you feeling empowered — not like you're falling short:

>> **"Don't talk to a man first" — the rule that left everyone single:** Raise your hand if you've ever stared at your phone waiting for someone to text you first. Now, keep your hand up if that person *never did*. Exactly.

   The idea that you should wait around for someone to approach you is like hoping Uber will magically show up without you opening the app. If you want something, *go for it*. If someone's interested, they'll respond. And if they're not? You just saved yourself time.

>> **"Never have sex on the first date if you want a relationship" — the biggest lie ever told:** Sex doesn't determine commitment. If it did, one-night stands wouldn't turn into marriages, and people who "waited" wouldn't get ghosted.

   The real rule should be: *Have sex when* you *feel comfortable, not when outdated advice tells you to.* If that's the first date? Great. If it's six months in? Amazing. Just make sure it's what *you* want, not what you think you "should" do.

>> **"People will only like you at a certain size" — the ultimate confidence killer:** If dating success was based on a number on the scale, every gym would double as a matchmaking service.

   What actually makes you attractive is confidence, not fitting into an unrealistic beauty standard. The rule here? Date when you feel good in your own skin, not when you've hit some imaginary goal weight. Because someone who truly likes you isn't going to care whether you're a size 2 or a size 22.

>> **"Men should always pay for the date" — the financial fairy tale:** Look, splitting the bill doesn't mean chivalry is dead. And expecting someone else to pay for every meal doesn't mean you're a gold digger.

The new rule: *Decide what works for you.* Some people love treating their partner, some prefer to split, and some feel strongly that the person who initiated the date should pay. The key is balance, respect, and doing what makes sense for you — not what your grandma told you was "proper."

>> **"Play hard to get" — the fastest way to confuse everyone, including yourself:** Playing hard to get might have worked in *Pride and Prejudice*, but this is the 21st century, and we have *read receipts* now. If you like someone, show them. If they like you back, great. If they don't, *next!*

There's nothing cute about pretending to be too busy when you're really just rewatching *Bridgerton* for the third time.

Building Your Own Dating Rules

Now that we've trashed the outdated nonsense, let's focus on creating rules that actually work for *you*.

>> **Be honest about what you want.**

If you're looking for something serious, say so. If you just want something casual, be upfront. Stop trying to mold yourself into what you think someone else wants.

>> **If they like you, you'll know.**

No one is "too busy" to text back. No one is "too emotionally unavailable" to show they care. If they want to be with you, they will make it obvious. Stop accepting mixed signals and start demanding clarity.

>> **Date on your timeline, not theirs.**

There's no magic formula for when to sleep with someone, when to define the relationship, or when to get engaged. Some couples meet and marry in six months; others take years. Do what feels right for *you*.

>> **Define success on your terms.**

A relationship isn't successful just because it lasts forever. Sometimes, success is recognizing when something *isn't* right and walking away.

> **Have fun, seriously.**
>
> If dating feels like a chore, you're doing it wrong. The point isn't just to "win" at dating — it's to enjoy the process while finding someone who genuinely adds to your happiness.

TIFF SAYS

Forget everything you've been told about how dating "should" be. The only thing that truly matters is this: Do what makes *you* happy. The best relationships don't come from following a set of outdated rules — they come from being yourself, knowing what you want, and refusing to settle for anything less.

2
Meeting Someone and Setting Up a Date

IN THIS PART . . .

Remember how to flirt and grab someone's attention.

Find out how to get off the dating apps and meet people in real life.

Ask for a date (or rejecting an unwanted dating invitation).

Pick the perfect spot for your date.

Look out for some red flags when setting up a date.

Navigate check etiquette while avoiding awkwardness.

> **IN THIS CHAPTER**
> » Getting over your fear of rejection
> » Flirting by text and/or social media
> » Practicing good, old-fashioned in-person flirting

Chapter **6**

Flirting 101: The Flirtation Formula to Get 'Em Hooked

We all know that charming person in our lives — or in every romantic comedy — who somehow has the perfect thing to say at exactly the right time. They joke around just enough to keep things light, but they're also magnetic, sexy, and desirable, as though the gods of flirting hand-crafted them for an epic dating life. But here's a little secret: They didn't go to university for a PhD in flirting. They simply learned to be fearless about rejection and figured out that their self-worth isn't tied to whether someone else likes them.

Now, I don't work on Wall Street, and I'm not a dating economist, but flirting and dating is simply a numbers game. Flirt with ten people; maybe half reject you, half give you their number, and out of those, two might go on a date with you. Compared to zero dates because you're scared they won't like you or you think they're out of your league — now those odds are looking pretty good, my friend. You've got to shoot your shot, because getting rejected hurts a lot less than knowing you never tried and let the future love of your life walk by because you were too afraid to say hi.

If flirting still feels as terrifying and confusing as your last relationship, don't worry! In this chapter, I guide you with conversation starters for dating apps and social media, along with pro tips on how to walk up to anyone in a bar, restaurant, yoga class, or even that cute barista at the coffee shop and secure a date.

> **REMEMBER:** There is no right or wrong way to flirt; there's only owning your personal flirting style.

Flirting with Rejection

The first thing you need to know about dating is that you'll never get a date if you don't ask. They say the squeaky wheel gets the grease, but in dating it's the most fearless person who gets the date.

One inevitable reality of dating is that, at some point, you'll get rejected. But one reality that doesn't have to be true is rejecting yourself with thoughts like "Someone like that would never want me," or "They're way out of my league," or "That person probably thinks I look like Shrek." We are the stories we tell ourselves, so if you're going to create a narrative, why not make it a positive one? Why not tell yourself that they'd totally like you and think you're a 10! The first step to not fearing rejection is accepting yourself and knowing that anyone would be lucky to date you. Just because a few people (or even a few dozen) turned you down doesn't mean everyone will. To start dating, you have to believe you're worth dating.

In a dating world full of ghosting, people taking 10–12 business days to respond to texts, and dating profiles with too few likes, it's easy to feel rejected. But the key to success is not focusing on those who don't like you. You can't lose if you don't stop putting yourself out there and flirting. You don't get your big date night by playing it safe.

> **TIP:** The next time you're scared to flirt or approach your crush, remind yourself: *No matter what their response, this will make for great brunch talk.* Do it for the story! It will either be the beginning of your love story or a funny story to share with friends over cocktails. Embarrassment is a choice, but what's truly embarrassing is wanting an exciting, fulfilling dating life yet staying home on the couch, telling yourself that people won't like you.

DOING THE FLIRTY FRIDAY THING

I always say, *a rejection a day is a slay,* and you should be proud of yourself for having the courage to go after the love life you want. There was a time in my life when I went to a bar in NYC with my friends every Friday for what we called "Flirty Fridays." We'd go "future hubby hunting." One of those nights, one of my favorite actors — my ultimate heartthrob — was waiting in line next to me for the bathroom. Terrified but determined, I asked him if his dating life was as good as it seemed in the movies. I knew I'd never forgive myself if I let my fear of rejection stop me, so there I was, flirting with my celebrity crush in a bathroom line! Against all odds, I got his number, and we even went out to dinner. Sure, he didn't end up being my forever leading man, but at least I got to play a supporting role for one night. None of it would've happened if I'd been too scared to put myself out there.

The Texting Playbook: Tips for Flirty and Fun Chats

Flirting via text is an art form — equal parts wit, charm, and strategically placed emojis. Done right, it can build excitement, spark a connection, and set the stage for an amazing date. Done wrong, and . . . well, let's just say "k" is not going to win you any hearts.

This section is your guide to mastering the fine art of texting and social media flirting, complete with good openers, playful techniques, and just the right amount of sass.

Knowing the rules of flirting via text

Before diving into your phone like it's a digital dating dance-off, remember these key rules:

- **»** **Be playful, not creepy.** Compliments are great, but keep it classy. "Your smile is amazing" is charming. "I dreamt about your elbows" is . . . not.
- **»** **Match their vibe.** If they're sending long, thoughtful texts, don't reply with one-word answers. If they're dropping memes, fire one back.

>> **Timing is key.** Don't wait five days to reply, but also don't triple-text if they haven't responded in five minutes. Play it cool.

Kicking things off with a good opener

Starting the conversation can feel intimidating, but a solid opener can break the ice and set the tone for some flirty fun. Here are some go-to options:

>> **The playful question:** Great for starting a conversation and immediately showing off your sense of humor.

"So, what's the most ridiculous thing you've ever done for free food?"

>> **The fun observation:** Tease them a little — playful banter is key.

"Your profile says you love hiking. Is that real hiking or Instagram hiking?"

>> **The hobby or interest question:** It's engaging and personal, showing you're paying attention.

"So, is that coffee in your profile photo just for the aesthetic, or are you a true caffeine connoisseur?" This works for coffee, pets, travel pics, or anything specific in their photos. "Tell me about your dog — is it the kind that loves belly rubs or secretly runs the household?"

>> **The compliment (done right):** A little flattering, a little cheeky.

"You have great taste in [insert their favorite music/book/show]. Clearly, you're a genius. Teach me your ways."

Keeping it fun with flirty techniques

Once the conversation's rolling, keep the momentum with these playful strategies:

>> **Tease them (nicely).** A little light teasing goes a long way. If they say they're bad at something, respond with "Good thing you're cute — because wow."

>> **Use emojis wisely.** Emojis are like seasoning: Use just enough to spice things up but not so much that it's overwhelming. A well-placed wink or smile can turn a simple text into a flirty one.

- **Create inside jokes.** If they mention something funny, reference it later. For example, if they tell you they love pizza, you can say, "So what's the best pizza in the world, according to the expert?" It shows you're paying attention and adds a personal touch.
- **Drop a playful challenge.** Challenges are fun, flirty, and spark a little competition. "Bet you can't name three good rom-coms that aren't *The Notebook*."
- **Give subtle compliments.** Instead of gushing, keep it cool: "You've got a way with words — are you secretly a poet or something?"

Handling social media flirting

Social media is its own flirting playground, where likes, comments, and DMs can all send a message. Here's how to play the game:

- **The strategic like:** Don't like *every* photo they've ever posted — that's borderline stalker territory. Instead, like a few recent posts to show you're interested without going overboard.
- **Comment game strong:** Keep it light and playful. If they post a food pic, comment, "So when's my invite?" If it's a travel shot: "I hope you at least brought me back a souvenir."
- **Slide into the DMs (smoothly):** Reply to their Instagram story with something witty: "Is this your official audition for cutest dog-owner duo? Because you're winning." Stories are the easiest way to start a convo without it feeling forced.

Avoiding texting pitfalls

Even the best texter can trip up if they're not careful. Avoid these common mistakes:

- **Don't overuse "haha."** If every text you send ends with "haha," they might think you're in a constant state of nervous laughter.
- **Don't overthink it.** Don't analyze every word they send. Flirting is supposed to be fun, not a puzzle to solve.

>> **Don't be too eager.** It's okay to like someone, but triple-texting or responding in .02 seconds every time might make you seem desperate.

Knowing when to transition to real life

The ultimate goal of flirting via text is to lead to an in-person connection. Once the banter is flowing and the chemistry is obvious, don't let the momentum fizzle out. Say something like the following:

"I feel like this convo deserves to be continued over coffee — what's your schedule like?"

"Okay, you're too fun to just text. Let's grab a drink and see if you're this cool in person."

Tailored Texting That Matches Your Vibe

Texting is like a virtual first impression — why send generic messages when you can stand out by showcasing your unique flirty personality? Whether you're witty, nerdy, romantic, or effortlessly cool, your texts should reflect *you*. Ultimately, flirting is just saying something you like and connecting it back to the person you're interested in.

Here's how to tailor your messages to your vibe with examples that'll make your match smile, laugh, and hit reply instantly.

>> **The witty texter:** You're quick on your feet and love a clever comeback. For you, texting is a chance to show off your humor and keep the energy light and playful. For example:
- "So, what's your go-to karaoke song? No pressure, but your answer will determine if this conversation continues."
- "Quick question: If we were both in a zombie apocalypse, would you save me or steal my snacks?"

>> **The sweet romantic:** You're all about the charm and a touch of heartfelt emotion. Your texts leave people smiling and feeling a little extra special. For example:

- "I saw something today that reminded me of you . . . it was ridiculously cute."
- "I'm not saying you're the best part of my day, but I've definitely smiled more since we started talking."

>> **The adventurer:** You love life and want your match to feel that excitement. Your texts are full of energy and invitations to try something new. For example:

- "You seem like someone who could totally pull off axe throwing. Let's find out — what's your schedule this week?"
- "So, what's something wild you've always wanted to try? Asking for date inspiration . . ."

>> **The nerdy charmer:** You're smart, curious, and maybe a little obsessed with your favorite fandom or topic. Use your passions to connect in a fun and relatable way. For example:

- "Be honest — if we were both Hogwarts students, which house would you sort me into?"
- "I feel like this is the perfect time to ask: Marvel or DC? Your answer may lead to a heated debate, fair warning."

>> **The cool and mysterious:** You're effortlessly chill and keep things simple yet intriguing. You like to create a little mystery while keeping the vibe smooth. For example:

- "So, do I get to guess your favorite food, or are you going to save me the embarrassment?"
- "I was going to come up with a clever opening line, but you already seem like the kind of person who'd be fun to talk to."

>> **The deep thinker:** You thrive on meaningful conversations and enjoy getting to know someone on a deeper level. Your texts show genuine interest. For example:

- "What's one thing you're really passionate about that people wouldn't guess right away?"
- "If you could live anywhere in the world for a year, where would you go — and why?"

>> **The straightforward connector:** You don't like games, and you're all about being honest and direct while keeping things casual and kind. For example:

- "Hey, I've really enjoyed chatting — what do you think about grabbing coffee sometime soon?"

- "So, do we keep texting, or are we going to meet up and see if this banter is just as good in person?"

TIP

Want to make sure your texts match your vibe? Here's how:

- **Use your strengths.** If you're funny, lean into humor. If you're kindhearted, let that show.
- **Pay attention to their style.** Mirror their texting energy to build connection without losing your voice.
- **Be authentic.** Don't overthink it. The best texts sound natural and true to who you are.
- **Add personal touches.** Reference something unique from your conversations, whether it's a shared interest or a joke you've created together.

In-Person Flirting: Turning a Smile into a Date

Now that you've mastered the art of flirting on dating apps, it's time to log off, touch some grass (as the kids say), and bring that charm into the real world. IRL flirting? Whole different manual — but don't worry, I've got you.

Flirting is just yapping and seeing where it goes. It's as simple as that! Look for signs of interest through context clues such as eye contact and laughter at your jokes. When you see someone at a party, workout class, or group event, start by making eye contact and smiling. If they smile back and hold eye contact, that's your green light to make your way over. If it's someone you know or see often, kick things off with a compliment.

REMEMBER

Compliments create connection. Try something like "I love your blazer; where did you get it?" or "That drink looks amazing; what is it?" The key is a subtle compliment or a simple conversation starter. If they reply with one-word answers or seem closed-off, it's time to gracefully move on.

PART 2 Meeting Someone and Setting Up a Date

Flirting in the wild: Fun and playful examples for in-person encounters

Flirting in person isn't about rehearsed one-liners — it's about being present, playful, and charmingly bold (without veering into cringe territory). Whether you're at a coffee shop, a party, or randomly crossing paths with someone cute, here are some flirty examples to help you break the ice and keep things light and fun.

REMEMBER

It's less about what you say and more about how you deliver this, so make sure eye contact and relaxed welcoming energy is in full effect!

At the coffee shop

Spotted someone cute in line? Use your surroundings to spark a playful conversation.

Playful observation: "Wow, you're really committing to the triple-shot espresso. Should I be impressed or concerned?"

Teasing guess: "Let me guess . . . you're a latte person with extra foam? No? Okay, now you have to tell me."

At a party or event

Parties are perfect for casual banter — use the vibe of the event to connect.

Compliment with a twist: "You look way too cool to be at this party. Are you undercover, or am I just lucky to run into you?"

Shared experience: "This playlist is wild — do you think the DJ is secretly trying to ruin our night, or just has very questionable taste?"

When you're out and about

Random encounters at grocery stores, parks, or even waiting in line are prime flirting opportunities.

Playful comment: "I see you're eyeing the last loaf of sourdough. Do we need to battle it out, or are you going to share?"

Compliment their choices: "You've got great taste in [wine/snacks/etc.]. Is this your secret to impressing people?"

At a gym or fitness class

Flirting at the gym is tricky — keep it light and respectful.

Light tease: "Okay, you're making the rest of us look bad with that form. What's your secret?"

Ask for advice: "I'm trying to figure out this machine — any chance you're a personal trainer in disguise?"

At a bookstore or library

If you spot someone browsing the shelves, use their book choice as a conversation starter.

Book-based tease: "Ooh, that's a bold choice. Are you really into [genre], or are you just trying to look intellectual?"

Ask for a recommendation: "I've been looking for something good to read — do you have any life-changing suggestions, or should I keep wandering aimlessly?"

When walking a dog (yours or theirs)

Dogs are the ultimate conversation starters — use them to your advantage.

Dog compliment: "Your dog is adorable! Is it as well-behaved as it looks, or is this just a good moment?"

Light joke: "Okay, your dog clearly has better style than me. Where do you shop for them?"

When you're in a group setting

If you're in a group and want to focus on someone, make them feel special without being over the top.

Subtle attention: "I feel like you're the funniest person here. Care to prove me right?"

Call them out (playfully): "I noticed you've been holding back on the jokes — are you saving your best material for later?"

At a bar or social hangout

Bars are classic flirting grounds, so why not lean into the fun?

Drink-related flirt: "Okay, you just ordered the most sophisticated drink here. Should I be intimidated or ask you for recommendations?"

Direct but playful: "I was trying to come up with a clever way to say hi, but here we are. So . . . hi!"

Keeping the vibes going

Starting a conversation is one thing, but keeping the vibe alive is where the magic happens. Witty banter is key! I call this the "volleyball method": They share something, and you bounce back a connection. If they mention they love Greece, even if you haven't been, you can say, "Wow, it looks amazing! I've been dying to go. What's your favorite island?" This works for any topic — travel, food, activities. If they've been to a place or tried something you're curious about, casually mention, "We should check it out together sometime."

REMEMBER

People find you interesting when you show genuine interest in them. Listen actively, add to the conversation, and let them feel like the most fascinating person in the room. Show your charm without dominating the conversation. Don't fear a slight pause; sometimes, giving space allows them to contribute and keeps things feeling relaxed. If the conversation feels stilted, it could just be nerves or maybe a mismatch in energy — give it a little time to unfold.

Avoiding the interview trap

Instead of "What do you do for work?" try "What's something you're passionate about?" Instead of "What's your hobby?" go for "What's been exciting you lately?" When in doubt, ask questions and show genuine curiosity. Curiosity may have killed the cat, but it definitely won't kill the romantic vibe.

The playful roast method: Tease just enough to leave them wanting more

If the conversation is going well, a great way to keep the energy playful is by teasing them in a silly, lighthearted way. This shows that you're comfortable enough to laugh together and keeps things fun. The playful roast can work after you've shared a bit about each other, like favorite sports teams, interests, or TV shows.

For example:

> "Wow, coming from someone who thought the movie was *The Devil Wears Macy's* instead of Prada, I'm not sure I'll be trusting your fashion tips!"

> "Oh, you're a Yankees fan? After this season, you might be the last one left in the city."

A little teasing shows confidence, proving you're not intimidated and that you're willing to challenge them. Just remember to stay in the sweet spot of casual and fun — accidentally crossing the line and calling it flirting is never a good look. I learned this the hard way! One time, I thought this guy was super attractive, and he kept his hat on all night. I joked, "What's with the hat? Are you hiding a bald spot under there or something?" Turns out, he actually was bald. Oops!

REMEMBER

Stick to light topics and avoid personal or sensitive subjects like religion, race, or looks. Keeping it playful without getting too personal will keep the vibe just right.

QUICK ONE-LINERS FOR FLIRTING IN PERSON

Need something flirty but straight to the point? Here are ten one-liners to spark a conversation and keep the vibe light and fun:

"I was going to say something clever to impress you, but you're kind of distracting."

"Do you believe in love at first sight, or should I walk by again?"

"I don't usually approach strangers, but you looked like someone worth breaking the rules for."

"Are you always this charming, or is it just because I'm here?"

"You look like you know all the cool spots around here — care to share your secrets?"

"You look way too interesting to be standing here alone — what's your story?"

"I feel like we're vibing, but I'll need confirmation over coffee or drinks."

"Do you come here often, or is this just the universe being ridiculously kind to me today?"

"I noticed you from across the room and had to come over before I started overthinking it."

"Hi, I'm [Your Name]. What's your name, or should I just call you 'the highlight of my day?'"

Dipping out gracefully and securing the date

Flirting is all about building excitement, but knowing *when and how* to exit the conversation is the key to leaving them intrigued and wanting more. Think of it like a good cliffhanger — just enough mystery to keep them thinking about you, but no awkward overstay. Here's how to master the art of the graceful exit while seamlessly transitioning to securing the date. And yes, we're making it funny because flirting should be fun, not a corporate pitch.

Time it right — don't linger too long

There's a golden window in every flirtatious conversation where the vibe is at its peak. Leave too soon, and you seem disinterested. Stay too long, and you risk being *that person* who just won't walk away. The trick? Exit when the energy is high, and the banter is flowing. Think of it like leaving a party before the snacks run out.

What to say:

> "Okay, I've officially taken up way too much of your time, but this was fun."

> "I should let you get back to your [activity/errand], but I'm glad we chatted!"

Drop hints that say "date me" without spelling it out

Before you walk away, casually mention something that plants the seed for a future hangout. Subtlety is your friend here — don't hit them with "*So when are we getting married!?*"

Examples:

> "I've been dying to try that new sushi place downtown. Have you been yet?"

> "You seem like the type who'd be amazing at trivia — I could use a teammate sometime."

If they're into you, they'll pick up on the hint. If they're not . . . well, you're off the hook before things get awkward.

The contact test: Seal the deal smoothly

You've built the vibe, dropped the hints, and now it's time to transition to exchanging contact info without it feeling forced. The goal is to make it casual, like you're doing *them* a favor by staying in touch.

How to ask for their number:

> "You're fun — I feel like we'd have a good time grabbing [coffee/drinks]. Want to swap numbers?"

> "I'd hate for this conversation to be a one-time thing. What's the best way to keep in touch?"

If you're feeling bold:

> "Okay, I'm calling dibs on your next free evening. Let me get your number so I can prove I'm as cool in person as I am right now."

Social media move: If asking for a number feels too soon, go for Instagram or another platform:

> "Are you on Instagram? Let's connect there so I can send you that meme I mentioned."

End on a high note

Your exit should leave them smiling and excited to hear from you. Make it clear you're interested, but don't overdo it — let them imagine the next step.

Parting lines:

> "Well, I'll let you go, but I'm definitely going to hold you to trying that trivia night with me."

> "This was fun. Don't forget about that coffee — you owe me a drink now."

REMEMBER

Here's the secret: Everything you need to be good at flirting is already inside you. Flirting is just like a muscle — the more you use it, the stronger it gets. (And hey, unlike leg day, this is actually fun!) The key to being successful at flirting is knowing — *really knowing* — that you're an interesting, exciting person with a lot to share. But here's the twist: The best flirts aren't just talking about themselves — they're curious and genuinely interested in learning about others too.

FLIRTING IS ALL ABOUT LUCK AND LOCATION

You can't control who you'll meet, but you can control where you go and how often. Ideally, your chances of meeting someone like-minded will increase by going to places that genuinely interest you. If you love theater, join a theater group; if you're into ancient philosophy, join a study group; and if you're a clown at heart, well . . . join the circus and find your perfect juggling partner!

On the other hand, if you're a heavy drinker, maybe don't look for love in an AA meeting. And if you're all about fitness, try joining a running club instead of hitting the club every night. To up your chances of meeting the right person to flirt with, choose three of your favorite places that reflect your interests and go as often as possible. Establish a relationship with these places so that the people who work or organize there can play matchmaker. For example, if you frequent a favorite bar once a week, friendly Joey the bartender might help

(continued)

(continued)

introduce you to that cutie at the end of the bar in a much more natural way than a cold approach.

If you don't know someone, try positioning yourself in closer proximity to them while respecting their space. If there's an open seat next to your crush in a class, stop hiding in the back and take it! While I can't promise you'll start a conversation, I can promise you won't make any connection if they can't even see you.

When life gives you a little dating luck — like an empty seat next to someone interesting or a chance encounter in the grocery line — take it as a sign that you're in the right place at the right time. And if it's a situation where you may not see them again or it's a quick encounter, end the flirting by casually asking if they'd like to exchange info, whether that's Instagram or a phone number. That way, you can pick up where you left off digitally.

> **IN THIS CHAPTER**
>
> » Knowing where to find the best spots to meet IRL
>
> » Getting a little help from professional Cupids
>
> » Finding love on the go
>
> » Going on a solo date

Chapter 7
No Wi-Fi Needed: Where and How to Meet People in Person

If you've ever eavesdropped during happy hour (and let's be honest, who hasn't?), you've probably heard a group of friends lamenting how impossible it is to meet people in person anymore. They'll go on about how everyone is glued to their phones, swiping on apps, and how the old-school approach to dating feels as outdated as VHS tapes and dial-up internet.

The two real requirements for meeting people in person are simple:

- » You actually have to leave your house.
- » You need to be open to conversation.

We're all craving connection, but it takes a little courage and a lot less scrolling. This chapter shows you how to ditch your phone, embrace the wild unknown, and find someone who makes you feel a connection stronger than Wi-Fi.

CHAPTER 7 **No Wi-Fi Needed: Where and How to Meet People in Person** 69

Finding the Best Places to Be Single and Mingle

Whether you're a certified homebody or the life of the party, let's get one thing straight. If you're serious about getting a date, you can't keep doing the same things and expect different results. Think about it — how's that "grocery store to gym to Netflix" routine been working for you? Exactly. It's time to shake things up.

Meeting people isn't just about showing up — it's about showing up with purpose. My secret weapon? The Q&C method: Questions and Compliments. Start with a simple question ("What's that drink you ordered?") or toss out a compliment ("I love your sweater, even though it reminds me of my grandma's curtains — it totally works!"). It's playful, it's fun, and most importantly, it's a conversation starter.

TIFF SAYS

Prioritize going to the same places more than once. Your chances of meeting someone — and creating an opportunity to connect — increase dramatically when you become a familiar face. People are more likely to strike up a conversation or feel comfortable around someone they've seen a couple of times. So don't just try a new place once and write it off — make it a regular spot and watch the magic unfold as you bump into the same person more than once.

Now, let's talk about the best places to put this into action and start turning those familiar faces into real connections:

- **Run clubs:** I always say, never chase someone . . . unless you're in a running club. These are perfect for connecting with people while pretending you're not out of breath. And the best part? Many running clubs end with happy hours, giving you the chance to flirt over a beer instead of gasping for air after a 20-mile run.

- **The park, beach, hiking trail, or neighborhood stroll:** Bring your dog, your yoga mat, or just your sparkling personality. Parks are prime real estate for meeting someone who might share your fresh-air vibe. Bonus points if you "accidentally" drop your Frisbee near a cute stranger.

- **The gym:** Flirting at the gym can be tricky — sometimes it's more like I'm dying than I'm thriving. But if the opportunity strikes (like you're both waiting for the same machine or standing side by side on treadmills), casually admire their workout set or ask how to lift more than the baby weights (asking for a "friend," of course). Just keep it light — you're here to make gains, not give cringe.

» **The club, bars, and nightlife:** Finding love under a disco ball isn't impossible — it just takes the right moves (both on and off the dance floor). Sure, there are plenty of people just looking for a good time, but if you're all about the nightlife, it's a great way to meet someone who matches your energy. Channel your inner Saturday Night Fever and find your dance partner!

TIFF SAYS

Pick a bar, club, or social spot where you can get to know the staff. Your bartender can double as your matchmaker. If you're a regular, they probably know the other regulars who'd vibe with you. It's like having your own personal Cupid behind the counter, and they're armed with cocktails and insider knowledge! Let them work their magic while you focus on your killer dance moves (or just trying not to spill your drink).

» **Church (or your spiritual home):** Whether it's Sunday service, hot yoga, or that "community group" that feels suspiciously cultlike but is full of hot, nice people, spiritual spaces are amazing for meeting like-minded singles. Plus, there's nothing sexier than shared values (and a cute downward dog).

» **Take a class (French cooking, painting, salsa dancing — anything):** Nothing says "potential soulmate" like chasing a goal you've been putting off for years and meeting someone who's doing the same. Whether it's learning to whip up a perfect soufflé or nailing your two-step, you'll bond over shared experiences and mutual awkwardness. Who knows? You might just end the class with a chef's kiss — both literally and figuratively.

» **Leagues (softball, dodgeball, poker — whatever floats your boat):** Joining a league is like hitting the social jackpot. You'll see the same people regularly, which makes it easier to connect. Plus, there's nothing more flirty than mock outrage when someone beats you at dodgeball.

» **Coffee shops:** Coffee shops are romantic classics for a reason. Grab your latte, compliment someone's laptop stickers, or ask what they're reading. Let the flirtation brew while you both wait for that soy foam to finish forming.

>> **Bookstores and learning collectives:** Who doesn't love pretending to be mysterious while holding a book you've only read two pages of? Bookstores and literary events are perfect for meeting people who appreciate a good story — and who knows, you might just start writing one of your own.

>> **Volunteering:** What's hotter than making the world a better place *and* meeting someone with a heart of gold? Whether you're rescuing puppies, planting trees, or handing out meals, volunteering is a prime spot to connect with like-minded, compassionate people. Plus, "We met while saving kittens" is a way better love story than "We matched on Hinge during my lunch break."

REMEMBER Finding someone special doesn't have to be complicated — or involve endless scrolling. Whether you're chasing goals in a cooking class, saving the world through volunteering, or just making small talk over coffee, the magic happens when you show up, stay present, and let things unfold. Your next connection might be closer than you think.

Choosing the Best Professional Cupids

At this point, *everyone* is trying to set you up — the deli guy knows a "nice nephew," your Uber driver's got a cousin who "just got out of a situation," and even your mom is stopping strangers in Trader Joe's like it's a casting call. Here's how to choose your matchmaker *wisely* (because not everyone with a pulse and a plus-one is your soulmate).

Finding your match(maker)

Now, I know you've got a whole lineup of self-appointed matchmakers in your life. Your aunt, for example, who starts every holiday dinner with "Why are you still single?" before launching into how she met a "great catch" in the produce aisle who just happens to be perfect for you. While family matchmaking is a national pastime, there's also a whole world of professional matchmakers and firms out there, claiming to be able to find you your dream person. Beware, though — some of these online matchmakers will promise you a soulmate and leave you with nothing but heartbreak and a maxed-out credit card.

Matchmaking can work wonders. I've personally matchmade over 100 people, and let me tell you, sometimes it takes someone outside your bubble to see the bigger picture. A good matchmaker listens to what you think you want while sneakily introducing you to what you actually need. It's like dating therapy — because let's face it, even surgeons can't perform surgery on themselves, and therapists need therapists. Sometimes, you just need a coach to help you navigate the wild world of ghosting, catfishing, and exes who still watch your Instagram stories.

If you're considering a matchmaker, shop around like you're on *Love Island*. Find someone who vibes with your personality and isn't draining your bank account faster than your last Bumble premium subscription. Matchmakers can be especially helpful if you're looking for something specific, like a shared religion, culture, or community. From Jewish matchmakers to Indian matchmakers, they're like human dating apps but with actual effort and no algorithms involved.

TIP: Think of it this way: Instead of wasting hours Googling "[Insert Religion Here] Singles Near Me" or enduring another awkward "maybe he'll text back" situation, matchmakers do all the legwork. They sift through the sea of potential partners, filter out the flakes, and present you with the cream of the crop. All you have to do is show up, sip your cocktail, and see if sparks fly. It's dating with a personal assistant — a luxury and, let's be honest, a relief.

Speed dating: Rapid-fire romance?

Now, with the merging of social media and our primal desire for IRL connections, speed dating has gotten a major glow-up. And no, I'm not talking about your grandma's speed dating, with awkward name tags in a church basement that felt more like Singles Anonymous than Eligible Partner Central. These days, there are apps and events that take over the hottest restaurants in the city, give you a killer ambiance, and let the sparks fly from there.

I'm a big fan of speed dating because, even if you don't walk away with a match, it's like a bootcamp for your confidence. You learn how to talk about yourself under pressure (and not sound like you're pitching a *Shark Tank* product), meet new people, and remember that, yes, good single people do exist. Boiling your entire personality down to five minutes isn't easy — it's basically a dating app bio in real life — but it's a great push to get yourself out there. Plus, even if you don't find "the one," you'll probably get some great stories.

Once, I went to a speed dating event where, at the end, you wrote down who you wanted to see again, and the company texted you if it was a match. Spoiler: I didn't get a match. But you know what I did get? Clarity. I realized a lot about what I want — and definitely don't want — in a romantic partner. Sometimes, you don't get a date, but you do get data. And that's basically a speed pass to skipping all the people who will waste your time.

TIP If you've been out of the dating game for a while, I cannot recommend speed dating enough. Why wait around for a chance when there's a fast track to connection? Who knows, you might just find "the one" in five minutes — or at least a solid lead for a second date.

Blind dates and asking your friends to set you up

Asking your friends to play Cupid can feel as awkward as trying to parallel park while everyone's watching, but honestly, why not give it a shot? If your friends love you (and they'd better if you're calling them friends), they should be more than willing to help you find love. It's a simple numbers game: The squeaky wheel gets the oil. How is anyone supposed to know you're looking for love if all you do is complain that "there are no good singles left" instead of actually strategizing and using your network?

It might feel awkward, but asking for help is not a sign of weakness. A simple "Hey, do you know anyone cool from work or that art class you're in? Also, what's the deal with your brother's hot friend from fantasy football night?" can go a long way. Guys, this works for you, too. A casual "Does your sister have any single friends?" or "What about that girl you were talking to at trivia night — does she have a friend for me?" is all it takes to plant the seed. You've got to approach this like trying to get on the guest list for the hottest party in town — be bold, confident, and just annoying enough that people pay attention. Chances are, your friends have connections they wouldn't have thought about until you asked.

WARNING

That said, proceed with caution when it comes to being set up with people too close to your friends — like their siblings, bosses, or anyone who's going to show up at Thanksgiving dinner. If things go sideways, you don't want to be the reason the holiday gravy gets awkward. But all in all, getting your besties involved in your dating life is one of the easiest ways to fix the mess without diving headfirst into yet another app. Plus, who better to help you find love than the people who already love you (and are also tired of hearing you complain about being single)?

Passport to Connection: Finding Love in New Places

People often think they're the problem when, honestly, the real issue might be their location. Every city has a culture, a vibe, and its own beauty standards — not to mention its preferred hobbies and lifestyles. It's not that you can't find love outside of the norm, but let's be real: If you're a city person who thrives on late nights at martini bars and Broadway shows, you're probably not going to vibe with a small-town scene where beer and bull riding reign supreme. On the flip side, if your idea of a good time is horseback riding and tending to your organic veggie garden, you're not exactly going to swoon over someone who thinks "getting into nature" means a rooftop party with bottle service.

So ask yourself: Do you actually like where you live? Do you vibe with the culture? Can you see yourself building a life with the kind of people you've met there? If the answer is a resounding no, it might be time to shake things up. And by shake things up, I mean pack your bags — or at least fire up Tinder Passport — and start exploring new horizons.

If you can't hop on a plane just yet, go digital. Tinder Passport lets you match with people anywhere in the world — Paris? Tokyo? A small Swiss village with hot farmers? The possibilities are endless. And if you can book a trip, why not go to that city you've always daydreamed about living in? Who knows, you might leave the baggage of your current city behind and find someone who makes you want to unpack and stay awhile.

REMEMBER: Sometimes, love isn't about changing who you are — it's about changing where you are. So whether it's a weekend getaway or a one-way ticket, the right location might just lead you to the right person. Because let's face it, your soulmate is probably not stuck in the same traffic jam you've been cursing for years. Time to change your scenery and maybe even your love story!

Mastering the Art of the Solo Date

A simple trick that can often lead you to a date? Taking yourself out on a date. Yep, just you. No entourage, no hype squad, and definitely no paparazzi — unless you count the random guy at the bar who keeps snapping pics of his martini. Society has convinced us that being alone in public is somehow tragic, like you've been shunned and forced into exile. But guess what? That mindset needs to go. Taking yourself out solo isn't embarrassing — it's bold, it's confident, and honestly, it's a great way to find someone who matches your vibe.

Start with places you feel comfortable. Bring a book to your neighborhood coffee shop and casually glance up (bonus points if it's from behind glasses you don't even need). Hit up that swanky hotel bar with the $20 peanuts — why not? Or treat yourself to that restaurant with the world's best mac and cheese that's allegedly meant for two. Who cares if you eat the whole thing by yourself? You deserve it.

REMEMBER: Here's the thing: If you want to find someone who's into you for you, you've got to stop worrying about what strangers think. No one's judging you for sipping a cocktail solo — they're too busy deciding if they have room for dessert. If you want to meet people in real life, it might be time to cut the safety net of the 20-person group chat and take a solo night on the town. Who knows? You might just discover that the best company you can bring to the table is your own — and maybe someone amazing will want to join you there.

IN THIS CHAPTER

» Navigating whether to make the first move

» Overcoming nerves and just going for it

» Asking someone out in person

» Asking someone out digitally

» Making sure the person is really someone you should date

» Declining a date with grace and kindness

Chapter **8**
How to Ask for or Reject a Date Invitation

The only thing more stressful than going on a date is wondering if someone actually wants to date you. It's a tale as old as time: "They love me, they love me not . . ." except now it's more like, "Will they DM me, or should I just shoot my shot?"

Similarly, we spend what feels like centuries crushing on someone — analyzing their every move, wondering if they like us, hate us, or even know we exist. We build them up in our minds as mythical Greek gods: impossibly beautiful, unattainable, and completely out of our league. Instead of wasting your precious time wondering, go find out — and all that fear and questioning will vanish just as fast as the last person who ghosted you.

The only thing worse than being rejected is rejecting yourself and never getting an answer. In this chapter, you'll learn that the worst thing they can say is "no," and it's better to hear that than to spend your life wondering what could have been.

We'll dive into all the ways you can ask someone out and how to gracefully accept (or extend) a date invitation. We'll talk about getting over rejection, figuring out the perfect time and place to ask someone out — whether digitally or in person — and even explore when a crush might be better left as a fantasy (yes, that includes co-workers, close friends, or, gasp, your best friend's ex).

By the end of this chapter, you'll spend less time worrying if they like you and more time planning the perfect date ahead of you!

Should You Make the First Move?

No magical love story begins with two people sitting silently in their respective corners, waiting for the other to make a move. Vulnerability is the price of admission for dating, and yes, it's risky. But like gamblers might say, the bigger the risk, the bigger the reward. And when it comes to dating, the reward is literally the only thing that can happen. Think about it: You didn't have that person in your life yesterday, so what's the harm in trying to get to know them today? The worst-case scenario is rejection, but the best case? A chance at something great. You miss 100 percent of the shots you don't take, and you'll definitely never kiss your crush if they're living in your head rent-free.

Navigating who should ask who out first

This age-old question has been debated longer than whether a hot dog is technically a sandwich. For centuries, women waited around, hoping someone would give them the affection they needed, while men agonized over whether she was just being nice or actually liked them. And let's not even get started on non-heteronormative relationships — first, you have to figure out their sexuality, and then take the leap of finding out if they're into *you*. It's like a romantic game of Clue with no instructions.

Here's the deal: There's no one-size-fits-all rule about who should make the first move, and the regret of *not* talking to that cute person on the subway or your pottery class crush will haunt you way longer than the sting of rejection. (Seriously, rejection fades, but regret? That's the emotional equivalent of gum stuck on your shoe — hard to get rid of and always annoying.)

IF THEY WANTED TO . . . WOULD THEY REALLY?

Ah, the infamous *if they wanted to, they would* — the mantra that's launched a thousand group chat debates. Sure, in an ideal world, everyone would be bold, clear, and straightforward. But guess what? We live in the real world, where people overthink, second-guess, and sometimes chicken out harder than a middle schooler at their first slow dance. The truth is, waiting for someone to make the first move because "if they wanted to, they would" is like assuming a pizza will show up at your door just because you're hungry — sometimes, you've got to pick up the phone and order it yourself. People have their own insecurities and fears of rejection, and while their hesitance might not mean they're not interested, it does mean you're stuck in a staring contest of *who blinks first.* So why not break the stalemate? If you're interested, make the move — you've got nothing to lose and maybe everything to gain.

When's too long to ask someone out?

If you've been waiting for someone to make the first move and it's starting to feel like you're in a Shakespearean tragedy, it's time to channel your inner risk-taker. For strangers, a compliment or a simple "Hey, what are you reading?" works wonders. If you want to level up with someone you know, invite them to that new trendy restaurant or casually suggest seeing a show together.

Bottom line? Stop waiting for Cupid to hit them with an arrow or for their phone to magically text you back. Life is too short to wonder "what if?" Risk it, ask them out, and worst case? You get clarity. Best case? You get love. And isn't that worth the gamble?

WARNING
The longer you wait to ask someone out, the more you risk becoming their go-to "person they talk to when their real crush isn't responding." Yikes.

If you've been strategizing for weeks, waiting for the perfect moment, here's the hard truth: The perfect moment doesn't exist. Life isn't a rom-com where everything aligns, the music swells, and they magically realize you're "The One." If you've been rehearsing your one-liners and stalking their Instagram like it's a full-time job, take a deep breath and just ask them out already. Because waiting too long? That's how you go from potential love interest to "Oh yeah, I forgot about them" in the blink of an eye.

Nerves and Courage: How to Be Nervous and Do It Anyway

You can be scared out of your mind and still have the courage to ask someone out. Because courage isn't the absence of fear — it's doing the thing even when you're terrified.

So, how do you build that courage? Here are some tips:

- » **Reframe rejection.** Instead of treating rejection like it's a personal attack (it's not), think of it as a game of "matchmaking roulette." Sometimes it's a hit, sometimes it's a miss. And that's okay. It's literally not about you — it's about the vibe, the timing, the universe, or maybe they just really don't enjoy pineapple as much as you do. You'll never know, and that's fine. Once you accept that not everyone is going to like you, you can be free to know you like you and find others that do. Just because one person doesn't want to be with you *does not* mean that nobody wants to be with you.

- » **Be your own cheerleader.** When those nerves start creeping in, fight back with some self-compassion. Would you talk to your best friend the way you talk to yourself when you're nervous? No? Then stop being mean to yourself! It's normal to feel shaky. You're stepping outside your comfort zone, and that's a big deal. So take a moment to tell yourself: "I'm funny, cool, and why wouldn't someone want to be with someone as legendary as me!" Nerves are a sign that you're growing, not failing.

- » **Preparation is key.** Okay, okay, I'm not saying you need to rehearse your lines like you're auditioning for a blockbuster film, but having a simple plan can help calm your nerves. Something like "Hey, I really enjoy hanging out with you. Would you want to grab coffee sometime?" Keep it short, sweet, and simple. You don't need to win an Oscar for this — it's just a date, not a TED Talk.

>> **Own it like a pro.** Once you've asked them out, the hard part is done. Seriously. After that, it's just a matter of sitting back and letting fate take over. If they say yes, awesome! If they say no, no sweat — just keep your cool and smile like you're the most charming human on Earth. Because, guess what? You are.

>> **Remember that it's not the end of the world.** When you put yourself out there, you're testing the waters. Will you get a yes? Maybe. Will you get a no? Maybe. But either way, the world keeps turning. You're not going to drop off the planet if someone says, "thanks but no thanks." You're still you, and that's *more than enough*. If you didn't ask, you'd never know.

How to Smoothly Ask Someone Out on a Date in Person

There isn't one perfect way to ask someone out, and not every attempt will go the same. But with a few tips, you can make the process way less nerve-racking — no matter the relationship or context. Here's how to navigate the art of the ask:

1. **Start with eye contact.**

   Eye contact is your secret weapon. I always say, the best way to get a glimpse at your future is to glance at the person you think is cute. If they meet your gaze and smile or give any sign of acknowledgment, that's your green light to approach. It's simple, natural, and it shows confidence without saying a word.

2. **Keep it contextual.**

   When you start the conversation, let the setting or shared activity guide you. This makes the interaction feel natural and less like a random leap of faith. If you're both at a bookstore, a gym, or a coffee shop, use your surroundings to your advantage. (See the nearby sidebar for more on what to say versus what *not* to say.)

SAY THIS, NOT THAT

You wanna keep it smooth, not cringe or creepy. Here's a quick guide to what to say versus what *not* to say:

What to Say	What Not to Say
"I noticed you like [specific thing]. Would you want to check out [related activity] together sometime?"	"You're hot. Want to go out?"
"I saw you picking up [item]. That's my favorite! Want to grab a coffee and chat about it?"	"Do you believe in love at first sight?"
"Wow, you're killing it in this [class/run/workout]! Would you ever want to team up?"	"You're so strong. Can you bench me?"
"I overheard you talking about [topic]. I'm into that too. Want to grab a drink and share recommendations?"	"Hey. You're cute. Let's date."

3. **Be light and playful.**

    The key to a successful approach is keeping the tone fun and low-pressure. Think of it as inviting them into a conversation, not issuing a life-or-death challenge. A little humor or creativity goes a long way. For example:

    - **At a bookstore:** "So are you team Hemingway or Fitzgerald? Because if you're a Fitzgerald fan, I might need to buy you a coffee to talk you out of it."
    - **At the gym:** "You make this look way too easy. Any chance you'd be up for showing me your secret workout routine over a smoothie sometime?"
    - **At a coffee shop:** "Okay, so you're clearly the kind of person who knows how to order coffee. Want to join me in my quest to find the city's best latte?"

4. **Avoid aggressive or pressuring energy.**

    Confidence is attractive, but aggression is not. You want the person to feel excited about the idea, not trapped into it. Keep the interaction casual and respectful, and always be ready to gracefully accept a no. If they hesitate or politely decline, respond with something like "No worries, it was nice chatting with you anyway!" and leave it at that.

5. **Know when to walk away.**

   Not every attempt will lead to a date, and that's okay! If they're giving one-word answers, avoiding eye contact, or looking like they're just trying to escape, take the hint and move on. Walking away with grace is just as important as making the ask.

REMEMBER

Timing is key when asking someone out. You don't want to shoot your shot while they're stressed, frantic, or dealing with life's chaos. Instead, you want to catch someone when their "cab light" is on — when they're open to connecting. Think relaxed environments, like after striking up a fun conversation at an improv class, a concert, or a cozy café. That's when you naturally integrate your ask, like "This was fun. Want to grab a drink sometime?" It feels effortless and not like you've been rehearsing in your head for hours.

How to Ask Out a Friend or Colleague Without Making It Awkward

Getting out of the friend zone can feel as impossible as trying to put together IKEA furniture without an instruction manual. And asking your cubicle crush on a date? That's basically Fear Factor: Office Edition. Why is it so intimidating? Because unlike a cute stranger on the street, this person already knows you. And you like them for more than just the romantic fantasy — they've made it past the first round of "could we actually get along?" auditions. But don't worry — it's totally doable, and I'm here to help.

Here are some different approaches you can take:

>> **The "test the waters" approach:** Before diving into full-on date mode, start by gauging their interest in hanging out one-on-one. Casually suggest something low-stakes that doesn't scream "Date!" but opens the door for quality time together.

Example: "Hey, I saw that new [movie/restaurant/event] is happening this weekend. Want to check it out together?"

Why it works: It's casual, nonthreatening, and gives you a chance to feel out their vibe.

» **The compliment and pivot:** Drop a genuine compliment to let them know you see them in a different light, then smoothly pivot to an invitation.

Example: "You have such a good sense of humor — it's one of my favorite things about you. We should grab a drink sometime. I think we'd have a lot of fun."

Why it works: It shows you've noticed something specific about them and sets a positive tone for asking them out.

» **The nostalgia trick:** If you've already had a great time together in a group setting, use that to your advantage.

Example: "Remember how much fun we had at [event]? We should totally re-create that — just us this time."

Why it works: It draws on a shared positive experience and makes the idea of spending time together feel natural.

» **The "help me out" gambit:** Ask them to join you for something that aligns with their interests or strengths.

Example: "You're always talking about how much you love [activity/hobby]. Want to show me the ropes this weekend? I could use a pro."

Why it works: People love sharing their passions, and it gives them an excuse to say yes without overthinking it.

» **The playful roast:** If you already have an easygoing, banter-filled dynamic, lean into it with a playful challenge.

Example: "Okay, you clearly think you're the [board game/coffee/snack] expert. Let's put it to the test — winner buys the loser dinner."

Why it works: It keeps things light and fun while sneaking in a casual date idea.

» **The direct approach:** Sometimes, the best way is just to go for it. Be honest and straightforward — no gimmicks, no tricks. Just you shooting your shot and letting them know your feelings.

Example: "I really enjoy spending time with you, and I think we'd have fun on a date. What do you think?"

Why it works: It's clear, respectful, and gives them space to respond without pressure.

> **The shared hobby setup:** If you share a hobby or regular activity, use that as a launching pad for something more personal.
>
> **Example:** "We always have so much fun at [hobby or class], Want to grab a drink after next time? I'd love to hang out outside of [context]."
>
> **Why it works:** It's an easy transition from something familiar to something new.

TIFF SAYS

Always remember: The goal isn't to walk away with a date *every* time. The goal is to show confidence, be respectful, and leave them with a positive impression. Whether they say yes or no, you've succeeded just by putting yourself out there.

How to Ask Someone Out Digitally

Dating apps are just the starting line, not the finish. The goal is to move the conversation from digital to real life before you turn into a pen pal. So don't overthink it — be bold, make your move, and remember that they swiped right for a reason.

TIP

A great way to ask someone out is to mention a restaurant, bar, or activity you like and ask if they've tried it. If they show interest, invite them to do it together. Keep it casual and conversational — it's not a marriage proposal! Also, and this is crucial: Move the conversation to texting ASAP. Staying in the app too long increases your risk of being forgotten or lost in their sea of matches. Nobody wants to be "Oh yeah, I meant to reply to them" material.

When I first moved to New York, I was *so* over the endless cycle of boring small talk on dating apps. You know the type: "Hey, how's your day going?" "Good, you?" Riveting stuff. I decided to take matters into my own hands and break free from the small-talk purgatory. At the time, I had about ten matches, so I sent them all the same message:

> "Hey, I'm on a mission to find the best hot chocolate in the city. Want to join me? I'm going [insert date here]."

And guess what? Over 50 percent said yes. Not only did I end up on some really fun in-person dates, but I also found some of the sweetest hot chocolate (and met some pretty sweet guys) along the way. Moral of the story? Sometimes all it takes is ditching the small talk and inviting someone to drink hot cocoa with you. Bold moves pay off — especially when there are sweet treats involved.

This approach works for just about anything — a movie that just hit theaters, your favorite band, or even a modern art museum filled with pieces you'll pretend to understand while secretly Googling what "postmodernism" means. Just throw out an activity and see what sticks. You'd be surprised — most people are just as excited as you are to break free from their screens and have some actual in-person connection.

Once you've matched, aim to schedule a date within two weeks of talking — the sooner, the better. Why? Because the longer you wait, the more likely you are to build a fantasy version of them in your head, only to find out they're the total opposite. You have no time to waste dreaming; you need to go out and find your person in real life.

REMEMBER

Make your invitation specific and time-bound. Instead of the classic "We should hang out some time," try "How about drinks this Thursday at [specific place]?" It shows initiative, and — let's be real — nothing says "I'm serious about meeting you" like having an actual plan that doesn't involve vague, wishy-washy timelines. You're not scheduling a dentist appointment; you're asking someone out!

The rejections you face today will eventually become the funny stories you tell your friends over brunch. And who knows? By the end of this book, you might need a calendar app to keep track of how thriving your dating life is.

When should you take your digital relationship into the real world?

Dating apps are great for matching, chatting, and exchanging witty banter, but at some point you need to move the relationship from swipes to something that doesn't involve a screen. So how do you know when it's time to ask them out? Well, let me save you from spending another week debating whether their "LOL" actually means they like you or if they're just polite. Here's how to tell when it's time to make your move — and some tips to ensure the timing is just right:

- **You've got the banter going strong.** If you've been chatting for 48 hours or more and the conversation is flowing like a Netflix binge with no awkward pauses, it's a green light. You've shared some laughs, exchanged fun facts about your favorite TV shows or brunch spots, and maybe even discussed something deeper than "What's your favorite color?" If they're matching your energy and the jokes are flying, it's time to suggest meeting in person.

  Pro-tip: Look for signs that they're genuinely engaged — like thoughtful replies, follow-up questions, or playful teasing. If their messages feel curated and not just as generic as a spam email, you're golden.

- **Responses are prompt and enthusiastic.** If they're responding to your messages faster than you can swipe right again, that's a major win. Bonus points if their responses aren't just one-word answers. (Because let's be real, no one has time for "hey" or "cool." We're looking for *substance* here, people.) If their texts have effort behind them — think emojis, full sentences, and maybe even GIFs — they're showing interest and investment.

  Pro-tip: If you've sent a meme and they replied with a meme of equal or greater value, that's a soulmate move. Plan the date.

- **There's a shared activity coming up.** If there's something happening that aligns with their interests (or yours), like a new movie release, a trivia night, or a seasonal activity (pumpkin patches, anyone?), use that as an icebreaker to suggest meeting up. "Hey, I saw there's an outdoor market this weekend — want to check it out?" is way smoother than "Wanna hang out?"

  Pro-tip: Be specific with your date idea. Instead of the vague "Let's hang out some time," give them a clear plan. People love confidence and clarity.

- **You've moved beyond the app.** If you're chatting on the app and it's going well, suggest moving to texting or another platform like Instagram. Why? It's not just about making communication easier — it also helps you confirm they're a real person. Plus, following each other on social media lets you get a sneak peek into their life, interests, and *possibly* their pet (a bonus if you're a dog lover).

Pro-tip: Social media stalking is fine — *light stalking*. Don't go five years deep into their Instagram and accidentally like a photo from 2018. That's not a "cute oops"; that's a "call the cops."

- **They're dropping hints.** Pay attention to whether they're hinting at meeting up. Comments like "I've been wanting to check out that new bar" or "This would be so much fun to do in person" are basically invitations. Don't overthink it — take the hint and suggest a date.

Pro-tip: If they've mentioned their favorite food or hobby, use it to plan the date. For example, "You mentioned you love sushi — want to try that new place downtown?" Personalizing your date idea shows you're paying attention.

- **They're actually available.** If they're consistently responding, showing interest, and actively engaging in conversation, they're likely open to meeting. On the flip side, if their responses are sporadic, filled with "Sorry, I've been busy," or so dry you feel like you're texting a robot, it might be time to reevaluate.

Pro-tip: If they cancel plans once but reschedule immediately, that's fine. If they're constantly dodging the idea of meeting up, move on — you deserve someone who's excited to meet you.

- **Trust your gut.** If everything's clicking and you feel ready, trust your instincts. Don't let fear hold you back. The worst that happens? They say they're not ready yet, and you move on. But if they're matching your vibe and seem genuinely interested, there's a good chance they'll be thrilled you asked.

PROS AND CONS OF A ZOOM/FaceTime PRE-DATE

Jumping on a Zoom or FaceTime before a first date can feel like a mini audition, but it's not without its perks. On the plus side, it's a great way to confirm that your match is, in fact, a real human being and not a 2015 photo of someone who vaguely resembles Chris Evans. You also get to gauge their vibe — are they charming, funny, or one of those people who breathes too heavily into the mic? And let's not forget, you can do all of this from the comfort of your couch, rocking sweatpants and strategically hiding the pile of laundry behind your laptop.

But here's the downside: Video calls can sometimes be painfully awkward. Your Wi-Fi might freeze at the exact moment you're making a weird face, or you'll spend half the call wondering if they're judging your plant that's clearly dying in the background. Plus, too much chatting before the date can kill the excitement of meeting in person — like when you accidentally watch all the movie trailers and feel like you've already seen the whole film.

Bottom line: A pre-date call can help you filter out the weirdos, but if the idea makes you cringe, skip it and dive straight into the real thing (with safety precautions, of course).

From screen to reality: Ensuring a safe first offline date

Meeting someone IRL for the first time can feel like walking into the unknown, but there are plenty of ways to make sure you stay safe, smart, and *actually able* to focus on whether they're as cool as their profile suggests. The following sections offer some pro-tips to keep your heart protected — and your body out of sketchy situations.

Verify they're a real human being

First things first, make sure your date is actually who they say they are. Catfishing isn't just a plotline for bad TV — it's a real thing. How can you tell?

>> **Ask for their social media.** No, you're not stalking, you're investigating. A quick glance at their Instagram or LinkedIn can confirm that they're a legitimate person and not a cardboard cutout of someone else's life. Bonus points if they have actual friends commenting on their posts.

>> **Do a video chat first.** Suggest a quick FaceTime or Zoom before the date. Not only does this confirm they're not a scam artist using photos from Google Images, but it also helps ease those first-date nerves. Plus, it's a great way to make sure their "6'2" profile claim isn't more of a *creative interpretation*.

CHAPTER 8 How to Ask for or Reject a Date Invitation   89

Meet in a public place

I don't care how amazing their playlist is or how much they say their dog would love you — you are not meeting them at their house for date one. Public places are nonnegotiable.

Choose a coffee shop, a busy bar, or a well-lit restaurant where there are plenty of people around. Worst-case scenario, if they're not your vibe, you can order something delicious and politely escape.

WARNING

If they suggest a "chill" first date at their apartment? Nope. Politely redirect to a neutral spot, or just unmatch them. We're here for safety, not Netflix and bad decisions.

Tell someone where you're going

Your friends aren't just for hyping you up before the date — they're your safety net. Text a trusted friend where you're going, who you're meeting (yes, include their name, photo, and any app profile info), and what time you expect to be back.

TIP

Use apps like Find My Friends or Life360 to share your location in real time. Sure, it feels a little extra, but isn't it better to have your BFF tracking you than starring in a *Dateline* special?

Set up a backup plan

Sometimes you just need an escape route — whether it's because the vibe is off or they're giving you major red-flag energy. Here's what to do:

>> **Have a fake emergency text ready.** Enlist a friend to call you with a "sudden crisis" if things go south. Something like, "Oh no, your goldfish is having an existential crisis? I'll be right there!"

>> **Trust your gut.** If you're feeling uneasy, don't worry about being polite. Excuse yourself, call a ride, and get out. Your safety is more important than their feelings.

Don't rely on them for transportation

Having control over your own arrival and departure is key. Drive yourself, take public transit, or use a ride-share app to get there. If things go sideways, you don't want to be stuck waiting for them to "drop you off."

ASKING OUT SOMEONE WHO ALREADY LIKES YOU

So, you know someone likes you — congrats! You're already halfway there, but let's not blow it. Here's how to handle it like a pro (and not a walking rom-com disaster):

- **Crush check-in.** Before you make a move, ask the million-dollar question: *Do I actually like them, or am I just flattered by their undying love for me?* If it's the latter, don't fake a romance just because you love the idea of a personal hype person or you're lonely. If you do like them, great! Proceed to step two.
- **Keep it simple; you're not Shakespeare.** You don't need to recite a sonnet or orchestrate a flash mob to ask them out. They already like you — this isn't a sales pitch; save the PowerPoint presentation for school. Something like, "Hey, I really enjoy hanging out with you. Want to make it official and grab dinner?" works well.
- **Have a game plan.** Don't just hit them with "Let's hang out sometime." Be specific — this isn't a mystery novel. You don't want your future date feeling like Nancy Drew trying to figure out when they will see you.
- **Play it cool.** Remember, this isn't a marriage proposal. Keep the tone light and fun. The key to attraction is showing you desire them but that you are not desperate for them.

> **TIP:** If you're using a ride-share app, let a friend know when you're headed home and track your trip. Some apps even let you share your ride details with others, which is a bonus.

Proceed with Caution: Should You Ask This Person Out?

When it comes to dating, the stakes can feel high — especially when the person you're eyeing is carrying emotional baggage, going through big life changes, or happens to share your office printer. Before you ask someone out, take a moment to check for potential risks. While there's no way to predict every outcome, doing a little due diligence can save you from unnecessary drama (and a lot of awkward small talk later).

Emotional baggage check: Are they really ready?

If they've recently escaped the fiery wreckage of a breakup or are navigating a major life change (new job, family drama, a move across the country), it's worth asking: Are they emotionally available, or are you about to board a roller coaster with no seatbelt? Sure, everyone has baggage, but there's a difference between a cute carry-on and a 15-piece luggage set.

Tips:

- Ask open-ended questions like "What are you looking for right now?" If they respond with something vague like "I'm just going with the flow," that's your cue to tread carefully.
- Pay attention to how they talk about their ex. If their ex's name comes up more than their own hobbies, you may want to pause and reassess.

Baggage check: Are lingering issues going to derail you?

Nobody's perfect, but lingering issues can weigh down your shiny new potential relationship. Whether it's unresolved drama with an ex, financial instability, or life chaos, it's worth doing a little investigative work before committing to a first date.

Tips:

- Look for red flags in their conversations: Are they constantly talking about "complicated situations" or do they seem like their life is one long cliffhanger?
- Trust your gut. If they seem chaotic in their texts, they'll probably bring that chaos to your life too.

Goal alignment: Do your futures even match?

Before you swipe right on someone's life, ask yourself: Do their career ambitions, life goals, and general plans line up with yours? If you're dreaming of a quiet life in the suburbs and they're planning to backpack through Europe for the next five years, it's worth reconsidering.

Tips:

> » Early conversations can reveal a lot. If they mention that their five-year plan includes living out of a van and yours involves kids and a mortgage, don't ignore the signs.
>
> » Compatibility doesn't mean being identical, but there should be some overlap in your big-picture goals.

Single status: Are they really unattached?

This one's a no-brainer, but you'd be surprised how many people forget to confirm it. Before you get too emotionally invested, make sure they're not still entangled in a relationship or using dating apps as a coping mechanism.

Tips:

> » Subtly ask about their dating history, something like "When was your last relationship?" can be a smooth way to find out if they're actually single.
>
> » Social media can be your friend (but don't go full FBI). Look for red flags like mysterious "best friend" tags or too many couple-y photos with no explanations.

Cubicle Cupids: The risks of dating in shared spaces

Dating someone in your office, apartment building, or other shared space might sound convenient, but it comes with its own unique set of risks. If things go south, you could end up avoiding the break room — or awkwardly bumping into them every time you check your mail.

Tips:

> » Before diving in, ask yourself, "If this doesn't work out, will it make my life miserable?"

» Keep it discreet in the early stages. Don't broadcast your potential romance to co-workers or neighbors until you're sure it's going somewhere.

» Be prepared to handle the fallout professionally or politely if things don't work out.

How to Delicately Decline a Date Invitation

So someone asked you out, and while you're flattered, you're just not feeling it. No need to panic or fake your own death — declining a date doesn't have to be as dramatic as an episode of *Grey's Anatomy*. Here's how to gracefully let them down so smoothly they might even think it was their idea not to see each other.

REMEMBER I've seen hundreds of rejections — both personally and through my matchmaking adventures — and here's the truth. Sometimes people in a relationship can be like gasoline and fire: two things that may be perfectly great on their own but absolutely disastrous together.

When you're in the hot seat, the key is to let someone down kindly and respectfully. Even though they may hate to hear the dreaded "let's just be friends," try to handle it the way you'd want someone to treat your best friend — with dignity, clarity, and kindness. That way you leave the situation with your integrity intact, and who knows — they might even thank you for it (after crying in the back of an Uber to Lana Del Rey; we've all been there).

Be honest, but don't go full brutal

They don't need your life story or a list of reasons why you're saying no. Keep it kind, clear, and light.

Example: "I think you're great, but I don't see us in a romantic way. I'd love to do a bestie hang one day!"

What *not* to say: "I'd rather get hit by a bus than talk to you for another second. Or did you really think you had a shot with me?" (Remember you're not trying to be the main character in their future therapy sessions.)

Blame it on timing, not on them

Although this is one of the oldest excuses in the book, it's still used because it works. It shifts the rejection from you to the timing, making them think that no matter who asked you out, the answer would be the same. It takes the personalization out of the rejection, which can soften the blow. But here's the thing: While the timing excuse might actually be true, don't leave them with false hope. You don't want them waiting by the phone while you're busy getting adjusted to your new job promotion, finishing your yoga certification, or finally learning French.

What to say: "Thank you for the invite, but I'm not dating right now — I'm really focusing on my career and myself."

What *not* to say: "I'm just super busy right now, but maybe after I cure cancer, climb Everest, and build a space colony on Mars, I'll call you."

REMEMBER

If you're not interested, close the conversation for good. Avoid words like someday, maybe, or in the future. Sure, time changes some things — like hairstyles and fashion trends — but it rarely changes whether you're attracted to someone. Let them be free to find someone who's excited about them instead of stuck waiting around while you're "finding yourself."

Don't become Caspar the Unfriendly Ghost

If you haven't been ghosted, you haven't been dating enough. Your dating life may feel as scary as *The Conjuring,* but you are not a ghost and if you don't like someone, give them the common decency of letting them know. Ghosting is the cowardly thing to when it comes to dating, and the reason you're reading this book is to become better at dating, which starts with being accountable for your own feelings, and the feelings of others to an extent. If you don't like someone, let them know via text after the date or pull them aside at work or at the gym and say you had a great time but you don't see it going anywhere.

IN THIS CHAPTER

» Choosing the right romantic setting

» Choosing a place you can both afford

» Avoiding potentially awkward spots

Chapter **9**
Right Place, Right Vibe: Nailing the Perfect Date Location

A good date starts with a good activity, and no, that doesn't necessarily mean the most expensive restaurant in town or flying someone out to Bora Bora. It just means keeping the date not bora boring. The key to impressing your date is to give effort and attention to what they say they like and also showing your own interests. It's also just as important to know where *not* to go when planning for the big night.

This chapter is your first-date guidebook to help make sure the first-date spot will leave you having to pick your second-date location.

Love's Launchpad: Finding the Perfect Place for Your First Date

I know the pressure of a first date spot can be overwhelming, but a first date shouldn't feel like a job interview or a dinner with your tax guy. Whether you're aiming for flirty and fun or mysterious and memorable, the *where* matters just as much as the *who*. Following are some tips for picking the perfect first date spot for you — intentions, budget, and romance guaranteed:

» **Noise level:** Aim for a venue where the noise level is just right — not so loud that you're shouting like auctioneers, but not so quiet that every awkward pause echoes like a pin drop in a monastery. Think lively café, not silent library. Avoid concerts, sports games, movies, or plays on a first date; save those for after the second date when you're more familiar.

» **Ambiance check:** The setting should match the mood you're aiming for. A cozy wine bar exudes intimacy, while a bustling arcade screams fun. Choose what reflects both your personalities; you don't want to end up at a winery when your date doesn't drink or a BBQ joint when your date is vegetarian.

» **Activity level:** Venues offering interactive experiences, like cooking classes or mini-golf, can ease first-date jitters and provide natural conversation starters. Plus, nothing says "romance" like a friendly competition over who can avoid the windmill on the mini-golf course.

» **Location:** Choose a spot that's convenient for both parties. You don't want your date traveling longer than a Starbucks line at 8 a.m., but also avoid picking a place right across the street from your apartment — that screams "preplanned booty call" rather than "potential future together."

» **Do your first-date diligence:** Utilize apps and websites to gather intel on potential spots. Work smarter, not harder, and whatever you do, please avoid walk-in-only places. Make a reservation first; you don't want to be awkwardly standing, waiting for a table, running out of conversation topics before the date even starts.

» **Personal touch:** Choose a location that reflects something you've discussed — like a mutual love for a specific cocktail, a favorite show filmed in a bar you know, or a museum that houses that one piece of art you actually know about. These little touches make your first date stand out and show that you took the time to make the person feel special.

TIFF SAYS: I always say, even if it's not a good date, make sure you have a good meal (or drinks, or both). Typically, if you enjoy the same location, you're on the way to an exciting dating destination.

Choosing a Date Night Spot That Fits Your Budget

In an era where social media flaunts first dates on private jets and luxury yachts, it's easy to wonder if your favorite local cocktail bar stands a chance. But let's be real: You don't need to empty your bank account to make a memorable impression. While money can add sparkle to romance, it can't buy genuine love. So focus on creating authentic connections in settings that reflect who you truly are — minus the distractions and the debt. After all, you don't need to apply for a personal loan to get personal with someone.

The following sections cover some ways to be rich with connection so you won't have to call your parents from the restaurant bathroom to Venmo you money to cover the bill.

BEING AUTHENTIC WITH YOUR BUDGET

Stay true to yourself. If you start with lavish dates that rival a billionaire's lifestyle, you might find yourself swapping caviar for drive-thru fish filets sooner than you'd like. Authenticity is key; you want your date to appreciate you for who you are, not for the luxury facade you can't maintain.

Avoid "money fishing." Pretending to have deep pockets when you're budgeting isn't sustainable. It's like casting a line with counterfeit bait; eventually the truth surfaces, and nobody likes a bait-and-switch.

For Those with Deeper Pockets:

Keep it real: Even if your wallet rivals a small nation's GDP, going overboard can attract those more interested in your assets than your

(continued)

CHAPTER 9 **Right Place, Right Vibe: Nailing the Perfect Date Location**

(continued)

personality. Remember, you want someone to connect with *you*, not your private jet.

Meaningful gestures over flashiness: Sometimes a thoughtful, less extravagant date can speak volumes more than a flashy, expensive outing. It's about creating genuine connections, not just showcasing wealth. Investing in a magical date is great — just make sure it relates to the person you are taking out and isn't just about you getting an ego boost because someone is falling in love with your lifestyle instead of you.

REMEMBER: While it's tempting to pull out all the stops to impress, sustainable and sincere dating means keeping your plans true to who you are — wallet included.

Happy hours lead to happy dating

If you're ballin' on a budget but still want to impress your date with a trip to that viral cocktail bar — the one with gold-plated chicken wings or a Taylor Swift sighting on its résumé — then happy hour is your new best friend. Almost every trendy spot has one, but here's the golden rule: Whatever you do, don't let on that you're going because of the discounts. Say something like, "Oh, I love hitting this place after work — it's got such a cool vibe!" instead of "Their martinis are only $7 from 4 to 6 p.m.!"

Whether you're rolling in cash or rolling pennies, the *worst* thing you can do on a date is complain about prices. No one wants to hear about your sticker shock when they're trying to enjoy their truffle fries. So do your homework, scope out the deals, and avoid looking like you just saw your bank account in real time. Happy hours are basically luxury dates at half the price — what's not to love? It's smart, suave, and your wallet will thank you for keeping it classy without going broke.

Free museum or park show days

Who needs a million dollars when you can look at million-dollar art for free? Many cities have free museum days or outdoor shows that let you soak up culture without soaking your wallet.

Reinventing the coffee date

The coffee date often gets roasted (pun intended) for being low-effort or, worse, downright cheap. And trust me, I've been there. Once I showed up to what I thought was a coffee date, only to realize I was actually on a coffee interview. Yes, I excused myself to the bathroom, wiped off my red lipstick, and swapped "flirty and fun" for my best LinkedIn energy.

Now, I get it — coffee dates can sometimes feel like a warm-up act instead of the main event. But that doesn't mean they can't be romantic! If you're opting for a coffee date, elevate it. Pick a spot near something fun — a farmers' market, a park, an art fair, or even a body of water. This way, the date feels more like an adventure and less like a pre-date "vibe check" because you weren't sure you wanted to commit to dinner yet. And look, it's fine if Starbucks is your go-to — just don't make it seem like you're doing it because you have no bucks. A little thought and creativity can turn even the humblest coffee date into something memorable (and no one will confuse it with a job interview this time).

BYOB restaurants and cafés

Ah, the beauty of BYOB — where you can channel your inner sommelier without needing a second mortgage. These gems let you skip the fear-inducing moment of nervously flipping through a wine list and trying to pronounce "Châteauneuf-du-Pape" without breaking a sweat. Instead, you can waltz in with your $20 bottle from the grocery store, pour it into a glass, and suddenly you're a wine snob who "detects notes of blackberry and just a hint of budget-conscious genius."

It's the ultimate life hack: enjoy a luxurious meal while avoiding the bill that makes you wonder if you accidentally paid for the waiter's student loans. So drink smarter, not harder — because nothing says romance like pairing a Michelin-starred dish with wine you bought on sale at Trader Joe's. Cheers!

The picnic is the ultimate pick

I've asked over 500 singles about their dream date, and right after "dinner and drinks," you'll always hear "picnic" — because nothing says rom-com vibes like a cheese board lovingly arranged by someone who Googled "how to assemble a cheese board" five minutes beforehand. A picnic is the perfect way to say, "I'm thoughtful, romantic, and definitely not trying to drop $200 on a restaurant where the portions are smaller than my dating pool."

The beauty of the picnic is its flexibility: You can ball out with fancy charcuterie or keep it chill with a $5 baguette and some Brie that's been in your fridge for a week (no judgment). Throw in a blanket, some sparkling water (or a bottle of $12 wine because we're fancy like that), and voilà — you've created a Hallmark movie moment on a Dollar Tree budget.

Plus, picnics hit the sweet spot of effort: enough to impress but not so much that it looks like you're overcompensating. Your date will feel like the main character in a love story while your accountant sighs with relief that you're not plotting financial destruction. Romance doesn't have to cost a fortune — just pack some snacks, pick a scenic spot, and let the sparks fly (preferably not from the broken lighter you brought for the candle).

Steering Clear of Date Spots That Can Lead to Awkward Moments

First dates are all about making a good impression, but the location can make or break the vibe. Some spots might seem okay in theory but can quickly spiral into a "never again" situation. Here's your guide to the first-date spots that are guaranteed to make things awkward, uncomfortable, or just plain weird.

>> **The movie theater:** Sure, it sounds romantic in the romcoms, but let's be real — sitting in silence for two hours in a dark room isn't exactly sparking conversation. Plus, do you really want your first-date memories tied to overpriced popcorn and the loud guy sneezing in the third row? Unless you plan on writing your questions on napkins and passing them back and forth, maybe skip this one.

>> **The gym:** Unless your idea of flirting involves grunting through squats and praying your deodorant holds up, the gym is a hard pass. Nothing says romance like beet-red faces, awkward eye contact during lunges, and someone shouting, "One more rep!" in the background. Save the fitness bonding for date three — or, honestly, never.

- **Family dinner:** Ah yes, nothing screams, "I'm super chill" like inviting someone to meet your entire family on date one. Your great-aunt asking, "So, what are your intentions?" isn't exactly the foundation for a romantic connection. Save the introductions for when they've at least learned your last name.

- **A club:** Sure, a club sounds fun if you're in the mood for loud music and questionable dance moves, but it's the worst for getting to know someone. Imagine shouting, "What's your favorite movie?" over the bass drop, only for them to hear, "Do you like gravy?" Just don't.

- **Fast food drive-thru:** Unless you're both 16 or starring in an ironic rom-com, a drive-thru isn't exactly date material. Sure, the fries are hot, but the vibe is cold. If you want to show effort, at least spring for a sit-down meal. (Bonus: no awkward car tray balancing required.)

- **A wedding:** You might think bringing a date to a wedding is a genius move (dancing! free food!), but it's a lot to throw at someone who barely knows you. Between drunk uncles, bouquet toss pressure, and "So, how long have you two been together?" questions, it's a disaster waiting to happen.

- **Extreme sports:** Rock climbing, skydiving, or anything that involves helmets and harnesses sounds fun . . . until you realize screaming for your life isn't cute. First dates should focus on getting to know each other, not wondering if this is how it all ends.

- **Their place:** Meeting at someone's home for the first date might seem convenient, but it's a big no-no. It's way too soon for such an intimate setting, not to mention it can come across as lazy or even unsafe. First dates are about neutral, public spaces where you can focus on conversation, not whether their couch has seen better days. Save the home visits for when you actually know their last name — and no, their Instagram handle doesn't count.

- **Sporting events:** Unless you both have a mutual love for overpriced nachos and yelling at referees, skip the stadium. Sporting events are loud, chaotic, and full of distractions — not ideal for getting to know someone. Plus, nothing kills a romantic vibe faster than a heated argument about whose team is better.

- **》 The laundromat:** If you're thinking, "Hey, it's quirky and low-key," let me stop you right there. Sure, multitasking is great, but folding your underwear while trying to flirt? That's a vibe no one signed up for.

- **》 Spots that are a trek for either of you:** First dates shouldn't feel like a cross-country road trip. If the spot you've chosen is a 90-minute drive or requires three bus transfers, you're already setting the tone for a hassle-filled evening. Keep it simple and convenient for both of you. The last thing you want is someone showing up frazzled and late because they had to navigate rush-hour traffic just to meet you.

REMEMBER

At the end of the day, it's not about Michelin stars, Instagrammable backdrops, or having the world's most original idea. It's about creating a space where you both feel comfortable, can laugh, and maybe share a basket of fries without judgment. So relax, pick somewhere you'd actually enjoy, and remember: The best date spots are the ones where the conversation flows, the awkwardness fades, and you both leave thinking, "Let's do that again."

> **IN THIS CHAPTER**
>
> » Stating your expectations clearly up front
> » Reevaluating if they insist on meeting privately without reason
> » Identifying when someone isn't valuing your time
> » Being wary of rushed commitments or emotional manipulation

Chapter **10**

Plan with Caution: Spotting and Avoiding Red Flags When Setting Up a Date

You've probably been told to watch for red flags on a first date, but the way someone plans (or doesn't plan) a date can reveal more flags than a referee at a playoff game. Here's the deal: If someone's genuinely interested, they'll prioritize locking in plans. Think about it — if a diehard Justin Bieber fan got the chance to hang with him at his favorite restaurant, would they reply with a halfhearted "maybe" or "soon"? Absolutely not! They'd be typing back faster than a teenager about to lose their Snapchat streak, already planning their outfit and telling all their friends.

In this analogy, you are Justin Bieber (yes, you're that iconic), and your date should be thrilled at the opportunity to meet you. If someone's excited, there won't be delays or cryptic one-word answers. They'll want to know when, where, and, most importantly, if you're team sushi or burgers.

TIP: How someone handles planning a date isn't just about logistics — it's a sneak peek into how they might handle you. Are they thoughtful? Respectful? Invested? Or are they just looking for a pen pal or a casual hangout? Keep your eyes open because when it comes to setting up the date, the signs are there if you know what to look for.

This chapter covers what you need to know to spot those red flags and avoid wasting your time.

Setting Clear Expectations

There's nothing worse than prepping for a date all week, only to realize you never actually nailed down a time. So you send that dreaded "Are we still on for tonight?" text, and *bam* — you're sent straight into texting purgatory. For hours, you nervously check your phone, only to finally get a half-hearted reply like "Yeah, sure, want to grab a drink?" or the classic "Sorry, got caught up at work."

Let me tell you something: That's not just bad communication — it's downright disrespectful. Sure, life happens, but if they can't give you the courtesy of a simple heads-up or carve out real time for you, that's a major red flag. A date, no matter how casual, should have some level of sacredness. At the very least, it should feel like they're excited to see you — not like they're squeezing you in between work emails and a pregame for the club.

TIFF SAYS: Here's my golden rule: If you don't have a confirmed time and place at least three days in advance, assume the date is off. Send one polite follow-up text to check in, but if you're met with silence, let it go. Don't stoop to playing detective, scrolling through their social media trying to figure out why they can't lock in plans. You're not auditioning for "CSI: Ghosted Edition."

The sad truth? Some people will text and chat endlessly but have zero intention of meeting in real life. (Yes, *Catfish* is a whole show about this.) Your time is way too precious for that nonsense. Whether you're looking for a fling or forever love, you deserve someone who makes their interest clear, not someone who makes you feel like an unpaid event planner.

THE INTEREST INTERPRETER: HOW TO KNOW IF THEY'RE COMMITTED TO A FIRST DATE

You've swapped flirty texts, maybe even a voice note or two, and now the convo's circling around "we should hang out sometime." But are they actually planning a date — or just stringing you along with calendar invites that never come? Here's how to tell if they're committed to a first date or just committed to wasting your time:

- "Let's hang soon!" (Spoiler: "Soon" means never.)
- "I'd love to, but I'm super busy right now." (Translation: They're busy scrolling Instagram.)
- Taking hours — or days — to respond, especially when you ask about a date. (If it's taking this long to confirm drinks, imagine planning a vacation.)
- "We could chill somewhere?" (Netflix and who dis?)
- "I'll have to ask my friends if we're doing something." (Since when does your date need a committee vote?)
- "Sounds fun, but it's kinda far." (Odysseus spent ten years trying to get home to Penelope. They can take an Uber.)

REMEMBER The key to love is locking in the date. Set clear expectations, and if someone isn't meeting them, it's time to swipe left on their nonsense and move on. You're the main character — don't settle for someone who treats you like an extra on their set.

Netflix and Not Chill: Dates Should Be Public First, Private Later

If you've been in the dating game long enough, you've likely gotten the infamous "wyd?" text at 11 p.m. Translation: "What are you doing right now, and can you come over to my place?" Or worse, "Can I come to yours?" Spoiler alert: If someone's only idea of a "date" involves their couch and no witnesses, it's not a date — it's a hookup with a side of potential red flags. Let's be real; there are only two reasons someone invites you to their house on a first date: *sex* and, yep, *sex*.

I've been there. I've fallen for the "I'll cook you a romantic dinner" line, only to find myself listening to some guy butcher "Wonderwall" on his guitar while I feasted on a "gourmet" spread of Lunchables and day-old beer. Not exactly the rom-com I had in mind. If they can't state your favorite color or your middle name, they definitely shouldn't know your address.

A real date involves effort — dressing up, going out, and making memories somewhere with decent lighting and zero roommates. You deserve more than sharing a bag of Cheetos while someone tries to convince you their SoundCloud mixtape is Grammy-worthy. It's not romantic; it's lazy and, frankly, unsafe.

REMEMBER

Safety first, always. If you're tempted (because hey, martinis and flirting happen), here's my survival guide to make sure your first date doesn't land you on the evening news:

- Share your location with three to five friends before going.
- Avoid giving out your address or going to theirs, especially on the first meet.
- If they call a rideshare for you, set the destination a block or two from your home.
- If they insist on hosting you at their place, politely decline and suggest a public spot instead.

Now, no judgment if a one-night stand is what you're after — just make sure the vibes (and safety measures) are in check. But trust me, meeting in public first for a drink or coffee will tell you if they're the American dream or American Psycho.

Bottom line: If you're serious about leveling up your dating life, it's time to kick the couch potatoes to the curb. You deserve someone who wants to watch *you* over a glass of wine, not someone who only wants to watch Netflix and "chill." Upgrade your standards and hold out for someone who's excited to plan a real date — not just press play on their streaming queue. Trust me, the right person will want to wine and dine you, not just recline and deprive you of a real date.

Time-Wasters 101: How to Spot the People Who'll Never Commit to a First Date

We all know the type — they pop up sporadically, like a bad pimple right before picture day. They text just enough to keep you hanging on but vanish as soon as any real plan is mentioned. These are the people who only hit you up when they're bored or, worse, could be serial daters who've booked 15 first dates but never intend to follow through. They talk about elaborate date ideas — private jet rides, secret speakeasies, or a wine-tasting under the stars — but they never actually make it happen. If they're more "when I get back from this trip" than "let's meet at 7 on Friday," you need to cut them loose. You deserve someone who values your time, not someone who treats you like their emotional Netflix queue.

Then there's the infamous Good Morning Texter. They'll send you a "GM, beautiful" every day, like they've got stock in motivational quotes. They'll ask about your favorite color, your dog's name, and your childhood trauma but somehow never mention an actual date. Congratulations — you've got yourself a pen pal, not a partner. They want to feel connected digitally while leaving you perpetually stuck in "flirting purgatory." If they're more interested in emojis than espresso martinis, it's time to move on.

Other classic time-wasters? Let's not forget:

>> **The Procrastinator Extraordinaire:** They'll keep pushing off plans like they're auditioning for a role in *Groundhog Day*. If you've been "planning" this date since 2022, accept that it's never going to happen.

>> **The Double-Booker:** They'll schedule something amazing . . . only to ghost you because they "forgot" they had another commitment. (Spoiler alert: That other commitment might be another date.)

>> **The Excuse Machine:** "I have a big work project," "My cousin's wedding is next year," "Mercury is in retrograde." They have a reason for everything, except showing up.

TIFF SAYS: If someone's wasting your time with empty texts, endless excuses, and zero effort, they're not serious about you — or dating in general. Toss the time-wasters and find someone who actually gets excited about making plans with you. Your time is valuable, and your love life deserves more than "GM" and ghosting.

Love Bombers and Text Overload: When Enthusiasm Becomes a Red Flag

Ah, the overly eager first-date whirlwind — also known as Captain Too Much, Too Soon. These are the people who'll send you 47 texts before lunch, including three good morning selfies, a poem about your smile (that they've never seen in person), and a playlist they made "just for you." Love bombing doesn't even begin to describe it — it's like they're auditioning for a role in your future wedding slideshow before you've even met for coffee. And don't get me started on the constant follow-ups: "Did you get my text?" "Are you mad at me?" "Just thinking about how amazing Thursday will be." Remember you're just grabbing a latte, not eloping in Vegas.

WARNING: Sure, enthusiasm is great, but when someone's coming on stronger than your aunt trying to set you up at Thanksgiving, it's a red flag. Look out for love bombing disguised as charm: over-the-top compliments, constant texting, or grand gestures that feel more overwhelming than sweet. It's not romance; it's emotional suffocation with a side of desperation. And here's the kicker: If they're already exhausting you before you've even met, imagine the energy they'll bring to an actual relationship. Run, don't walk. Or better yet — block, don't respond. You want a partner, not a stalker.

110   PART 2 Meeting Someone and Setting Up a Date

IN THIS CHAPTER

» Figuring out where you stand on the payment issue

» Looking at common payment etiquette questions and debates

» Dating on a budget

» Spotting red flags when it comes to paying the bill

» Surviving unexpected and embarrassing situations

» Dating someone who has way more (or way less) money than you do

Chapter 11
Who's Got the Bill? Navigating the Check Etiquette

J Lo once said, "My love don't cost a thing," but clearly she hasn't been on a date in these times of inflation and the eternal confusion about who's actually supposed to pay. Who pays used to be simple: Men paid, and women laughed at their bad jokes because, hey, it was a free meal at the best restaurant in town. But now? Welcome to the exciting (and slightly confusing) era of individual beliefs and dating systems, where there's no one-size-fits-all approach to who picks up the tab.

Money is a hard thing to navigate in dating, and it gets even more complicated as you grow a relationship and finances grow together. Figuring out how you approach a first-date check can be a great sign as to how you both will navigate finances in the future.

This chapter offers some ways to make sure you feel confident on payment so you can pay attention to your amazing date.

Knowing Your Standards on Payment Before the Date

There's no wrong answer when it comes to splitting the bill — except not knowing your answer ahead of time. Depending on your gender, there may be societal expectations about who should pay, but ultimately, it's all about communication and confidence.

For the most part, the two most common unwritten rules are these: Whoever asked the other out should pay, or the man always pays.

Around 50–60 percent of people in heterosexual relationships believe the person who asked for the date should pay. Many younger couples, especially Millennials and Gen Z, lean toward splitting the bill 50/50 as a norm. Both are fine, as long as you know where you stand and can back it up without turning the check into a philosophical debate. One time I thought I met the love of my life. He was perfect and we had so much fun together. I thought he was taking care of the bills from our lavish dates, but after about ten dates I got an email with a not so romantic invoice — yes, an *invoice* — for the month of dates split down the middle. It was to be paid in net 30, and our relationship only lasted net 30 too.

For the Straight Man: If you're very interested in someone, it never hurts to pick up the bill (unless they adamantly insist on splitting, which you should respect). Often, the issue isn't about the money itself but what it signals. For example, many people subconsciously evaluate generosity as a sign of future compatibility — like "If he's not taking care of this now, how's he going to help me raise a family or afford a houseplant, let alone a mortgage?"

However, if you're more of a "we should split things equally" kind of guy, express that before the date to avoid the awkward "So . . . how are we doing this?" moment after dessert.

REMEMBER Transparency is key — it's not about whether you can afford to pay, but about being upfront with your intentions. You might say something like "Hey, just so you know, I usually prefer to split finances on dates. Does that work for you?" Boom — problem solved, awkwardness avoided.

And if that honesty results in them ghosting you? Well, congratulations! You dodged someone who doesn't align with your values. Better to figure that out early than to face money fights later in a relationship. Proactive communication about finances now can save you from bigger headaches later, like splitting half your assets instead of just splitting the bill.

REMEMBER It's not just about who pays — it's about finding someone who matches your lifestyle, values, and maybe even your love for a good budget-friendly happy hour.

NO DISHWASHING DATES: THE CASE FOR BRINGING YOUR WALLET

Who doesn't love to be wined and dined? This girl sure does — but let me tell you, it's not always the fairytale you hope for. Case in point: 2021, fresh out of college, wide-eyed and optimistic, I went on a date with a guy named David. I thought he was my Mr. Big, but turns out he was just my *big* mistake. Mid-date, he ran into his ex, and — wait for it — he *left* with her, sticking me with the bill. Thankfully, it was just cocktails (hallelujah for small mercies), and I had enough on my broke college budget to cover it without having to wash dishes. Not that I could've scrubbed a plate anyway, considering I'd just spent my last pennies on a fresh manicure for the occasion. Priorities, right?

The lesson here: Always be prepared to cover the bill if needed. You never know when you'll encounter a David — or someone who insists on splitting the check because they "believe in equality" but really just don't want to pay for that second margarita you clearly deserved. Even if you're a traditionalist who expects the man to pay, it's wise to have a backup plan in case he doesn't deliver. And if you do pay, just tell yourself it's an investment in never having to see him again.

Breaking Down Payment Options and Debates on a Date

When it comes to who picks up the bill on a date, opinions vary widely — and it's not always as simple as "the guy pays." This section explores different schools of thought on payment etiquette, how gender roles influence expectations, and important considerations for LGBTQ+ daters navigating these conversations.

The great debate: Who should pay the bill?

Ah, the check: dating's final boss. It shows up at the end of a perfectly good date and turns the whole thing into a social standoff. Who reaches for it? Who awkwardly pretends not to see it? Who loses their wallet "by accident"? The following sections break down the most common bill debates and adds a little humor to this age-old battle of wits.

>> **The "you asked, you pay" rule:** This one's straightforward. If you did the asking, you're footing the bill. It's like sending an invitation to a party — you don't charge people for snacks when they show up (unless you're a monster).

>> **Pro:** It's clear, easy, and makes you look generous.

>> **Con:** What if you're both so "laid back" that neither remembers who technically asked? Cue the awkward silence.

>> **The "men should pay" old-school standard:** This classic tradition says men always cover the bill. Somewhere, a 1950s etiquette guide is nodding approvingly.

>> **Pro:** It can feel chivalrous and romantic — like you're starring in an Audrey Hepburn movie.

>> **Con:** It's 2025, and no one brought their monocle. Plus, what happens if you ordered the $18 avocado toast? Fair? Debatable.

>> **The 50/50 split camp:** This team says equality is sexy. Both people enjoyed the meal, so both people should pony up.

>> **Pro:** Nobody feels like they "owe" the other person, and it's pretty straightforward.

> **Con:** Venmoing someone $4.37 for your share of the fries kills the romance faster than discussing your ex on date one.

» **The "who reaches first wins" gambit:** This one's all about reflexes. Whoever grabs the check first gets to pay, end of story.

> **Pro:** It's spontaneous and avoids unnecessary conversation.
>
> **Con:** It's also how some people fake "forgetting" their wallet. If they're moving slower than a sloth on sedatives, you know what's up.

» **The income-based theory:** Whoever makes more money should pay. That's the logic here: If one person earns more, they should "invest" in the meal.

> **Pro:** It's thoughtful and keeps things proportional.
>
> **Con:** Unless they brought their tax returns, how exactly do you figure this out without sounding like an IRS agent?

» **First round's free, next one's on you:** This group believes in taking turns. Whoever pays for the first date gets a free pass next time.

> **Pro:** It shows mutual interest and effort.
>
> **Con:** This only works if there *is* a next date. Otherwise, congrats, you're out $75 and they're ghosting.

» **The cultural norm card:** In many cultures, one person (often the man) is expected to pay as a sign of respect or tradition.

> **Pro:** It feels natural and aligns with shared values — no awkward negotiation.
>
> **Con:** If your date isn't familiar with this, you might end up explaining your traditions *and* covering their dessert.

» **The "impress me" clause:** Some people believe whoever's trying to win the other over should pay. Think of it as a dinner-based audition for their affection.

> **Pro:** It's a bold way to show interest and effort.
>
> **Con:** It's also how you end up staring at a $150 seafood bill, wondering if love is really worth this much lobster.

- **The "who cares?" method:** This group doesn't overthink it. Whoever grabs the check first pays, and if there's a problem, they figure it out later.

   Pro: It's casual and stress-free.

   Con: It only works until both of you assume the other person is covering it, and suddenly you're playing chicken with the waiter.

- **The "pay your own way" independence plan.** This argument says everyone should cover their own costs. Financial independence for the win!

   Pro: No one feels obligated, and it keeps things simple.

   Con: Splitting a bill for coffee feels fine, but itemizing a fancy dinner? Hello, buzzkill.

REMEMBER

Bottom line (pun intended), communicate or prepare for chaos. Let's be honest: There's no universal rule for who pays the bill. It all comes down to preferences, expectations, and whether or not someone mysteriously "forgets" their wallet every time. The key is to communicate — ideally before dessert arrives. Whether you split, treat, or switch off, the most important thing is that you both feel respected. And if they're still debating their share after 20 minutes? Congratulations, you've just discovered your deal-breaker. If the check is causing you stress about how you both align, that may be the ultimate check-in that you both are not the ones for each other.

Paying the bill in LGBTQIA+ dating: Communication over assumptions

When it comes to LGBTQIA+ dating and paying the bill, it's just like any other relationship — communication is key, but it's not tied to outdated gender roles. Without those societal expectations dictating behavior, the dynamics can be more flexible. That doesn't mean it's always straightforward, though. Awkward moments around the check can pop up for anyone, no matter who's at the table.

Typically, the bill can go one of three ways: The person who initiates the date picks it up, it's split evenly, or the two alternate paying. It's less about who "should" pay and more about finding a rhythm that works for both people. If someone loves treating their date as part of their personality or values, that's great! If splitting feels fairer and more balanced, that works too. What matters is that there's clarity and mutual respect in the moment.

Of course, the check can still bring out unexpected assumptions. Maybe one person thought the initiator was paying, while the other assumed they'd split. To avoid turning the date into a silent standoff over who reaches first, it's helpful to casually address it. A simple "How do you usually like to handle the bill?" keeps things easy and prevents any awkward misunderstandings.

TIFF SAYS

Ultimately, it's not about the specifics of who pays — it's about the effort, respect, and intention behind the gesture. Whether one person treats, both contribute, or the decision changes based on the vibe, the key is to approach it with honesty and a little grace. Because at the end of the day, the bill is just a small detail in the much bigger story of how you treat each other. And if they're as generous with their humor and kindness as they are with the check? That's the real win.

PAYMENT PREFERENCES TO PONDER

Let me give you a few examples of how you might handle the check from my wildly diverse group of friends. First, there's Tia, who went on a date with a guy who spent the whole evening reminding her how expensive everything was. He didn't order an entrée, insisted on splitting the bill, and then asked her to Venmo him $2.50 the next day because he calculated the tax wrong. Of course, she ghosted him faster than he could say "money request."

Then there's Bailey, who wouldn't dream of pretending to pay. She's so bold she skips the fake wallet reach entirely and just waits for the check to be handled like the queen she is. Her idea of splitting involves her partner's net worth, not the bill.

Now let's talk about Jake, who's a total gentleman but also prefers to go Dutch. He feels it sets the tone for equality and avoids any weird power dynamics. On one date, his date insisted he pay for everything, which made him feel like an ATM instead of a potential partner.

(continued)

(continued)

> Needless to say, there wasn't a second date, and now Jake always politely brings up splitting before the check arrives to avoid awkwardness.
>
> And finally, there's Emily, a powerhouse CEO at a major law firm. She insists on paying for first dates because, as she says, "I don't want to owe anyone anything." Respect, Emily.
>
> The point is, there's no universal rule for who should pay on a date, and honestly, there doesn't need to be. What does matter is that you figure out what feels right for you, communicate it clearly, and avoid letting payment etiquette ruin an otherwise great evening. Oh, and one final tip: Whatever your payment method, just make sure it doesn't get declined. Nothing kills the vibe like your card getting rejected after ordering the filet mignon.

Red Flags When Splitting the Bill

Navigating the bill at the end of a date can be tricky, but certain behaviors go beyond awkward and into full-on red flag territory. Here's what to watch out for when someone's true colors come out just as the check arrives:

- **The Houdini act:** This is the classic disappearing act where your date suddenly needs to "use the restroom" or "take an urgent call" the moment the check hits the table. If they come back just in time to say, "Oh, you got it? Great, thanks!" it's a clear sign they're not serious about being a partner — or a decent human being.

- **The itemized accountant:** Beware of the person who whips out their calculator and starts dividing the bill to the last penny, insisting you owe exactly $14.73 because you dared to order the extra guac. While fairness is great, this level of nitpicking shows they might be more invested in their wallet than in you.

- **The "forgot my wallet" move:** If the infamous "oops, I forgot my wallet" excuse happens once, sure, maybe it's an honest mistake. But if it feels rehearsed or they conveniently only realize it after eating their entire meal, you're likely dealing with someone who has zero intentions of contributing.

» **The Venmo vigilante:** You thought the date went well until the next day, when you get a Venmo request for half the tip, a share of the tax, or — gasp — the $2.50 you didn't even know was missing. This kind of behavior screams petty and can leave a bad taste in your mouth, no matter how good the dinner was.

» **The complainer:** They spend the whole meal complaining about how expensive the menu is, making you feel guilty for every bite you take. Then, when it's time to pay, they casually suggest you split — even though you ordered a water and they indulged in a cocktail. It's less about the money and more about the lack of generosity and self-awareness.

» **The guilt-tripper:** This person doesn't directly ask you to pay but lays on the sob story about how tough their financial situation is right now. By the end of their tale, you feel like a villain for even considering splitting the bill. While empathy is great, guilt-tripping isn't a sustainable relationship strategy.

» **The silent splitter:** If they stay completely silent when the check arrives and just stare at you with those "Well, what are you going to do?" eyes, it's a sign they're avoiding the topic altogether. Communication is key — even about the bill — and someone who can't handle that may struggle with bigger conversations down the line.

» **The over-orderer who opts out:** They go all out — ordering appetizers, cocktails, and dessert — but when the check comes, they suddenly suggest splitting the bill evenly, leaving you paying for half their indulgence. This is less about sharing and more about exploitation.

WARNING

While one red flag might just indicate an off night, consistent patterns around money are worth noting. The way someone handles the bill says a lot about their attitude toward fairness, respect, and generosity — traits that will carry over into other areas of a relationship. Always trust your instincts and remember that no amount of great conversation or shared appetizers is worth tolerating bad behavior when the check comes.

REMEMBER

Whether you're treating, splitting, or negotiating dessert duty, it's less about the cash and more about the connection. If they're dodging the bill, acting like a human Venmo request, or over-calculating down to the last crumb of bread, it's not just a red flag — it's a full parade. The goal isn't just to survive the check

CHAPTER 11 **Who's Got the Bill? Navigating the Check Etiquette** 119 moment but to find someone who brings the same energy to the relationship as they do to paying the tab (hopefully without itemizing it). It's your dating life, and you get to decide how you feel most comfortable handling the bill. Ultimately, you're looking for someone who checks all your boxes — including how they handle the check.

When the Bill Doesn't Go as Planned: A Survival Guide

The food was delicious, the conversation was flowing, and you're already thinking this date could be a success. Then the bill arrives, and suddenly everything falls apart faster than your faith in humanity when you realize they didn't even *pretend* to reach for their wallet. Whether it's an awkward misunderstanding, a blatant expectation that you're footing the bill, or just a wild twist you weren't prepared for, here's what to do when the check-paying doesn't go as planned — and how to handle it like a pro.

Scenario 1: The "Oh, I forgot my wallet" move

This classic excuse is the red flag equivalent of a parade. If they're truly embarrassed and fumbling for a solution, it might just be an honest mistake (after all, we're all human). But if they're sitting back like they've just won a free meal contest, it's time to assess.

What to do: Smile politely, pay the bill (if you're able), and mentally file this under "People I'll Never See Again." If you're feeling cheeky, say something like "Don't worry, I've got this — just promise me you'll grab the next one!" If they offer zero remorse or effort to make it up to you? Consider this meal your tuition for the lesson of knowing when to leave someone behind.

Scenario 2: The surprise split request

You thought they were paying. They thought you were paying. And now they're pushing the check your way while suggesting a split. Awkward? Sure. The end of the world? Not quite.

What to do: If you're caught off guard but can manage to pay your share, go for it — but don't let this moment sour the whole evening. You can laugh it off with something like "Oh, so we're going Dutch tonight! Good to know for next time." If splitting wasn't in your budget, be honest: "I wasn't prepared to split tonight, but I can Venmo you later."

That said, if splitting isn't something you're comfortable with, always come prepared with enough cash or a card just in case — because no one wants to end their date washing dishes in the back. Then use the moment to communicate your preferences: "I've typically dated people who prefer to provide for the first date, but I understand everyone has their own style." Again, it's all about personal preferences — there's no "right or wrong" here, just a need for clear communication. If it's a dealbreaker for either of you, at least you'll both know early on.

Scenario 3: The silent bill stare-off

The waiter drops the check, and . . . nothing. They're staring at it like it's a sudoku puzzle they don't want to solve. The silence is deafening. Are they waiting for you to grab it? Are you waiting for them? This could go on forever.

What to do: Break the tension by addressing it head on, but keep it light: "So, how are we handling this? Want to split it?" If they're weird about it, that's their problem — not yours. No one should have to sit through an Olympic-level waiting game over who pays.

Scenario 4: They assume you're paying

They didn't even try to reach for their wallet. Maybe they think you invited them, so you're paying. Maybe they think you're their personal meal sponsor. Either way, it's awkward.

What to do: If you're fine paying the bill, no problem — just pay it and move on. Sometimes it's easier to avoid the awkwardness altogether if the meal was great and you feel like it's worth covering. However, if you're not okay with the assumption and feel it's unfair, this is where communication comes in. Try something like "I don't mind taking care of this, but in the future I'd prefer we share the cost." If they bristle at that, it's a sign you may have mismatched values.

Scenario 5: The cultural or personal expectation

For some people, paying the bill isn't just a courtesy — it's an expectation rooted in their culture, upbringing, or personal values. Maybe you were raised to believe that whoever initiates the date should pay, or perhaps it's important to you that your date demonstrates generosity by covering the bill. Whatever the case, it's valid to feel a certain way about this situation — but communication is key.

What to do: If footing the bill (or expecting someone else to) is part of your worldview, own it with confidence and grace. Say something like "Just so we're on the same page, I was raised to believe the person who initiates should take care of the bill — it's just what I'm used to." Or "I really appreciate when someone provides on the first date — it's how I feel valued." On the flip side, if you love covering the bill, let them know: "I like to treat — it's something I enjoy doing."

Ultimately, there's no right or wrong here; it's about understanding each other's preferences and finding common ground. If your values don't align, that's okay too. It's better to find out sooner rather than later.

Scenario 6: The overly generous offer

On the flip side, sometimes someone insists on paying, and you're left feeling weird about it — maybe it's too soon for them to foot the whole bill, or you wanted to contribute but they shut you down.

What to do: Graciously accept if they're genuinely offering, but let them know you'll get the next one: *"That's so kind of you — thank you! I'll make sure to grab the check next time."* A little generosity on either side is a nice gesture, but it should feel mutual over time.

Champagne Taste on a Beer Budget: Dating Across Income Brackets

Dating someone with a different income level can feel like mixing a fancy bottle of champagne with a can of budget soda — it might work, but only if you shake things up the right way. Whether you're the one splurging on dinner while your date subtly Googles "how to split appetizers," or you're the one budgeting while they casually suggest a weekend in Santorini, income differences are less about math and more about managing expectations. This section breaks down the highs, the lows, and the downright hilarious moments of dating across income brackets.

TIFF SAYS

You don't need to be in the same tax bracket to build a great relationship — just the same page about what matters. And if they can laugh with you over cheap wine or let you sneak them into a free museum day? That's a partner worth keeping — no matter what's in their bank account. However, if dating expectations are that you are on the same income page and earning the same amount, make that clear at the first check so you don't waste your time and your savings.

Weighing the positives and challenges

Dating someone with a different income can bring unique challenges — like navigating who pays for what without awkwardness or assumptions. The key is finding balance through open communication, respect, and understanding. The following list offers some positives that can result from dating someone with a different income:

- » **You'll experience things you never would have before.** If your partner earns more, you might suddenly find yourself at a $100-per-plate dinner wondering how to pronounce *amuse-bouche*. If you're the higher earner, you might discover the joys of thrift store dates or picnic sandwiches that taste way better than overpriced caviar. Bonus: You'll each get a peek into a world you wouldn't have entered on your own.

- » **You learn that fun is priceless.** A sunset hike costs nothing, and a backyard movie night is basically free. If you're both creative, you'll realize the best memories aren't tied to price tags. Who needs a luxury yacht when you've got a two-person kayak and questionable steering skills?

- » **You'll hone your communication skills (quickly).** Budgeting dates or adjusting to new experiences requires a lot of talking — and we're not just talking about ordering drinks. Conversations about money may feel awkward at first, but they're great practice for building trust. And trust me, you'll get good at casually suggesting, "Let's try the special pizza deal!" without actually saying you're broke.

Dating across different incomes can lead to awkward money talks, unbalanced expectations, and stress. Here's what to look out for:

- **Lifestyle clashes:** They suggest a Michelin-star restaurant, and you're thinking, "Does Taco Bell count as fine dining?" These differences can lead to some head-scratching moments. The trick? Middle ground. Maybe you alternate — one fancy night, one low-key food truck crawl. (And yes, food trucks are objectively cooler.)

- **Guilt or awkwardness:** The higher earner might feel bad for suggesting costly activities, while the lower earner may feel like they need to "keep up." If your date casually drops, "Let's do Paris next month," and your bank account laughs out loud, it's okay to say, "How about Paris . . . Texas? I hear it's got great BBQ."

- **Misaligned spending habits:** If one person's idea of "treating themselves" is a $300 spa day and the other's is a $3 iced coffee, things can get tricky. Communicate early: "I'm more of a frugal foodie. How do you like to approach spending?" Keep it light, because nothing kills the vibe like a heated debate over splitting guac.

Beyond those challenges, there are some possible red flag situations and behaviors to watch out for:

WARNING

- **Power dynamics:** If one person starts calling all the shots because they're footing the bill, it's a red flag, not a romantic gesture. Being treated is lovely, but being steamrolled? Not so much.

- **Budget-shaming:** If they make jokes like, "Aw, you've never flown first class? That's cute," you don't need to laugh — you need to leave. Respect for each other's finances is nonnegotiable.

- **Incompatibility in financial goals:** One person saving for a down payment while the other's impulse-buying NFTs might not be a great match long-term. You don't need to have identical spending habits, but similar goals can save you both headaches (and wallets).

How to make it work without losing your mind (or savings)

When your wallets don't match, just remember — relationship points aren't earned by who drops the most cash, but by who laughs at the waiter's jokes first. Keep it light, keep it honest, and the rest will follow. Here's how to make it work:

- » **Talk about it, but make it chill.** No need for a PowerPoint on your finances. Just say, "That sounds fun, but I'm trying to stick to a budget right now. Any chance we could try [cheaper activity] instead?" Confidence is sexy, and so is knowing your financial limits.

- » **Balance generosity and budgeting.** If they pick up a pricey dinner, surprise them later with something thoughtful like cooking their favorite meal or planning a free outing. Generosity isn't about money; it's about effort.

- » **Laugh at the differences.** Dating someone from a different income bracket means you'll both get out of your comfort zone. Embrace the weird moments, like when they explain what "dry-aged steak" is while you introduce them to the dollar menu's finest.

BUDGETING AND LOVE: FINDING BALANCE IN THE DATING ECONOMY

The only thing harder than knowing your value in the dating market is affording three dates a week in this economy. While it's important to be generous and make your date feel appreciated, you also don't want to end up in dating debt. No one wants to explain to their credit card company why "romantic sushi night" is now a recurring problem.

Set a monthly dating budget that works for you — think of it as an investment in your love life. Once you've figured out your financial comfort zone, explore payment strategies that align with your values. Whether you're splitting the bill, treating your date, or alternating who pays, the key is to make it work for you. Because let's face it, love might be priceless, but dinner and drinks definitely aren't.

Dating Without Breaking the Bank

Dating should leave you full of connection but often can leave your bank account empty. If you are struggling with your finances, you don't have to give up dating; you need to rethink how you date and meet someone who is willing to grow with you. The good news? Being broke doesn't mean you can't be generous or creative in dating. It just requires honesty, effort, and a touch of resourcefulness. Here's how to date like a pro — even when your budget is tighter than skinny jeans after a big meal:

- **Be honest about your finances (without oversharing).** You don't need to hand your date a printout of your bank statement, but being upfront about your budget can save a lot of awkwardness later. If they suggest a pricey restaurant or activity that's out of your range, try saying, "That sounds amazing, but I'm on a tighter budget right now. How about we try [alternative suggestion] instead?" This shows you're not only thoughtful but also good at problem-solving — a bonus in any relationship.

- **Creativity is free.** Some of the best dates don't cost a thing. Suggest a walk in the park, a sunset hike, or a cozy night of cooking at home (if you're comfortable with that level of intimacy). A scavenger hunt around your city or a visit to a free museum can be way more memorable than an overpriced meal. Effort and thoughtfulness always trump money when it comes to making an impression.

- **Reframe "generosity."** Being generous doesn't always mean spending money. It can be about your time, attention, and thoughtfulness. Write them a note, create a playlist, or plan a date that incorporates something they've mentioned loving. Generosity is about showing you care, not about maxing out your credit card.

- **Pick spots that fit your budget.** If you're planning the date, choose affordable places where you feel comfortable. A trendy food truck, a quirky coffee shop, or even a local dive bar can be great alternatives to a pricey restaurant. Your vibe and conversation matter far more than the backdrop.

- **Don't make it weird.** If your budget becomes a topic, own it without shame. Say something like "Right now, I'm focusing on saving, but I'd love to still find ways for us to have fun." Confidence and openness can turn what might feel like a vulnerability into a strength.

3
Swipe Right to Date Night: The Ultimate GRWM Playbook for Your First Date

IN THIS PART . . .

Look and feel your best for a first date.

Master mental hacks to feel confident for a first date.

Find some flirting tips to keep the date fun and exciting.

> **IN THIS CHAPTER**
> - » Looking your best for a first date
> - » The fresh and flawless hygiene checklist
> - » Authenticity: Showing your style, not playing pretend
> - » The power of a signature scent: Smelling like success
> - » Posture and presence: Making an entrance that turns heads

Chapter **12**

From Outfit to Attitude: Making a Great First Impression

To have a good date, you need to feel good — and that starts with feeling like you look good. There's nothing worse than already being nervous about a first date and realizing halfway through that you're still radiating onion bagel from lunch or suffering in those "lucky pants" that haven't fit right since the first season of *Stranger Things*. Let's face it: Nobody feels confident when they're distracted by bad breath or wondering if their waistband is plotting against them.

Before any date, it's crucial to run through a hygiene checklist. Even if you're the nicest, best-looking person on the planet, you'll make your dating journey a lot harder if your vibe screams, "I came straight from spin class and forgot deodorant." This chapter is here to help you show up authentic but elevated — polished without pretending. From clothes to posture to a foolproof hygiene routine, these tips will have you feeling as put together as prom night and ready to enjoy your date, knowing the only thing turning heads is your charm.

Looking Your Best for a First Date

I always say, never compare yourself to how other people look — because to compare is to despair. Instead of spiraling over the fact that you're not a famous supermodel or landing on *People*'s Sexiest Person Alive list (it's rigged anyway), focus on working with what you've got. The right person will think you're a supermodel in their eyes, no matter what.

TIFF SAYS

Take it from me — I've never been a size 2, and I've been told by "experts" (and, let's be honest, *really wrong* TV dating coaches) that no high-value person would ever want someone who wasn't skinny. Spoiler: They were full of it. I broke that brainwashing, tossed out those toxic ideas, and ended up dating more *GQ* cover-worthy men than I can count. Why? Because I've learned that looking good is subjective, confidence is sexy, and there's no one-size-fits-all formula for beauty.

Sure, if you 100 percent fit the mainstream beauty standard, you might get more dates, but let's be real: You're not trying to sell out Madison Square Garden with potential suitors. You're just trying to find *your person*. So, instead of obsessing over what you're not, focus on what you are — and what you can tweak to feel like your best self.

TIP

Grab a notebook (or your notes app, if you're feeling modern), and make two lists:

>> **What's already gorgeous about you:** Yes, this is a brag session. Do it.

>> **What could use a little glow-up:** No judgment — just things *you* want to improve.

Be honest: Are you steaming your clothes or just hoping the wrinkles scream "effortlessly cool"? Are your meals mostly McDonald's fries and Red Bull? (No shade, but maybe hydrate once in a while.) The goal isn't to become someone else overnight — it's about making small, subtle changes that help you feel better about yourself. The following sections can help you with that by focusing on glow-up strategies and picking out your most flattering first-date outfit.

REMEMBER

Confidence is the real glow-up. When you feel good, you look good. And when you look good, your vibe screams, "I'm the prize!" which, let's face it, you are.

The glow-up recipe: Turning insecurities into confidence

We all have those little insecurities that sneak in and steal our sparkle. But guess what? Confidence isn't something you're just born with — it's a skill you can build. The following tips can help you turn those doubts into your secret power:

- **Steam it, don't dream it.** Wrinkled clothes don't scream "effortlessly cool" — they just scream "I overslept." Invest in a steamer or use the shower trick to make sure your outfit looks as fresh as your vibe.

- **Hydrate like you mean it.** Your skin loves water almost as much as your soul loves gossip. Swap a soda (or, let's be honest, that fourth coffee) for a tall glass of H_2O and watch your complexion thank you.

- **Upgrade your posture.** Confidence starts with how you carry yourself — literally. Shoulders back, chin up, and strut like you're Beyoncé walking into Target.

- **Elevate your grooming game.** Whether it's a fresh haircut, beard trim, or finding the *perfect* signature scent, small tweaks to your grooming routine can make a big impact.

- **Nourish, don't punish.** Replace your McDonald's-and-Red-Bull diet (we see you) with a mix of actual vegetables, protein, and yes, still some fries. Balance is key.

- **Focus on your favorite features.** Love your eyes? Highlight them with a pop of color. Think your smile is great? Invest in some whitening strips. Lean into what makes you feel fabulous.

- **Sweat it out, but make it fun.** You don't have to become a gym rat to feel good — take a dance class, go for a hike, or do some yoga. Moving your body boosts your mood and gives you that post-workout glow.

- **Declutter your closet.** Ditch the clothes that don't make you feel amazing. Keep the items that fit well, reflect your personality, and make you excited to get dressed.

>> **Revamp your social media.** Unfollow the accounts that make you feel insecure and follow people who inspire you. Your feed should uplift you, not make you question your worth.

>> **Invest in self-care.** Whether it's a face mask, a long bath, or that book you've been meaning to read, take time to care for yourself. Self-love radiates outward.

>> **Practice gratitude for you.** Every morning (or whenever you're scrolling TikTok), write down one thing you love about yourself. Over time, you'll start to see just how great you really are.

>> **Surround yourself with hype people.** Your circle should be filled with people who cheer you on and remind you of your worth — because nothing kills insecurities like a solid support system.

>> **Dress for the date (and your confidence).** Wear something that makes you feel unstoppable. Forget trends — if you feel like a star in it, you'll radiate star energy.

>> **Smile like you mean it.** It's free, it's easy, and it's the ultimate confidence booster. Plus, smiling makes you look approachable and leaves a lasting impression.

>> **Own your insecurities.** Instead of hiding what makes you feel vulnerable, embrace it. Nervous laugh? It's charming. Slightly crooked teeth? Iconic. Your quirks make you memorable.

REMEMBER: The glow-up isn't about perfection — it's about showing up as the best version of yourself, feeling good, and making sure that the person across the table knows they're lucky to be there with *you*.

How to have the dream outfit for the dream date

The first step to loving your outfit is matching your fit to the activity you're doing. If you're going on a hike in the hills, skip the double-breasted suit unless you're filming *Mission Impossible: Outdoors Edition*. And if you're headed to an expensive French restaurant with all the menu items you can't pronounce, let's agree to leave the cargo shorts or mom jeans at home — French cuisine deserves a little respect (and your stretchy pants deserve a night off).

Next, your outfit is more than fabric — it's a sneak peek into your personality. Love neutrals and cool tones? Rock them confidently. Obsessed with cheetah print? Wear all 50 shades of it! The key is showcasing your style in a way that feels authentic *and* fits the vibe of the date.

TIFF SAYS

Above all, dress comfortably. I once wore the tightest dress I owned because I wanted to turn heads, and oh, I turned them — when the dress split at the table and I had to flee like I was auditioning for *Super Bowl Halftime Scandals: The Sequel*.

Here's the deal: Your outfit should make you feel like *you* — the best, most fabulous version of yourself. Not the "I'm pulling and tugging at my clothes every five seconds" version. So keep these tips in mind for the perfect date night look:

- **Know the venue.** Tailor your look to the setting. A cozy coffee shop calls for laid-back chic, while a fancy rooftop bar might need a touch of glamour.

- **Comfort is king (or queen).** If you can't walk, breathe, or sit without discomfort, it's not the right fit — literally.

- **Plan for weather.** Check the forecast! Nothing kills a vibe like freezing in your sleeveless dress or sweating through your blazer because you forgot it's July.

- **Pick the right shoes.** Avoid shoes that scream, "I'm about to file a complaint with my podiatrist." Cute *and* comfortable is always a win.

- **Don't overdo it.** Statement pieces are fun, but you don't need to wear all your bold accessories at once. Choose one standout piece and let it shine.

- **Think long-term.** Would this outfit survive the entire date? Whether you're sitting, standing, or doing something active, make sure your clothes can keep up with you.

REMEMBER

The best accessory to any outfit is your confidence. When you feel good about what you're wearing, it shows — and that's the vibe you want to bring to any date.

CHAPTER 12 From Outfit to Attitude: Making a Great First Impression

Fresh and Flawless: Your Pre-Date Hygiene Checklist

You want your date to remember *you* — not your breath. Good hygiene is the simplest way to make a great first impression without even trying. Follow this easy checklist to show up fresh, confident, and totally date-ready:

- **Banish the bad breath.** Brush, floss, and don't forget the tongue — it's where bad breath hides. Follow it up with mouthwash and stash mints or gum for a quick refresh before the date. Just don't chew gum like you're auditioning for a cow-themed TikTok dance.

- **Shower like you mean it.** This is nonnegotiable. Use your favorite soap, shampoo, and conditioner to feel squeaky clean. Don't forget to exfoliate — you want soft, touchable skin, not sandpaper elbows.

- **Deodorize and scent up.** Apply deodorant and a signature scent. A light spritz is perfect — don't turn yourself into a walking perfume counter. You want them leaning in, not leaning away.

- **Check your hands.** Clean, trimmed nails are a must. If you're shaking hands, holding hands, or giving a high-five (hey, you never know), you want those hands to be date-ready.

- **Tame the mane.** Fix your hair! Whether it's a fresh haircut, styled curls, or a well-groomed beard, take the time to make sure your hair game is on point. This also applies to any stray eyebrow or nose hairs.

- **Keep it fresh below the neck.** Clean clothes are a given, but fresh undergarments? Nonnegotiable. That's all we'll say on that.

- **Hydrate your skin.** Moisturizer isn't just for skincare junkies. Apply some to your face, hands, and any areas that might be showing. Glowing, hydrated skin is always in.

- **Check the details.** Are your shoes clean? Did you iron/steam your outfit? Are there any stains or lint that need handling?

- **Prep your smile.** Even if you're not a teeth-whitening enthusiast, make sure your teeth are clean and shiny. A great smile can make the whole date brighter.

>> **Pack your "confidence kit".** Toss these items into your bag or pocket:

- Mints or gum
- Lip balm
- A small comb or hair tie
- Tissues or wet wipes (you never know)

TIP Remember to give yourself a once-over in front of the mirror before you head out. Spin around, check for any wardrobe mishaps, and most importantly, give yourself a wink — you look amazing!

REMEMBER The key to hygiene is feeling good about yourself so you can focus on the date, not whether you remembered to use deodorant. When you're fresh, polished, and confident, you're unstoppable!

Presenting Yourself Authentically from the Jump

I get it — you want your date to like you. But the absolute worst thing you can do is show up pretending to be the person you think they'd like. This isn't Halloween, so leave the costumes and personas at home. If you're someone who loves wearing bright pink and glitter, don't show up dressed like Wednesday Addams just because your date plays bass in a goth rock band. Authenticity is key — because if they're not into the real you, why waste your time?

Here's the thing: If you're a smiley person who laughs loudly at dad jokes, don't try to morph into a brooding intellectual sipping black coffee while quoting Nietzsche. Your date will see right through it when you accidentally snort laughing at your own joke. And if you love athleisure because it's cozy and makes you feel like an off-duty Olympian, don't force yourself into heels or a tie that feels like a punishment. You want to show up looking like the best version of yourself, not a knockoff of someone else.

And let's talk about personality. If you're bubbly and enthusiastic, lean into that charm. If you're a bit more reserved, embrace your cool, mysterious side. The goal is to feel comfortable so that your personality can shine — not to waste energy putting on a performance.

REMEMBER: First dates are auditions for your real self, not a fictional character. If you spend the whole evening faking it, you'll either have to keep up the act forever or deal with the awkwardness of them realizing later that you actually hate hiking, don't listen to indie rock, and have no idea what kombucha even is.

So wear what you love, laugh how you laugh, and let your true vibe shine through. The right person will love you for exactly who you are — snorts, sequins, and all.

The Right Scent, Right Time

There's a special kind of confidence that comes with knowing you smell amazing. It's like having a personal halo of allure that follows you everywhere — except instead of glowing light, it's hints of lavender and citrus. Science even backs it up: Scent plays a huge role in attraction. Our noses are wired to pick up on subtle chemical signals called pheromones, which can influence how much someone vibes with you. So really, your signature scent isn't just a spritz — it's practically your dating superpower.

The right scent isn't about drowning yourself in the first bottle you grab; it's about choosing something that complements you. Whether it's a woodsy cologne, a playful floral, or something that smells like bottled-up confidence, the right fragrance can make you feel unstoppable. It sends the message, "I have my life together, and I smell like it, too." And let's be clear — you don't need to spend your rent money on an iconic designer perfume. Sometimes the perfect scent is just a quick spray of something that fits your vibe from the local drugstore.

WARNING: Your scent should whisper, not scream. You want your date to lean in closer, not turn away because they're trying to dodge a fog of "Eau de Overkill." And trust me, you do not want to smell like you walked out of an Abercrombie & Fitch store in 2002 or like a high school locker room that's been overrun by body spray. Subtlety is your best friend here — less is truly more.

The magic of a signature scent is its ability to leave a lasting impression. Studies show that scent is one of the most powerful memory triggers. Long after the date, they might catch a whiff of something similar and instantly think of you — and not just because you accidentally spilled some on their jacket. So take your time, test a few options, and when you find the one, spritz lightly and walk into your date knowing you smell as good as you look — possibly better.

PRE-DATE EMERGENCY KIT: BE PREPARED FOR ANYTHING

The following items are your secret weapon for looking polished, feeling confident, and being ready for whatever your date (or life) throws at you:

- **Breath mints or gum:** For when that onion bagel decides to make a comeback.
- **Lip balm:** Nobody likes dry, cracked lips — keep them kiss-ready.
- **Mini deodorant:** Because dates don't pair well with sweat anxiety.
- **Tissues or wet wipes:** For spills, smudges, or surprise sneezes.
- **Compact mirror:** Check your teeth, hair, and eyeliner before the date (or during a bathroom break).
- **Travel toothbrush/floss picks:** Just in case that spinach decides to hang out longer than it should.
- **Blotting papers:** Keep your face looking glowy, not greasy.
- **Safety pins:** For unexpected wardrobe malfunctions (hello, split seams).
- **Backup hair tie or clip:** For when your down-do isn't cooperating.
- **Mini perfume/cologne:** A quick spritz can work wonders for confidence.
- **Pain reliever (like ibuprofen):** For last-minute headaches or cramps.
- **Portable charger:** You don't want your phone dying before you can text your friend to say how it's going.
- **Cash or a card:** Always have enough to cover your part of the date or an escape Uber.
- **Band-aids:** For unexpected blisters from those "cute but cruel" shoes.
- **Lint roller:** Pet hair or lint ruining your sleek look? Not today.

(continued)

(continued)

- **Hand sanitizer:** For clean hands after touching door handles, menus, or escalator rails.
- **Breath spray:** A faster, subtler alternative to gum or mints.
- **Tampon or pad:** Even if you don't need it, you never know when someone else might.

Sit Up, Smile, and Slay: Posture Power for Your Date

Posture and presence are your silent wingmen on any date. Standing tall, keeping your shoulders back, and making eye contact doesn't just make you look confident — it actually helps you feel confident, even if your inner monologue is freaking out about whether you have spinach in your teeth.

TIP Remember, your date isn't expecting perfection; they're looking for someone who's happy to be there. So even if your nerves are doing cartwheels, focus on maintaining an open and relaxed body language. Smile, lean in (but not too much — this isn't a dentist appointment), and show genuine interest. A positive attitude is contagious, and when you radiate enthusiasm, it not only makes you more attractive but also helps put your date at ease. After all, the best first impression isn't about being flawless; it's about being present, engaged, and making the other person feel like they're worth your time and not that you're there to treat them like they're your therapist or because you were bored.

At the end of the day (or date), how you present yourself is all about feeling good and letting your authentic self shine through. From your outfit to your posture, your scent to your smile, the goal isn't perfection — it's confidence. When you feel great about how you look and carry yourself, that energy is magnetic. And remember, a date is about connection, not a fashion show or a job interview. So go out there, embrace your quirks, and show up as the best version of you. Because the right person isn't just looking for someone who looks good — they're looking for someone who feels good to be around. If you feel confident in your look, I'm confident your date will see all the amazing things you have to offer — almost as amazing as your outfit!

> **IN THIS CHAPTER**
> » Understanding why you get nervous on dates
> » Ditching the "what ifs" for what could be
> » Turning nerves into excitement
> » Getting a little hype from your friends
> » Staying present before and during a date
> » Knowing that every "no" is simply a detour
> » Debating whether to have that pre-date drink
> » Getting yourself hyped with some helpful affirmations

Chapter **13**

Bye-Bye Butterflies: How to Crush First Date Nerves and Boost Your Confidence

I've never understood why people call pre-date nerves "butterflies." It doesn't feel like a whimsical flutter of wings — it feels like a butter-die. You know, that heavy, stomach-churning panic, like you just chugged three energy drinks on an empty stomach while debating if your date will like you, hate you, or spend the night eating an entire rack of ribs while oversharing about their ex. The world of possibilities is endless, and that's the beauty and the chaos of dating.

But nerves are normal! They're just your body's way of saying, "Hey, this could be something big." Think of them as the same adrenaline that pop stars feel before they step onto a stage for their sold-out world tour. The trick is not letting the nerves stop you from performing — and by performing, I mean showing up and being your amazing self.

You may not be able to control the outcome of the date, but you can control the effort and energy you bring to the table. When you realize the dating gods have already scheduled more people in your life than you could possibly swipe through, you stop stressing about one date and start focusing on having fun. This chapter helps you tackle those nerves step by step. Because once you shake them off, you'll go from nervous wreck to receiving your award in the dating hall of fame. And trust me, when you're busy juggling all the second dates begging for your attention, you'll laugh at how anxious you used to feel about the first one.

Why Do We Get Nervous Before a Date?

Getting nervous before a date is as universal as wondering why the waiter always gives the other person the check. It's a mix of biology, psychology, and the pure, unrelenting fear of embarrassing yourself in front of someone you might like. At its core, nerves are just your body's way of saying, "Hey, this could be important!" — even if your brain is screaming, "Run away, this could be a disaster!"

Scientifically speaking, pre-date nerves are tied to your body's fight-or-flight response. When faced with the uncertainty of whether your date is your soulmate or someone who chews with their mouth open, your brain floods your system with adrenaline. This is great if you're about to escape a tiger, but less helpful when you're deciding whether to order the burger or the pasta. Your heart races, your palms sweat, and suddenly you're hyper-aware of every tiny flaw you think you have. Thanks, evolution.

Psychologists also point out that dating taps into a primal fear of rejection, which dates back to when being kicked out of the tribe could mean literal risk to survival. In today's world, getting ghosted won't lead to starvation, but your brain hasn't quite caught up. Instead, it overreacts, making a simple dinner feel like you're presenting your entire life's worth in a job interview where the stakes are love, happiness, and your mother finally getting off your back about being single.

Nerves also mean you care. If you're feeling butterflies (or, as I prefer, butter-dies), it's because you're stepping out of your comfort zone and taking a risk. That's a good thing! Being nervous before a date doesn't mean you're doomed; it means you're human. So embrace the shaky hands and racing heart — you're about to dive headfirst into the wild, unpredictable adventure of connection. My hope is that your dates don't feel like a workout but, in the words of Nike, even if you're nervous, Just Do It.

Swapping the "What Ifs" for "What Could Be"

Changing your "what ifs" from doom-and-gloom scenarios to exciting possibilities is the ultimate pre-date mindset hack to help quell those nervous feelings. It's easy to spiral into thoughts like "What if I spill my drink? What if they don't like me? What if they secretly run a pyramid scheme and try to recruit me?" But here's the thing — these negative "what ifs" aren't just unproductive; they're also unfair to yourself and the other person. Psychology tells us that our brains have a negativity bias, meaning we're naturally wired to focus on potential disasters. But guess what? You can rewire that thinking with a little effort and a lot of humor.

Instead of "What if they think I'm boring?" flip it to, "What if they find me so fascinating they can't stop texting me after the date?" Instead of "What if I say something dumb?" try "What if my awkward joke is actually charming and makes them laugh?" The beauty of the "what if" game is that it works both ways, so why not rig it in your favor? After all, the worst-case scenario is usually far less likely than the best-case one.

TIP Studies show that practicing optimism can reduce stress and boost confidence — two things that are essential for a successful date. By shifting your "what ifs," you're not just being blindly positive; you're giving yourself the mental space to be open to good things happening. And let's be real: A date is a chance for connection, not a life-or-death situation. The stakes might feel high, but at the end of the day it's just two people sharing drinks, food, or awkward small talk.

Romance often involves a little faith and a touch of delusion. If you're going to daydream about scenarios that aren't real, make sure they're about candlelit dinners, surprise kisses, and epic stories of how you met — not rejection, spilled wine, or awkward silences. Because when you think about it, believing in the "what could be" is how all great love stories begin.

How to Turn Nerves into Excitement

Studies show that anxiety and excitement trigger similar responses in the body. It's why some people jump out of airplanes for fun. By reframing nerves as excitement, you can channel that energy into positive anticipation rather than paralyzing fear. Instead of thinking, "What if they don't like me?" think, "What if they do?"

Following are some tips for getting those nerves to actually work for you:

>> **Reframe your mindset.** Instead of thinking, "I'm so nervous," tell yourself, "I'm so excited!" Studies show that anxiety and excitement share similar physiological responses — heart racing, palms sweating, adrenaline pumping. By simply swapping the narrative in your head, you can trick your brain into viewing the date as an opportunity rather than a threat. Think of it as the difference between "I might fail" and "I might win!"

>> **Visualize the best-case scenario.** Take a moment to picture the date going really well. Imagine you're laughing over a shared joke, they're loving your stories, and the chemistry is undeniable. Visualization helps your brain focus on positive outcomes, which can naturally ease those nerves. And hey, if you're going to let your imagination run wild, why not make it a rom-com instead of a disaster flick?

>> **Move your body.** Channel that nervous energy into action. Jumping jacks, a quick walk, or even an impromptu dance party in your room can help burn off excess adrenaline. Plus, moving your body releases endorphins, those feel-good

chemicals that will have you feeling less "ahh" and more "aww I got this."

- **Breathe like you mean it.** Nervous breathing tends to be shallow and fast, which makes you feel even more panicked. Slow it down with the 4-7-8 technique: Inhale for four seconds, hold for seven seconds, and exhale for eight seconds. It calms your nervous system and gives you time to remember that you're not auditioning for *Survivor*.

- **Set a positive anchor.** Think of a song, quote, or mantra that makes you feel invincible. Maybe it's Lizzo telling you to "feel good as hell" or simply repeating, "I'm a catch, and they're lucky to meet me." Tap into something that gives you confidence and makes you feel unstoppable.

- **Shift focus off yourself.** Nerves often come from overthinking how you'll perform or be perceived. Instead, focus on them. Get curious about your date — what they like, what makes them laugh, what their go-to karaoke song is. Shifting your attention outward helps reduce self-consciousness and reminds you that dates are about connection, not perfection.

- **Have a go-to game plan.** Prep a few topics or questions in advance to keep the conversation flowing. Think of it as your cheat sheet: favorite travel spots, funny childhood stories, or even what they'd grab first in a zombie apocalypse. Knowing you have a few safe topics can take the pressure off.

- **Laugh at your nerves.** Nervous energy loses its power when you call it out. If your hands are shaking or you stumble over a word, laugh it off. "Wow, I must've had too much coffee — I'm jittery!" A little self-deprecating humor can break the ice and show your date you're human (and adorable).

- **Remind yourself what's at stake (spoiler: not much).** This is just one date. If it goes well, great! If not, it's a funny story for your group chat. You've survived bad haircuts, awkward presentations, and middle school gym class — this is nothing in comparison.

- **Celebrate afterward — no matter what.** Regardless of how the date goes, reward yourself. Go for dessert, call a friend, or treat yourself to a Netflix binge. Turning the experience into a win (just for showing up) helps you associate dates with positivity, making the next one even easier.

REMEMBER: The key to turning nerves into excitement is flipping the script. You're not "terrified" — you're thrilled. You're not "stressed" — you're ready. And honestly, isn't it kind of exciting to see where this wild, unpredictable ride of dating will take you next?

The SOS Call: Why Friends Always Have the Best (or Worst) Advice

Friends are like the lifeguards of your dating life — they're there to save you when you're drowning in nerves, doubts, or questionable outfit choices. Before a date, it's practically a rite of passage to call, text, or group chat your inner circle for advice. And honestly, no one hypes you up better than your friends. They're the ones who will tell you, "You're too good for them anyway," if things go south and will also gas you up like a Formula 1 car, reminding you how amazing you are before you even leave the house.

But let's be real: Friend advice is a mixed bag. One friend will tell you to "just be yourself," while another is out here suggesting you "play hard to get" or "accidentally" drop that you know how to make perfect risotto. The key is figuring out whose advice aligns with your values — and whose you should take with a salt-rimmed margarita.

REMEMBER: The real magic of friends isn't just in their advice but in their unwavering hype. They'll remind you why your date is lucky to spend time with you — not the other way around. So lean into that pre-date pep talk, let them gush about how good you look in that outfit, and take the hype with you. Because when you feel good about yourself, that energy is magnetic.

And hey, even if their advice turns out to be ridiculous ("Send them a meme before you leave for the date!"), you'll always have them to laugh with — or vent to — when the date's over. Friends may not always get it right, but their love and support will always have your back.

Tricks to Get Out of Your Head and Stay Present

Your mind loves to run wild with "what-ifs," but that just kills the vibe and your confidence. These simple tricks will help you hit pause on the overthinking and actually enjoy your date:

- **Pre-date prep: Channel your inner CEO.** Treat your nerves like an overzealous intern — give them something to do! Pick out your outfit, rehearse a few icebreakers, and mentally note where the bathrooms are (because drinks happen). Being prepared will make you feel like the main character, not someone fumbling through their lines.

- **Call the hype squad.** Phone a friend who hypes you up better than a reality TV reunion host. Let them remind you that you're a catch and the only thing your date should worry about is keeping up. Bonus: They'll distract you from spiraling into a black hole of "What if they hate me?"

- **Reframe the stakes.** Instead of worrying, "What if they don't like me?" flip it: "What if *I* don't like them?" You're not auditioning for a part — you're interviewing *them* for a role in your life. Shift the power dynamic, and suddenly you're the one holding the rose.

- **Get mindful, not mind-full.** Take a moment to breathe. Try the 5-4-3-2-1 trick: five things you can see, four you can touch, three you hear, two you smell, and one you taste (hopefully not the onion bagel from lunch). It'll keep you grounded and off the panic train to Overthinkingville.

- **Set a silly intention.** Instead of aiming for "perfect," aim for fun. Challenge yourself to make your date laugh, drop an obscure fact, or spot a neon sign with a misspelled word. Focus on the quirky little joys, not whether this is your future spouse.

- **Active listening is your secret weapon.** Instead of zoning out while you plan your next witty comment, actually *listen*. Not only does this make you look like a great conversationalist, but it also stops you from replaying that awkward joke you told three minutes ago. Bonus: You might learn something cool about them.

>> **Channel Beyoncé (or your inner rockstar).** Walk in like you own the place, even if your hands are shaking like a Jenga tower midgame. Confidence is like glitter — fake it, and eventually it's everywhere. Plus, nobody can tell you're nervous when you're grinning like you just won the lottery.

>> **Laugh at the awkward moments.** Awkward silences? Embrace them! Say, "Wow, we're both so lost in thought — we must be philosophers." You'll both laugh, and it's way better than panicking over why your joke about bread didn't land.

>> **Focus on the room, not your flaws.** If you start spiraling into "Is my hair weird?" or "Why did I wear this shirt?" distract yourself. Check out the decor, listen to the music, or admire how good you are at sitting upright. It's the little victories.

>> **Give yourself a little sweet treat.** Whether the date ends with sparks or a polite handshake, you win just for showing up. Reward yourself with dessert, a bubble bath, or a call to your bestie for the post-date breakdown. You're already crushing it by putting yourself out there.

Every "No" Is Just a Detour to Your Eventual "Yes"

Let's face it — rejection stings. But here's the twist: Every "no" isn't the end of your dating story; it's just the universe redirecting you to someone better. Rejection is just redirection. Think of rejection as GPS recalculating your route. Sure, it's annoying, but wouldn't you rather detour now than end up stuck in a dead-end relationship?

Sometimes nerves can hit before a date because deep down, you feel like you don't deserve them. Trust me, I've been there — feeling like my life would crumble if a man in a blue suit who wouldn't stop talking about stocks didn't think I was pretty. I spent so much time agonizing over what I said, what I ate, and whether I laughed too loud. And for what? A lukewarm guy who made me feel like I was auditioning for *Shark Tank* instead of going on a date?

WARNING: If you're walking into a date feeling like you're auditioning for someone's approval, that's your red flag. A date shouldn't feel like a battlefield — it should feel like you're a judge on *The Voice*, and every chair is turning for you. You're the prize, and anyone lucky enough to sit across from you should feel that way too.

Once you start viewing yourself as worthy of love and fully datable, the pressure melts away. If it works out, great! If it doesn't, they weren't your person. And remember this: You never had that person before the date, so no matter what happens, the only way to go is up.

So if they don't like you, that's okay, because you like you. You'll find someone who sees you for the star you are — no blue suits or stock talk required.

To Sip or Not to Sip: The Pre-Date Drink Debate

Ah, the million-dollar question: Should you pre-game your date? On one hand, a little drink can help take the edge off. On the other, you don't want to show up asking them, "How do you feel about love?" with the intensity of someone who's three martinis deep. The sweet spot? One drink — just enough to turn your nerves into charm without turning your charm into chaos.

Think of it like seasoning a dish: a dash of tequila? Perfect. A whole bottle of wine? You're about to burn the casserole and blame the oven. If you're using that pre-date drink to relax, great. But if you're tossing back shots to calm your jitters, maybe switch to chamomile tea — or call a friend for a pep talk instead. Alcohol will never cure the real issue of nerves — it's just a band aid. There's no problem with a date night drink, but it should never be used as a coping mechanism to feel more confident.

REMEMBER: You're trying to make a good impression, not an impression that you're about to be escorted out of the restaurant. Keep it classy, keep it light, and save the tequila dance for date number two. After all, no one's ever said, "You know what I loved most about them? The way they showed up already halfway to hung over." You want to be drunk in love, not drunk.

The Confidence Check-in: Affirmations to Combat Date Nerves

You've got to know your worth if your dating life is going to glow up. Here are some affirmations to help you be your own hype person — and show up confident, every time:

- **"I am worthy of love and connection."** A little self-love reminder goes a long way.
- **"I bring something special to the table (and it's not just my great taste in restaurants)."** You're the main course, not the side dish.
- **"This is just a conversation, not a performance."** No need to win an Oscar — just be you.
- **"If they don't like me, that's their loss."** Honestly, it's true.
- **"I have as much to offer as anyone else."** You're not auditioning; you're exploring possibilities.
- **"A single date doesn't define my worth."** It's one evening, not your life story.
- **"I am confident, charismatic, and capable."** Say it, believe it, own it.
- **"Rejection is just redirection."** A no just means making space for the right yes.
- **"I've got this, and if I don't, I'm doing it for the plot."** Worst-case scenario? Comedy gold for your friends.
- **"I am exactly the kind of person someone would want to date."** And that someone could very well be sitting across from you tonight.
- **"Awkward moments are funny brunch convo."** Seriously, what's a date without a little chaos?
- **"I am more than enough, exactly as I am."** Confidence, plain and simple.
- **"This is supposed to be fun, not stressful."** Dates are about possibilities, not perfection.
- **"I am allowed to enjoy myself without worrying about the outcome."** The journey is just as important as the destination.
- **"I am the prize."**

With this list of affirmations in hand, you're officially on your way to saying goodbye to pre-date jitters and hello to feeling like the fabulous, unstoppable version of yourself. Remember, you're not single because there's something wrong with you — unless you insist on debating pineapple's place on pizza during every conversation, in which case, maybe rethink that opener. And honestly, it's better to be single than stuck with someone who has the emotional range of a teaspoon or still claps when a plane lands.

Once you start seeing your worth, you'll realize you're not just a catch — you're the whole dang ocean. You're ready to share your incredible self with someone deserving, but you don't need anyone to validate your value. The future love of your life is already out there, possibly stuck in traffic or debating which shirt to wear, but they're on their way.

And as for those nerves? They're just a reminder that you're about to step into something exciting. Don't let them hold you back from the romance (or at least a free drink) waiting around the corner. Now go out there, shine bright, and show the world that you're ready for love — on your terms.

IN THIS CHAPTER

» Greetings and salutations

» Knowing what to say on a date

» What to avoid saying or eating on a first date

» What do if the date is going well or terrible

» How to secure a second date or gracefully exit

» How to leave a date with them wanting more

Chapter 14
Big Date Energy: Starting and Keeping the Date Fun and Flirty

You've finally made it to the big night — the first date. You've picked out the perfect outfit, spent an embarrassing amount of time deciding if your hair looks effortlessly cool or just messy, and maybe even rehearsed a few jokes in the mirror (we respect the dedication). But now, as you approach your date, a thousand tiny questions flood your brain: *Handshake, hug, or awkward little wave? What if there's nothing to talk about? What if they don't laugh at the dad joke I've been perfecting all day?*

Here's the thing — you've already done the work. Now it's time to enjoy it. First dates aren't meant to be a high-pressure performance or an audition for *The Bachelor*. They're about connection, fun, and seeing if you actually vibe with this person beyond their well-lit profile pics. So take a deep breath, let go of the *what-ifs*, and focus on what's actually happening *right now*.

This chapter covers everything from first impressions (hint: confidence is hotter than an expensive cologne), conversation starters that won't leave you both staring at your drinks in silence, and ways to end the date on a high note — aka leaving them thinking, "Wow, I hope we do this again." If you keep things optimistic, fun, and maybe just the right amount of flirty, you'll be well on your way to a second date. And if not? Well, at least you got a great story out of it (and hopefully a good drink).

Salutations: Greeting with Style

The first five seconds of a date can set the tone for the whole night, so you want to nail the greeting, without overthinking it into oblivion. Should you go in for a hug? A handshake? A casual wave from an awkwardly far distance like you're signaling a plane? Here's the golden rule: *Match their energy.* If they're leaning in for a hug, go with it. If they seem a little reserved, a confident but warm "Hey, it's so great to finally meet you!" and a smile will do just fine. Avoid the dreaded hesitation dance (where both of you move in, then out, then back in again like malfunctioning robots).

TIP

If you're unsure, default to a friendly side hug — it's approachable without being too much. And for the love of all things romantic, don't hit them with a business-like handshake unless you're signing a contract rather than ordering drinks.

TIFF SAYS

I always say the best way to make a first date *not* feel like a painfully staged job interview is to pretend like you already know them. No, I'm not saying act like you're long-lost soulmates (please, don't start with "So, do you think our future kids would have your nose or mine?"), but rather, approach them like a friend you haven't seen in a while.

Think about it — if you're meeting up with a close friend, you don't start with "So, what are your five-year goals?" You probably greet them with a warm "OMG, you actually exist outside of my phone screen!" or "Okay, tell me why you walked in here looking like a main character."

Keeping it casual and playful from the start instantly lowers the pressure for both of you. It makes your date feel like they're in familiar, comfortable territory, which means they're more likely to relax, open up, and actually enjoy the moment. Plus, confidence (even the fake-it-till-you-make-it kind) is attractive, and acting like you already belong in each other's lives — even in a lighthearted way — sets a fun, easygoing tone.

So instead of diving into "What are you looking for in a partner?" two minutes in, try something like this:

> "Alright, so what's something cool I should know about you that your dating profile didn't mention?"

> "I was going to say I'm excited to meet you, but I feel like I already know you. You're just my friend now — sorry, no take-backs."

> "I hope you're okay with being the more responsible one tonight because I have no idea how to read a cocktail menu properly."

REMEMBER

When you start with warmth, humor, and familiarity, your date won't feel like they're sitting through an interview — they'll feel like they're meeting someone they *actually* want to see again. And that? That's how you win the first date.

Once you've successfully closed the distance without tripping over your own feet, you need to break the ice fast. Here are a few go-to openers to start things off on a high note:

- **Playful confidence:** "Alright, so on a scale of one to 'My dating profile is a complete lie,' how close do I look to my photos?"
- **A lighthearted compliment:** "Okay, I see you — best-dressed award goes to you already."
- **Observational humor:** (If they arrive holding a coffee, jacket, and bag while juggling their phone) "Wow, showing up prepared for any possible scenario — I respect that level of organization."
- **The location tie-in:** (If you're meeting at a bar/restaurant) "So, be honest — did you pick this place because you love it, or did you Google 'best first date spots near me' five minutes ago?"
- **Self-deprecating humor (always a win if done right):** "You made it! And I made it! Look at us, already excelling at this dating thing."

The goal? Make them smile immediately. If you kick things off with warmth, humor, and ease, you're setting up the rest of the date for success. Worst case? You at least avoid the dreaded "Soo, you come here often?" opener, which feels more like a cheesy pickup line from the '80s rather than a romantic start to your night.

Relaxing and Engaging with Your Date

A great date isn't about saying the *perfect* thing or having a script — it's about making each other feel comfortable and actually enjoying the moment. The best conversations aren't forced; they flow naturally, creating real connections. Here's how to ditch the pressure, ask the right questions, and make sure your date feels more like a fun adventure than an awkward Q&A session:

» **Ditch the pressure.** First things first — remind yourself (and your date, if necessary) that this is not a high-stakes negotiation. You're just two people seeing if you vibe, not trying to sign a long-term contract. The moment you release the pressure to be *perfect*, you instantly become more fun to be around.

Instead of walking in thinking, "I need to impress them," try shifting your mindset to "Let's just see if we get along." When you focus on genuine connection instead of approval, the whole dynamic changes from stiff and anxious to light and enjoyable.

» **Talk about what excites you (and let them do the same!).** One of the easiest ways to break past small talk is to tap into excitement. Instead of the predictable "What do you do?" ask:

"What are you passionate about?"

"Do you have a hidden talent?"

People light up when they talk about things they love. If you're obsessed with your dodgeball team, don't be embarrassed — own it. Enthusiasm is contagious, and even if your date doesn't share the same passion, they'll be drawn in by your excitement. Even if you're talking about work, focus on the parts that excite you ("I love meeting new people") instead of the logistics ("I spend six hours a day dealing with Wi-Fi issues").

» **Pop culture is your friend.** Sometimes the smallest details lead to the biggest connections. If you love listening to the Smiths in the back of a taxi and pretending you're in a coming-of-age movie, share that. If you've been to every Green Day concert since 1996, own it. Maybe you think Sabrina Carpenter is an *icon* — say it with your chest.

Pop culture is a universal language — talking about movies, music, or random internet trends gives you instant common ground and can lead to fun, playful debates. ("Is *Die Hard* a Christmas movie?")

» **Talk about travel.** One of the easiest ways to spark a lively conversation is talking about travel. Ask:

"What's the best trip you've ever taken?"

"Where's one place you've always wanted to go?"

"Are you more of a 'lie on the beach' traveler or a 'let's hike a volcano' type?"

Even if you haven't traveled much, talking about places you want to go, bucket list experiences, or even hilarious road trip mishaps can keep the conversation flowing.

» **Talk about your favorite hobbies and activities.** People love talking about what they're passionate about — but be careful not to make it feel like an interrogation. Instead of the dreaded "What's your favorite song?" (the hardest question in the world under pressure), try these:

"What's a song you never skip?"

"What's the most unexpected thing you're really into?"

"What's the last thing you got way too obsessed with?"

This makes the conversation curious, not demanding. Whether they're into painting, marathon running, or competitive axe-throwing, learning about someone's hobbies makes for way more interesting conversation than a stale "So, how long have you lived here?"

Topics and Actions to Avoid on the Date

Some things are better left unsaid — or undone — on a first date. To avoid turning your night into a horror show, pay attention to the advice in the following sections on what to skip so that your date sticks around past the appetizers.

Avoiding trauma dumping

Now listen, I get it. After a few drinks, that little voice in your head might whisper, "Tell them everything. Let it all out. This is your moment." And suddenly, before you know it, you've trauma-dumped your entire life story — your childhood pet's mysterious disappearance, your ex's emotional unavailability, the fact that your co-worker Sarah microwaves fish in the office (again!). But here's the thing: You're looking for a better relationship, not BetterHelp.

TIFF SAYS

I once went on a date with a *perfect* lawyer — charming, well-dressed, *crushing it* in a navy suit. I was ready to be wooed. But the entire evening? One long rant about his boss, Jim, and how Jim had *personally* sabotaged his career. For *thirty full minutes*, I sat there listening to his corporate heartbreak like I was a LinkedIn recruiter, not a date. By the end of dinner, I didn't leave him with my number — I left him with my friend's contact info who works in career coaching because, honestly? He needed a business strategy more than a girlfriend.

REMEMBER

Here's the golden rule: Keep it light, keep it positive, and for the love of all things romantic, do not turn your date into an impromptu therapy session. Everyone has stress, a demanding job, and parking lot enemies, but your date does not need to carry that burden before they even know your middle name. Instead of unpacking *all* your baggage in one sitting, try talking about the fun, exciting things happening in your life right now. Trust me, you'll have plenty of time to bond over life's deep struggles — just maybe not before the appetizers arrive.

Avoiding talking about your exes

There are very few ways to make a first date instantly awkward, and bringing up your ex is at the top of the list. Nothing kills the romance faster than casually dropping, "Yeah, my ex used to love this place," or worse, "Wow, you actually remind me a lot of my ex." No one wants to feel like they're competing with a ghost from relationships past. Whether you're ranting about how toxic they were or reminiscing about how they *just didn't appreciate you the way they should have,* it's all a bad look.

Even if you swear you're *totally over it,* excessive ex-talk makes it seem like you're still mentally drafting texts you wish you had sent. Instead, focus on the person sitting in front of you! Ask about their favorite travel spots, their go-to comfort show, or the weirdest job they've ever had. Keep the vibe fresh and forward-thinking — because, trust me, nothing says, "I am absolutely still emotionally involved with my ex" like spending 20 minutes explaining why *you're not emotionally involved with your ex.*

TIFF SAYS

I once dated a guy in college who, from the first date onward, could not stop talking about how "crazy" his ex was. Now, one thing I've learned the hard way? If someone won't stop calling their ex *crazy,* chances are *they* were the ones making them crazy. But I overlooked it because, hey, maybe he was just venting? Maybe he was totally done with her? Nope. A few dates later, I got a text saying, "So sorry, I actually moved upstate with my ex." *Sir, what!?* Turns out he was just waiting for her to take him back and I was the halftime show in their romantic Super Bowl. Lesson learned: Excessive ex-talk doesn't just mean the ex is still in their head — it might mean you're the backup plan while they wait for their reunion tour.

Love bombing — When "too good to be true" is exactly that

Ah, love bombing — the oldest trick in the *fake romance* book. It's when someone you just met starts showering you with over-the-top affection, big promises, and dramatic declarations of "I've never felt this way before" — all before they even know your last name. If they spend date number one talking about planning your future vacations, introducing you to their mom, and calling you their soulmate, slow down, Romeo. Love bombing isn't romance — it's a red flag disguised as a dozen red roses.

The truth is, real love takes time. Someone who barely knows you shouldn't be making grand commitments like "I'd move anywhere for you" when they haven't even learned how you take your coffee. It's intoxicating at first — who wouldn't love being treated like the main character in a rom-com? But here's the catch: Love bombers aren't building a connection; they're setting the stage for control. They create an emotional high, then just as quickly pull back, leaving you wondering what went wrong.

So how do you spot it? Watch for intensity without foundation. If they're declaring their undying love before they've even asked about your favorite movie, take a step back. Real interest is about *getting to know you,* not throwing empty promises your way. And if they're planning a future with you before they've even memorized your number? That's not fate — that's fast-tracked fantasy.

Saving the spicy talk for later

Look, I get it — flirting is fun, chemistry is important, and you might already be wondering what they look like without that well-fitted jacket. But let's get one thing straight: Your first date is *not* an audition for an HBO after-dark special. Jumping into *highly sexual topics* too soon is like putting hot sauce on your pancakes — confusing, unnecessary, and more likely to make things awkward than exciting.

There's a fine line between playful, flirty banter and straight-up TMI territory. Saying, "You look amazing tonight"? Perfect. Saying, "I bet you look amazing without that outfit on"? Sir, this is a Chili's. A well-placed compliment? Charming. A full breakdown of your biggest kinks before the drinks even arrive? Absolutely not.

Not only does steering the conversation toward *sexy topics* too early make things weird, but it also signals that you're not actually interested in *them* — just in getting to the main event. And nothing kills the vibe faster than making someone feel like they're being fast-tracked to a hookup when they were just trying to enjoy their pasta.

So keep it light, keep it fun, and keep it **PG-13 at most** — because trust me, if the date goes well, there will be *plenty* of time for *that* conversation later.

Keeping your hands to yourself (until it feels right)

Listen, a little playful touch can be flirty and romantic — *eventually*. But on a first date? Less is more. A light touch on the arm during a laugh? Cute. Randomly playing with their hair like you're a hairstylist mid-shift? Please, no.

Not everyone has the same comfort level with touch, and you don't want to come across as *too much, too soon*. The goal is to leave them thinking, "I'd love to feel more of that," not "I need to file a personal space complaint." Think of physical touch on a first date like seasoning — just a sprinkle goes a long way. So maybe save the full-on hand-holding, excessive knee-grabbing, and surprise back rubs for *after* you know they actually like being touched. Because trust me, there's a big difference between "flirty" and "Why is this person playing footsie with me under the table five minutes in?"

Keep the first date light — Save the existential crises for later

Look, first dates should be fun, not feel like you accidentally wandered into a political debate or a late-night philosophy class. Dropping "So, what are your thoughts on the meaning of life?" before the drinks even arrive isn't exactly setting the mood. Heavy topics like religion, politics, family trauma, or the inevitable collapse of society might be great discussions down the road, but on a first date? Hard pass. Think of your conversation like a campfire — you want to keep adding little sparks to make it glow, not dump a bucket of gasoline and hope for the best.

Yes, it's important to know if your values align, but launching into "So, where do you see yourself on the spiritual spectrum?" before they even know your last name is a one-way ticket to Awkwardville. Instead, focus on light, engaging topics that give you a sense of their personality *without* making them feel like they're being cross-examined. There will be plenty of time for deep talks if the date goes well — so maybe, just maybe, let's hold off on solving world hunger until the second round of drinks.

TIFF SAYS

Now, having just said that, some things are deal-breakers and that's okay. If you know deep down that you'd rather be single forever than date someone who, say, votes for the opposite political party, has vastly different religious views, or doesn't believe in dogs (*yes, this is a red flag*), then it's better to know sooner rather than later. The key? Bring it up in a way that feels natural, not like you're launching an investigative report. Instead of aggressively leading with "So, where do you stand on [insert hot-button issue]?" before your drinks even hit the table, try something more open-ended like

> "I think it's really important to share certain values in a relationship. What are some of the things that matter most to you?"

"I try to keep an open mind about most things, but I do feel really strongly about [insert topic]. What about you?"

This way, you're gauging their perspective without making it feel like an interrogation. If you realize early on that their views are a complete no-go for you, you can gracefully keep the date short without wasting anyone's time (or pretending to laugh at their jokes while mentally plotting your exit). Just remember: The goal is to see if you're compatible, not to turn the evening into a political debate club meeting. If the date starts feeling more like a cable news segment than a fun night out, it's time to change the subject — or the exit strategy.

HOW YOU TREAT YOUR SERVER SAYS EVERYTHING ABOUT YOU

Let's get one thing straight — **being rude to the server is a major red flag.** No matter how charming, funny, or good-looking someone is, if they treat waitstaff like they're auditioning for *Hell's Kitchen*, the date is officially *over*.

Complaining about service, nitpicking the menu, or acting entitled ("Umm, I asked for extra ice, and this is clearly regular ice") is not a personality trait; it's a turnoff. If something is genuinely wrong with the meal, sure, politely mention it, but do not become the person who makes it their mission to humiliate the staff over a slightly slow refill.

And let's talk about the tip. A shockingly high number of dates have ended with one person watching in horror as the other leaves a sad, disrespectful tip — or worse, no tip at all (*gasps in moral outrage*). Look, if you can't afford to leave at least 20 percent, you shouldn't be dining out. If your date pulls a "Well, the service wasn't *that* great" excuse to justify stiffing the server, consider that a sneak preview into how they handle generosity, gratitude, and kindness in general.

So here's my pro tip: Watch how they treat their server, because that's a good indicator of how they'll treat you. A date who says, "thank you," makes eye contact, and doesn't act like the staff are invisible? Green flag. Someone who snaps their fingers, is unnecessarily demanding, or leaves pennies for a tip? Run.

The Graceful Exit: How to Leave a Bad Date without Drama

Not every date is going to be a rom-com moment. Sometimes you're stuck across from someone who won't stop talking about their ex, chewing loudly, or explaining why cryptocurrency is the future of society. Whatever the reason, you're ready to leave — but how do you do it smoothly? Here's how to make your exit without causing a scene (unless they *really* deserve one).

The emergency call: Your classic get-out-of-jail-free card

The oldest trick in the book — and for good reason. Before the date, have a friend ready to call or text with an excuse. It doesn't need to be dramatic (no need to fake a house fire), just simple and effective:

> "Oh no, my roommate just locked herself out — gotta run!"

> "Work emergency! I need to answer this, but let's catch up soon."

> "My dog is sick." (Even if you don't have a dog — who's going to question a mysterious, imaginary pet emergency?)

Bonus tip: If your friend is really committed, have them call you mid-date and loudly say, "You won't believe what just happened!" before you even speak. Instant drama, instant exit.

Being honest: When the vibes are off, just say it

If the date is just *meh*, but they're a nice person, you don't have to fake an emergency to escape. Being upfront is the grown-up move (even if it's awkward). Keep it short and kind:

> "Hey, I really appreciate meeting you, but I don't think we have that spark."

> "I've had a nice time, but I don't feel the connection I'm looking for."

"You seem great, but I think we might be looking for different things."

They might be bummed, but at least you're not ghosting them mid-appetizer.

Skip the "Irish exit" — unless they deserve it

Now, *technically*, you *could* just excuse yourself to the bathroom and never come back, but let's be real — unless your date is being super rude, that's not the move. However, if they're making you uncomfortable, disrespecting boundaries, or just being a full-on creep, then by all means, pull a Houdini and vanish like a magician at a kid's birthday party. No explanation needed.

Your comfort comes first — always

Bad dates happen, but your time and energy are valuable. If you're not vibing, or worse, feeling uneasy, leave. You don't need to have an elaborate excuse or to wait until they finish their long-winded story about their fantasy football league. A simple "Hey, I'm going to head out" is all it takes.

At the end of the day, dating should be fun — not an endurance test. So trust your gut, know your exit plan, and remember: You owe no one your time if it's not feeling right.

Date Night Finish Line: How to End on a High Note

A first date isn't just about making a great first impression — it's about ending things in a way that keeps the momentum going (or making a clean exit if it's *not* a match). Whether it was fireworks or just *fine*, how you handle the last few minutes can set the tone for what happens next. So let's break it down:

First date kiss: Hit or miss?

Ah, the age-old question: *To kiss or not to kiss?* The truth is that there's no right answer — it all depends on the vibe. If the chemistry is undeniable and you're both lingering like a rom-com finale, go for it. But if you're second-guessing or feel like you need a *flowchart* to decide, it's perfectly fine to wait until next time. A flirty "I had so much fun tonight" with a lingering goodbye glance can be just as effective as a kiss in leaving them wanting more.

If it was one of those movie-magic first dates, there's no shame in sharing a kiss in front of the subway entrance, outside the restaurant, or right at your front door — just hoping your roommates aren't watching through the window. But let's be real — there's a big difference between a romantic kiss and a full-on make-out session. Read the room. If you're clear on ending the night solo, keep it classy, charming, and short, and then keep it moving!

And let's not forget: Kisses are like a little physical test drive before deciding if you want the whole car. If the kiss is just as good as the date? You, my friend, might be onto something great.

Sex on the first date: A gamble, a game changer, or a trip to Situationshipville?

People love to say, "If you have sex on the first date, they'll lose respect for you." But let's be real — anyone who would lose respect for you over something they also did was never a quality person to begin with. Respect isn't lost over an act; it's lost over who they are as a person (and really, if they were the type to ghost, they were going to ghost whether or not you took your pants off).

Now, let's talk about the real risk. Having sex on a first date is a roll of the dice — you might end up with fireworks, fall in love, and get married, or you might wake up in permanent residency in Situationshipville, where the only commitment is to vague texting and last-minute plans. There's no right or wrong answer here. If the vibe is there and you genuinely want to do it, go for it. If you're unsure, there's also something to be said for a slow burn — sometimes waiting builds excitement, deepens the connection, and lets you see if this person is really worth your time (and your best sheets).

>> **Make sure it's your choice, not theirs.** If you're going to do it, do it because *you* want to, not because you think it will make them like you more, keep them interested, or magically turn them into a committed partner. Sex isn't a sales

pitch, and you don't need to prove your value by giving them a "free trial" of your affection.

>> **Chemistry is key — but so is clarity.** Ask yourself: *Is this just physical attraction, or do I actually like this person?* Because sometimes, a strong physical connection can make you ignore the red flags waving in the background like an inflatable tube man at a car dealership.

>> **Don't assume it means commitment.** Having sex early in dating doesn't automatically fast-track you to an exclusive relationship. Some people can separate sex and emotions, while others catch feelings the second they make eye contact mid-hookup. The key is knowing which type you are — and making sure you're not expecting one thing while they're on a completely different page.

>> **Always, always, always protect yourself.** Listen, safe sex is hot sex — point blank. Make sure you're using protection and prioritizing both your physical and emotional well-being. You don't want to be waiting on test results (or clarity on where you stand with them) just because you got caught up in the moment.

>> **Post-date reflection: What do *you* want?** Afterward, check in with yourself. Do you feel happy and confident about the decision? Or are you spiraling, rereading texts, and wondering if you made the right move? Your answer will tell you a lot about what feels right for you moving forward.

At the end of the day, when to have sex is all about your comfort level. If it feels right, own it. If you want to wait, own that too. Either way, one night doesn't define a relationship — your connection, communication, and mutual effort do.

WARNING

But let's get one thing straight — never sleep with someone just because you think it will make them want you more or prove you're "the one." If they need convincing, they're not the one. Taking a few dates to get to know someone never hurts, and believe it or not, it is totally possible to have great sex *and* keep them around *without* making them your ex.

SAFETY FIRST: WHY YOU MIGHT WANT TO SKIP THE RIDE HOME

Even if the date was *amazing*, it's always a good idea to take control of your own transportation. While it might seem romantic to accept a ride home, especially if they offer sweetly, having an independent exit keeps things on your terms. It's not about assuming the worst — it's just about staying in control of your own safety and comfort. If things go well, there will be plenty of time for romantic drives in the future.

"Can't wait to see you again": When to drop that line

If you actually want to see them again, don't play it cool — say it. A casual "I had a great time; let's do this again," or "Next time, I'm picking the spot," keeps things open and gives them a clear signal that you're interested. If you're *not* feeling it, a kind but firm "It was great meeting you" does the trick — no need for false hope or vague "let's see" energy.

Text timing: When to hit send after the date

No one likes the "should I text first?" anxiety spiral. Here's the truth: If you had a great time, just text them. A quick "I had such a great time tonight. Let's do it again soon!" takes zero effort and makes your interest clear. No games, no waiting three days, no pretending you're too busy doing *important things* (like scrolling through your dating apps again). If they're into it, you'll know. If they're not, congrats, you didn't waste three days waiting to find out.

Post-Date Check-in: Questions to Ask Yourself Afterward

Before you get too caught up in analyzing how *they* felt, check in with *yourself* first. Ask yourself:

- Did I actually enjoy my time, or was I just trying to impress them?
- Did the conversation feel fun and natural, or was I carrying the entire date?
- Do I genuinely want to see them again, or am I just caught up in the moment?

If it's a yes to all the good things, great! If not, don't force it. The whole point of dating is to find mutual connection — not just to make sure they like you.

How to Lock in That Second Date

So, you're on a date that actually *feels* like a date — not an awkward small-talk marathon or a forced networking event. The conversation is easy, the chemistry is there, and you're already thinking, "Okay, I'd actually like to see this person again." Now, let's make sure the night doesn't end with a vague "We should do this again sometime" that leads nowhere. If you're into them and want to keep the momentum going, here's how to set up that second date without making it weird.

- **Plant the seeds for a second date (subtly, of course).** If you're feeling it, start casually weaving in future plans so it doesn't feel like a high-pressure ask. Say something like:

    "You're into live music? We should check out that jazz bar sometime!"

    "Wait, you've never been to [cool local spot]? We have to fix that."

    This way, you're not just hinting at another date — you're already giving it a reason to happen.

» **Drop hints about places you'd love to go.** If they're picking up what you're putting down, mentioning a cool activity or restaurant you've been meaning to try gives them the chance to jump in with "Let's go!" For example:

> "I've been dying to try this rooftop bar everyone keeps raving about."

> "Next time, we should totally get dessert — I feel like we really missed out."

Suddenly, the idea of seeing each other again is already in motion, and you're not just leaving it up to fate.

» **Check their availability (without sounding like you're booking an appointment).** Instead of the vague "We should do this again sometime," try something more direct but still low-pressure, like

> "So, what's your week looking like?"

> "Are you usually around on weekends, or are you more of a weekday adventurer?"

If they're interested, they'll give you an answer that makes it easy to follow up. If they're *not*, well — at least you won't be left wondering.

» **Just say it: "I'd love to see you again."** If you had a great time, just be honest about it — because a little confidence is way more attractive than playing it cool. At the end of the night, try a simple

> "This was really fun. I'd love to do it again."

> "I had a great time with you — let's make sure this isn't a one-time thing."

Gives them a clear signal without feeling like a big, dramatic declaration. If they feel the same way, **boom — second date secured.** If not, hey, at least you know where you stand. Either way, you leave the date knowing you gave it your best shot!

4

Date or Fade? What Happens after the First Date

IN THIS PART . . .

Arrange a second date and beyond.

Learn how to get over it if you end up being ghosted or things just don't work out.

Move beyond the small talk and align on money, religion, ethics, and more.

IN THIS CHAPTER

» Planning your next moves: Key milestones after a date

» Next steps after a mediocre or bad first date

» Following the chemistry: When to make it physical

» Time to commit? Knowing when to focus on one person

Chapter **15**
Making the Most of Date Number Two and Beyond

So you survived the first date — congrats! You made it through the awkward small talk, the nerve-racking decision of whether to hug, handshake, or go full European cheek kiss, and maybe even a first-date kiss that didn't feel like a middle school slow dance. Now comes the next challenge: actually keeping the momentum going.

One of the biggest struggles in modern dating is the "one-and-done" phenomenon — you go on a five-hour marathon date, full of deep conversation, shared laughs, and actual *connection,* and then . . . radio silence. Why? Because options feel endless. Some people treat dating like a never-ending buffet, where instead of going back for seconds, they just grab a brand-new plate and try something else.

But here's the thing — the *real* magic of dating doesn't happen in the first-date highlight reel. It happens when you actually get to know someone past their *polished, curated "first-date self."* The second date is where things *shift from surface-level fun to actually seeing what's possible.* It's no longer just "What's your sign?" *and* "OMG, you like sushi and reality TV too?!" — it's where you figure out if this is just *a great first-date experience* or something worth exploring.

This chapter is all about navigating the second date and beyond — how to explore what you really want, keep the connection alive, and make sure you're not just another chapter in someone's *Serial First Dater* saga. Because let's be real: Dating is fun, but endless first dates? Exhausting. (Trust me, I should know. Before I learned these tricks it felt like I dated all of Manhattan, and some of New Jersey too.)

The Second Date: Where Compatibility Gets Real (or Reality Sets In)

One of the biggest mysteries in dating is mistaking surface-level similarities for compatibility. Sure, you both love sushi and have an unhealthy dedication to Bruce Springsteen karaoke, but does that mean you're *soulmates?* Not necessarily. The second date is where you start peeling back the layers — showing a little less of the rehearsed, polished "first-date you" and a little more of the real you (yes, even the part of you that sets 17 alarms but still sleeps through all of them).

So how do you make sure the second date actually helps you see if there's long-term potential? The following sections tell you what to focus on.

TIFF SAYS The second date is where the fun starts. If the first date is about impressing each other, the second date is about actually seeing if you like each other. So ditch the small talk, pick an activity that gives you real interaction, and start focusing on who they actually are — not just who they seemed to be after two margaritas and a well-timed joke. And remember: Dating is supposed to be fun. The goal isn't to find your forever person by the second date; it's to see if this is someone you want to keep learning about. And if not? Well, at least you got a fun story and another step closer to someone who is.

Making the date an activity, not just dinner and drinks

Look, drinks are fun. Dim lighting, a little wine, *boom*, instant chemistry. But is it real chemistry, or just a pinot noir illusion? The second date is a perfect time to do something that doesn't involve alcohol and late-night flirty eyes across the table.

Try a coffee date, a daytime picnic, or even a workout class — because if you still like them while sweating and slightly out of breath, that's a green flag.

Seeing someone in broad daylight, sober, and in a nonromantic setting helps you figure out if you're falling for *them* or just falling for the ambiance of dimly lit restaurants and fancy cocktails.

Asking questions that actually matter

We are *not* here for another two-hour round of "What's your favorite movie?" This is your chance to dig a little deeper. Nowadays, we do not have time to waste on the wrong people (inflation is too high to be buying dinner for people who don't align with your future).

Instead of just keeping things surface-level, ease into questions that actually help you understand if you're compatible:

> *"What's something you're really passionate about outside of work?"*
>
> *"What's a goal you have for the next year?"*
>
> *"How do you like to spend your weekends when you have zero plans?"*

No need to go full FBI interrogator — just keep it natural, but intentional.

Focusing the conversation on key topics

The second date is where you start figuring out if your long-term wants and lifestyles match up. Some key things to pay attention to:

- **Family and values:** Are they close to their family? What kind of environment did they grow up in?
- **Career and goals:** Are they ambitious? Do they love what they do, or are they figuring things out? (Either is fine, but knowing where they're at is important.)
- **Love languages and communication style:** Are they the type to send cute good morning texts, or are they more of a "see you when I see you" kind of person?
- **What they're looking for:** Are they dating for something serious or just vibing?

TIP: A second date is the perfect time to *gently* explore these things without making it feel like a job interview.

Do they have a "roster," or are they actually looking for something?

Dating these days is a sport, and some people have a full-blown team. If you're looking for something more serious, the second date is a good time to subtly figure out if you're talking to a free agent or someone with a full lineup of active players.

A couple of ways to get a sense of this:

> *"So, how has dating been for you lately?"* (A casual way to gauge if they're actively *seeing* multiple people)

> *"Are you the type of person who dates one person at a time or keeps things open until it gets serious?"* (Direct but not aggressive)

REMEMBER: This isn't about demanding exclusivity on date two, but it's about understanding if their dating style aligns with yours. If you're looking for something real, and they're out here trying to break the world record for most active Hinge matches, it's good to know sooner rather than later.

PART 4 Date or Fade? What Happens after the First Date

Are you getting comfortable or losing interest?

The first date is all about butterflies and excitement. The second date? This is when things start to settle.

Here's where you might start noticing things like:

- » Are conversations still flowing easily, or do you feel like you're pulling teeth?
- » Do you feel excited to see them again, or are you just going through the motions?
- » Are they just as engaged and curious about you, or do they seem a little too meh about making plans?

If the energy is still there, that's a great sign! But if you're already feeling yourself lose interest or struggling to connect, that's also important information. The second date is a checkpoint — sometimes it moves things forward, and sometimes it's where you realize you're just not feeling it.

Gauging their effort: Are they actually trying?

If your date is already showing signs of laziness or inconsistency, it's not going to get better.

Do they take days to respond to texts but claim they're "so into you"? Are they making you do all the planning, or do they contribute to making the date happen?

Do they seem interested in getting to know you, or is it feeling one-sided?

REMEMBER: Effort should be equal. If you're already having to *convince* them to make time for you, that's not someone who's actually serious about dating.

When Is It Time to Meet the Friends?

So you've had a few great dates, the chemistry is strong, and now the big question looms — when is the right time to introduce them to your friends? On one hand, meeting the squad can be a fun way to integrate someone into your world. On the other hand, bringing them in too soon can feel like throwing a new hire into a company holiday party before they even have an employee ID.

There's a fine balance between "Hey, come meet my favorite people!" and "So, I'm making you meet my inner circle, and their opinions will now dictate our future together." This section offers you some tips on how to figure out the right timing and avoid turning this milestone into an accidental relationship pressure cooker.

Consider the intent: Why are you introducing them?

Before deciding to introduce your date to your friends, ask yourself:

- » Is this just a casual hangout, or do I want my friends' input?
- » Am I excited to integrate them into my life, or am I doing this to get validation?
- » Do I see this going somewhere, or am I testing the waters before I commit?

If you're bringing them just because you feel like you *should* or because you're not sure how you feel and want your friends to decide for you, *pause*. Your friends' opinions matter, but you should have a sense of where this is headed before outsourcing the decision-making process.

The "too soon" zone: When to hold off on friend introductions

There are some clear red flags that indicate it's too early to make introductions:

- » **You're still figuring out if you like them.** If you're still undecided, don't use your friends as a focus group. Get clear on your own feelings first.
- » **You're only a few dates in.** If you haven't even had a real conversation about what you're looking for, bringing them into your friend circle might be premature.

- **The relationship has no direction yet.** If you have no clue where things are going, introducing them too soon can add unnecessary pressure.
- **They haven't earned a spot yet.** Your friends are VIPs in your life — bringing someone into that space should be reserved for people who actually deserve to be there.

REMEMBER: If you're still in the *fun-but-uncertain* stage, keep things between the two of you for now.

The right time: When it makes sense to introduce them

Now, let's talk about when it *actually* makes sense to introduce them to your friends:

- **You've been dating for a while and it's feeling solid.** If you've been seeing each other consistently and both feel good about it, it's probably a good time.
- **You've had conversations about where this is going.** If you've established some kind of mutual interest in the future, meeting the friends is a great next step.
- **It's a low-stakes setting.** The first meetup doesn't have to be a formal "so this is my future partner" situation. A casual group hangout, party, or brunch can be a less intense way to introduce them.
- **You actually want their opinions.** If your friends are an important part of your life, introducing your partner should feel like a natural integration, not a forced step.

TIP: A good rule of thumb? If you'd be embarrassed to introduce them yet, it's probably too soon.

How to make the introduction feel natural

If you're ready for the introduction, don't overthink it — keep it casual. Here's how:

- **Set the scene.** Let your friends know what to expect so they don't grill your date like a witness in a crime drama.

CHAPTER 15 **Making the Most of Date Number Two and Beyond** 177

> **Start with a group hang.** A larger setting (like a game night, casual dinner, or birthday party) is *way less intense* than a one-on-one dinner where your friends are all secretly analyzing them.

> **Don't make it weird.** Avoid saying things like "So, what do you guys think?" on the first meeting. Let things happen naturally.

What if it goes . . . horribly?

Say you take the plunge and . . . it's a mess. Maybe your friends aren't sold, your date feels awkward, or someone accidentally brings up your ex. (Why do friend groups always have that one person?)

If your friends don't like them, take their opinions into account, but trust your own instincts. If your date didn't vibe with your friends, don't panic — it might take a couple of meetups to warm up. If it was just uncomfortable, chalk it up to first-time awkwardness and try again in a different setting.

WARNING

If there are major red flags, pay attention to them. Friends often see things we don't.

TIFF SAYS

Meeting the friends shouldn't feel like a test or a chore — it should happen when it feels right. If it's too soon, there's no harm in waiting. And if it's the right time, set it up for success with low stakes and natural interaction.

When to Have Sex: The Ultimate Timing Debate

Let's get real — figuring out when to have sex with someone you're dating can feel like trying to solve a riddle with no answer. Some say the third date is the magic number, others insist you should wait until commitment, and then there are those who act like you need to sign a joint mortgage first. The reality? There's no universal timeline, but there are some key things to consider before you take things to the bedroom (or the car, or their couch, or wherever questionable decisions happen).

This section breaks it down.

The right time to have sex? Whenever YOU feel comfortable

Forget rules, societal pressures, or that one friend who swears by their "wait until date five" strategy. The only *right* time to have sex is when:

- **You actually want to** (not because you feel obligated, pressured, or need to "keep them interested").
- **You trust them enough to be naked with them** (if you can't even trust them to text back on time, maybe hold off).
- **You feel safe, both emotionally and physically** (because nothing ruins the moment like regret and an emergency Google search about STDs).

REMEMBER: Sex is not a milestone you have to hit; it's a choice. So whether it's the first date, third date, or after a tax return is filed together, do what makes sense for you.

Will they lose interest if you sleep with them?

Ah yes, the fear that if you sleep with someone "too soon," they'll mysteriously vanish into the abyss like a bad Tinder date. Here's the truth: Someone who is genuinely interested in you won't lose respect for you just because you had sex.

What will make them lose interest is:

- **A lack of emotional connection:** If your dynamic is purely physical, don't be shocked if they *only* hit you up at 2 a.m.
- **A lack of clear expectations:** If you never talked about what you both want, don't assume sex will make them suddenly see you as "the one."
- **Them being a trash person:** If someone ghosts you after sex, they were never serious in the first place. Sex wasn't the reason — they just showed you who they were faster.

REMEMBER: So instead of asking, "Will they lose interest?" ask yourself, "Am I sleeping with someone who actually values me?"

The third date rule: Still a thing or just dating mythology?

The third date rule has been around since the dinosaurs (okay, maybe just since the '90s), and while it's a convenient *guideline*, it's not a law. Some people need more time, some are down on the first night, and some prefer to wait until there's a clear emotional foundation.

The key takeaway? Sex should happen when both people are genuinely excited about it — not because an arbitrary rulebook says it's "time."

What if you're not sexually or mentally compatible?

This is a real concern because bad sex is, well, bad. What if the chemistry is amazing, but when the moment arrives, it's like two confused Sims trying to interact? Or worse, what if they make noises that sound like a dying animal and now you can never unhear it?

Some things to keep in mind:

>> **Sexual chemistry can take time to develop.** Awkward first encounters don't mean doom — it just means you might need to communicate more.

>> **If they're not willing to meet your needs, that's a problem.** If they treat sex like a solo performance rather than a duet, consider if that's something you can work with.

>> **Mental compatibility matters just as much.** If you love deep conversations and they only respond in memes, that connection *outside* the bedroom might not be strong enough to keep the attraction alive long-term.

How to make sure you won't regret it

Sex is supposed to be fun, not an emotionally draining gamble where you wake up questioning your life choices. Before you go there, ask yourself:

>> **Would I be okay if I never heard from them again?**
(If the answer is no, maybe slow it down.)

>> **Do I feel emotionally and physically safe with this person?** (Bare minimum.)

>> **Do I actually like them, or do I just like the attention?**
(Because that post-sex clarity is real.)

Sex should never feel like a test, a strategy, or a way to keep someone around. It should be something you both want, with zero regrets afterward.

TIFF SAYS There's no "right" time — just the right person and the right feeling. Whether you wait a few hours, a few dates, or a few months, sex is not what determines the success of a relationship — mutual respect, effort, and connection do.

So ditch the stress, listen to your gut, and make the decision that feels best for you — not one based on outdated dating myths or unnecessary pressure. Because when it's right, it won't be about the timing — it'll just feel natural.

When to Commit: Decoding the "What Are We?" Phase

Modern dating is a chaotic mix of rosters, situationships, soft launches, and full-on relationships — so how do you know when it's time to focus on one person? Should you delete the apps? Are you supposed to know their phone password? And how many people are too many before you need an Excel spreadsheet to keep track of them?

If you're trying to figure out where you stand, here's how to navigate the transition from casual dating to something more serious — without sending a "so . . . what are we?" text that makes you cringe the second you hit send.

Building a roster: How many people can you date at once?

If you're actively dating, chances are you've got a roster — aka a casual lineup of people you're seeing until something *clicks*. But at what point does it go from fun exploration to a full-time logistics nightmare?

- **One person:** Either you're super focused or already in love but pretending to be chill.
- **Two to three people:** The sweet spot for most casual daters — just enough variety to compare personalities without mixing up their names.
- **Four or more:** Either you're thriving, or you have so many overlapping convos that you accidentally text "good morning, sunshine" to someone you haven't actually met yet.

If you forget their favorite drink, double-book dates, or need a Google Doc to track their fun facts, it's time to trim the list.

Knowing when it's getting serious

There's always that moment in dating when things start to shift — where you go from "This is fun" to "Oh no, I think I actually like them." So how do you know when it's happening?

- You start canceling other dates (willingly, not because of scheduling conflicts).
- You text all day, every day, and not just for logistic planning.
- You miss them when they're not around (and not just because they pick the best restaurants).
- They come up in conversations with your friends — even when you're not talking about dating.
- You start thinking about future plans — not wedding bells, but things like "I bet they'd love this place."

If they've gone from *one of many* to *the one you're making time for*, you might be in the commitment danger zone.

How to tell if they're still seeing other people

If you're getting serious, you probably want to know if they're still seeing other people — without sounding like a detective. Some subtle clues:

> They are weirdly vague about their availability ("Let's see how the week goes." Okay, but why? What secret mission are you on?).

> You've never seen their apartment, and all dates are neutral territory — classic roster behavior.

> Their texting habits are wildly inconsistent — hot one week, ghost vibes the next.

> Their Instagram is full of mysterious group photos, and you have no idea who any of these people are.

Instead of playing FBI, just ask. If they dodge the question, there's your answer.

Sharing phone passwords and managing Instagram love

Welcome to the modern relationship milestone checklist: At what point is it normal to share passwords, post each other, and acknowledge your relationship online?

> **Phone passwords:** This shouldn't be a hostage negotiation. If they panic at the thought, *that's a discussion*.

> **Instagram and social media:** Not everyone loves a hard launch. But if they're *liking thirst traps and never posting you*, at least raise an eyebrow.

> **Following exes:** If they still interact with their ex's posts *daily*, remember that there's a difference between being friendly and being in denial.

> **Deleting the dating apps:** The real test of exclusivity. If they still have them "just in case," maybe you should too.

If you trust them in real life, don't spiral over online behavior. But if their phone is always face-down with notifications off, maybe trust your gut.

When to delete the dating apps for someone

Nothing says "I'm off the market" like deleting Hinge — but when should you do it?

Too soon: After one magical date. Relax.

Too late: If you've met their family but they're still swiping.

Just right: When you've both agreed to be exclusive — and not just because you saw them pop up on a friend's Bumble.

If you're ready but they're hesitant, ask why. If they hit you with "I just like meeting new people," congrats, you're dating a networking event.

When it's time to commit, it shouldn't feel like a guessing game. If you're constantly wondering where you stand, that might be your answer.

The right person won't leave you confused — they'll make it clear that they want you and only you. Until then, keep your options open, trust your gut, and never settle for someone who treats you like an option while you treat them like a priority.

If there's one thing to take away from all of this, it's that there's no magic formula, no universal dating playbook, and definitely no trophy for the person who finds love the fastest (if there was, we'd all be playing a lot harder). Whether you're navigating first dates, decoding text messages like you're solving a murder case, or debating whether to delete the apps or just "take a break," it's all just part of the ride.

> **IN THIS CHAPTER**
> - » Not sweating the post-date silence
> - » Surviving and moving on from a situationship
> - » Breaking up without the blow-up: How to end it with grace
> - » Handling ghosting: Moving on when they disappear
> - » Keeping cheaters and manipulators out of your life

Chapter 16
Ghosts, Goodbyes, and Getting Over It: Surviving the Heartbreak

If you're an active dater, chances are you've been ghosted so many times that you could star in your own haunted house. But before you start calling an exorcist (or sending a strongly worded text to that person who "just wasn't ready for a relationship" but is now engaged), let's talk about how to actually move on without letting heartbreak turn you into a bitter meme in human form.

Losing love — whether you're the one getting dumped, the one doing the dumping, or just the victim of a disappearing act — is never easy. It doesn't matter if it was one month, five years, or even a whole marriage. The hardest part isn't the breakup itself — it's not letting heartbreak break *you*. The dating world is full of mysteries: Why does the perfect first date sometimes turn into ghosting? How does someone who *checked all the boxes* still end up being the wrong fit? Why do connections fade, and how do people who *seemed* to care suddenly act like you never existed? All of these questions are enough to drive you into an existential crisis — but instead of spiraling, let's talk about how to recover and get to the ultimate dating glow-up.

Ditching the Wait: Stop Gluing Your Eyes to Your Phone

We've all been there. It was a magical date — laughter, deep convos, future plans, maybe even a romantic goodnight kiss. You're floating on a cloud, convinced you've finally cracked the dating code. Then . . . silence. Days pass, and suddenly, your phone is quieter than a library at 2 a.m.

At first, you try to be chill. *Maybe they're just busy.* Then you start analyzing: *Did I say something weird? Did I accidentally insult their dog?* And before you know it, you're refreshing your messages like it's your full-time job, hoping that, somehow, their text will appear if you just stare hard enough at your screen.

But here's the thing: If someone wants to see you again, they'll make it known. You won't need to send out a search party or become a detective analyzing their Instagram activity. (*They were online 15 minutes ago but haven't replied — what does it MEAN?!*)

And in case you need a reminder: Texting them more won't make them want you more. It'll just make them feel like they're being hunted. You deserve better than wasting your day refreshing your DMs. If they haven't texted back, go live your life! They could be busy, traveling, or just not that into you — and that's okay. The right person won't leave you questioning.

Here's how to handle the post-date silence (without losing your dignity):

TIP

>> **If they haven't texted, wait a reasonable amount of time.** Give it a day or two. No need to go full "I'm too cool to care" mode, but also don't act like your Wi-Fi will cut out if you don't send a text first.

- **If you want to follow up, keep it simple.** A light "Hey, I had a great time the other night!" is fine. What's *not* fine? A five-paragraph essay asking where things stand.
- **If they don't respond? Move on.** Ghosters don't deserve closure, they deserve to fade into irrelevance.
- **Don't let one bad experience turn you into a cynic.** No, *not all men suck.* No, *not all women are the worst.* The person meant for you won't vanish into the abyss.

TIFF SAYS

Don't keep knocking on a door that's not answering. If someone is truly interested, they'll show it. They won't leave you deciphering mixed signals like it's an ancient prophecy. If they ghost, thank them for removing themselves from your life early, and keep it moving. Because the truth is, the more time you waste waiting for the wrong person to text, the longer you're delaying meeting the right one.

Healing from a "Situationship": Getting Over Someone You Never Really Had

Sometimes it starts with one flirty DM and suddenly you're acting like you're married but without the title, the commitment, or even a toothbrush at their place. It's all the late-night convos and good morning texts, but none of the actual security. Congrats, you've landed in the romantic gray zone where vibes are high and clarity is low. It used to be as simple as asking, "What are we?" Now it's more like, "What was that?"

If you've found yourself caught up in the romance with none of the security, don't worry — you're not crazy, you're just in the suburbs of commitment. The following sections show you how to navigate your way out (with your dignity and playlist intact).

What are situationships?

If you're new to the dating space or have been blessed enough to be in a real relationship for most of the 2020s, you might not know what a *situationship* is. So let me break it down for you.

At its core, a situationship is one person wanting commitment, while the other is "not ready for anything serious right now."

It's the romantic equivalent of being put on a waitlist — you *kinda* have a spot, but there's no guarantee you'll ever actually get in.

Unlike a fling (which is fun, carefree, and usually has a clear expiration date), situationships are messy, undefined, and built on just enough emotional breadcrumbs to keep you hooked. You do all the relationship-y things — cuddling, deep talks, going to Trader Joe's together like an old married couple — but without any actual security. It's basically like signing an invisible contract that says, "We can ghost each other at any time, see other people, and technically neither of us can be mad because we never really defined what this was."

It's the Wild West of dating — where commitment is optional, communication is vague, and heartbreak is inevitable.

Getting over a situationship that didn't go as planned

So, you got stuck in the *Will they? Won't they?* vortex of a situationship, and — spoiler alert — it didn't turn into the relationship you were hoping for. What now?

» **Accept that it was never a relationship.** I know, I know — this is painful to hear. But the first step to moving on is realizing you were never actually in a real relationship. You had relationship moments, but moments don't equal commitment. And no, "But we had such a connection!" does not count as a binding agreement.

» **Stop romanticizing the "potential."** If you find yourself reminiscing about how great things could have been, stop. Situationships thrive on potential — what you imagined it could be, what you thought it might turn into. But if it was actually meant to be something real, it would have been.

» **Resist the urge to seek "closure."** There's no "big conversation" that will magically make them wake up and realize they love you. Situationships usually end with silence, mixed signals, or a casual "I'm just not in a place for something serious." Any attempt to get closure will likely just reopen the wound. The real closure? Them not stepping up was your answer.

- **Block, mute, unfollow, whatever it takes.** Situationships have a terrible habit of resurfacing — usually in the form of a 2 a.m. "I miss you" text or an accidental like on your Instagram story. Don't let them breadcrumb their way back into your life. If they couldn't commit before, they won't magically change just because they got bored.

- **Remind yourself that you deserve more than bare minimum effort.** One of the biggest traps of a situationship is feeling grateful for the smallest things:

    "But they texted me first today!"

    "They actually planned something instead of saying 'wanna hang?'"

    "They called me instead of just sending a Snap!"

    These are basic things, not grand gestures. If you have to celebrate the bare minimum, it's because you weren't getting enough in the first place.

- **Do something that reminds you who you are.** Nothing steals your confidence like waiting around for someone to pick you. Get back to doing the things that make you feel like you again — hobbies, gym, new experiences, even just wearing an outfit that reminds you you're *that* person. The goal? To feel so good that if they ever do come back, you genuinely don't care anymore.

- **Don't let one situation make you bitter.** It's easy to leave a failed situationship saying, "Dating is trash. People are the worst. Love is a scam." But one emotionally unavailable person does not represent the entire dating pool. Keep your standards high, your energy unbothered, and remember: Real relationships don't require convincing someone to want you.

TIFF SAYS

Situationships only win if you stay in them. The best revenge is moving on so hard that you forget you ever even had to Google "how to get over someone who was never really mine." Keep your standards up, your time protected, and your energy reserved for someone who's actually sure about you.

Rejection to Redirection: How to Grow Through the No

No matter how many times you've been rejected, there is no magical way to avoid the sting of someone you like not liking you back. And let's be real — rejection sucks. It's like ordering fries and realizing they forgot the sauce, except instead of ranch, it's your *self-esteem* that's missing.

But here's what I won't do: I won't sugarcoat it and tell you to just "stay positive" like you're a motivational quote on a TJ Maxx pillow. No, you deserve a full 24-hour period of feeling the pain. Go ahead — throw yourself a personal heartbreak film festival, cue up *When Harry Met Sally*, stare dramatically out the window while listening to sad songs, and let yourself think, *Wow, maybe I actually will be the perpetual bridesmaid/groomsman but never the one at the altar.*

But once that's done? We're getting back up. This section offers you strategies for doing just that.

Accepting that rejection is a normal part of dating

I know it *feels* personal when someone says, "I don't see this going anywhere," but let's flip the script.

Have *you* ever ghosted someone because you just weren't feeling it? Have *you* ever gone on a date with someone perfectly nice but with the personality of a saltine cracker? Have *you* ever swiped left because their profile gave off "I still live in my mom's basement" energy?

Exactly. Rejection isn't always about you — it's about them, their preferences, and what they're looking for. If someone's not interested, they're doing you a favor by making space for someone who will be.

Knowing that compatibility isn't about your worth

Here's the thing — you can be an amazing person and still not be the right fit for someone else. And that doesn't mean you're not lovable or that something is wrong with you. Compatibility is not a reflection of your worth — it's just two puzzle pieces that don't quite click.

Think of it this way: Coffee is amazing. So is pizza. But coffee and pizza together? Not exactly a match made in heaven. Just because two things are great individually doesn't mean they work together, and the same goes for dating.

So instead of thinking, *Why wasn't I good enough?* reframe it as *We just weren't the right fit, and that's okay.*

Stop trying to make the wrong person like you

We've all been there — obsessing over why they didn't like us, as if solving that mystery will magically make them change their mind. (Spoiler: It won't.)

Rejection only hurts more when you try to force something that isn't meant for you. Stop rereading their last text like it's a breakup autopsy. Stop convincing yourself that if you had just worn a different outfit, been a little funnier, or sent a perfectly casual-yet-intriguing follow-up text, things would have been different.

REMEMBER: If they wanted to be with you, they would be. That's the only answer you need.

Redirecting your energy into something better

You know what's worse than rejection? Wasting time on people who don't appreciate you. Instead of chasing someone who doesn't care, shift your focus:

- **Glow-up out of spite.** Get a new haircut. Go to the gym. Post a thirst trap that makes them regret their choices. (Is it petty? Maybe. Is it effective? Absolutely.)
- **Upgrade your dating strategy.** Maybe you need to stop going for emotionally unavailable people who text like they're sending messages via carrier pigeon.
- **Have fun.** Rejection isn't the end of your love life — it's just a plot twist. Take a break, enjoy your friends, and date with the energy of someone who knows their worth.

CHAPTER 16 **Ghosts, Goodbyes, and Getting Over It: Surviving the Heartbreak** 191

Remembering that the right person won't reject you

I know it's tempting to spiral and think, "Maybe I'm just undatable," but let's be clear: One person's no is not a universal no. Just because someone didn't see your value doesn't mean the next person won't. The right person will see you, choose you, and won't leave you questioning.

REMEMBER: Every rejection is just a redirection to the person who *will* appreciate you. So stop crying over people who were never really yours, stop dwelling on "what ifs," and start getting excited about who's coming next.

One day, you're going to look back and laugh at the fact that you were ever upset over someone who clearly wasn't on your level.

Surviving the Dating Chaos

Let's be real — dating in the modern world is like a never-ending reality show where you didn't sign up, but somehow keep getting cast. One day, you're on *The Bachelor*, getting wined and dined, and the next? You're on *Survivor*, trying to navigate mixed signals and avoid getting emotionally stranded.

Some dates feel like a scene from a rom-com, full of laughter, chemistry, and effortless conversation. Others? They feel like an episode of a true crime documentary waiting to happen. And then there are those dates that make you wonder, "Wait . . . am I actually being punk'd right now?"

TIFF SAYS: In my life, I've probably been on at least 300 dates (look, don't judge me — I'm just a girl looking for love, too, you know). While I've had my fair share of magical moments — romantic dinner dates, Broadway shows, and nights that made me feel like I was living my own version of *Breakfast at Tiffany's* — I've also been stood up, been on dates with guys who were fully blacked out, and even had someone bring his friend along to "judge" if I was hot enough. (Spoiler alert: The only thing *hot* that night was the meal because I left immediately.)

But here's the thing — no one is immune to the disaster date. We all get them. They're part of the package deal that comes with putting yourself out there. But after every hurricane comes a rainbow — isn't that what Katy Perry said?

So if you've ever left a date thinking, "What the actual hell just happened?" just know that you're not alone. And the best way to survive the chaos? Laugh through it, take the lesson, and remember that every bad date is just making for a better story when you finally find the right one.

In this section, I give you guidance on how to avoid dating burnout, recover from a disaster date, and know when to stop investing in someone who's just not that into you.

Avoiding dating burnout

Dating burnout is real. One minute you're excitedly swiping, planning cute date outfits, and feeling like love is just around the corner. The next? You're exhausted from small talk, convinced *everyone* is emotionally unavailable, and debating whether to just buy a cat and call it a day.

But here's the thing — love is still out there. It's just that sometimes you have to wade through the swamp of terrible first dates and ghosters to find it.

Following are some tips for keeping your energy up while dating:

- **Don't date like it's your full-time job.** If you're going on multiple dates a week with zero time for yourself, of course you're going to be exhausted. Take breaks when needed. Love is not an Amazon Prime package — you don't need to rush delivery.

- **Make dating fun again.** Plan unique dates, try new things, and stop treating dating like an obligation. If you're only meeting people for drinks at the same bar over and over again, of course it feels repetitive.

- **Lower the pressure.** Every date does not need to be "the one." Not every dinner needs to end in wedding bells. Sometimes it's just a nice conversation and a free meal.

- **Take a social media detox.** Seeing another engagement post when you're still swiping past people holding fish in their dating profiles? Yeah, that's frustrating. Take a break from the constant reminders.

> **Surround yourself with good energy.** Talk to friends who uplift you. Avoid the "dating is a dumpster fire" complainers — negativity is contagious.

Disaster date? Here's your next move

So you just survived the worst date of your life. Maybe they showed up late, spent the entire time talking about their ex, or confessed they think *birds aren't real*. Whatever it was, it was a train wreck.

How to recover from a bad date:

> **Laugh about it.** Seriously, disaster dates make for *great* stories. Call your best friend, spill every detail, and turn your suffering into entertainment.

> **Remind yourself: It's just one person.** A bad date does not mean dating as a whole is bad. It just means this person wasn't it.

> **Make an emergency exit plan for future dates.** Next time, have a go-to excuse ready (or a friend on standby to fake an emergency call).

> **Don't let it discourage you.** You don't quit eating because you had a bad meal. You don't quit shopping because you bought one ugly sweater. One bad date doesn't mean you stop dating.

> **Reward yourself.** Bad date? Treat yourself. Whether it's ice cream, retail therapy, or a solo movie night, celebrate the fact that you survived.

They're just not that into you: How to spot the signs early

Ah, the dreaded mixed signals. One day they're texting you nonstop. The next day you're getting one-word replies that feel like they were typed under duress. If you're wondering, "Are they into me, or am I just entertainment until someone else comes along?" you probably already know the answer.

Signs they're just not that into you:

- **You're always the one initiating.** If you disappeared, would they notice? Or would they just find another texting pen pal?
- **They're hot and cold.** One week they're planning the cutest date. The next? They're "super busy" and vanish like a magician.
- **They only make last-minute plans.** A person who likes you makes real plans. If they only text you at 10 p.m. asking "what's up," congrats, you're a backup plan.
- **You're confused.** If you're constantly asking yourself, "Do they actually like me?" they probably don't like you enough. Because when someone is really into you, there's no confusion.

What to do if you realize they're not into you:

- **Don't chase.** If they're not putting in effort, don't waste yours trying to change their mind.
- **Walk away gracefully.** No dramatic exit needed. Just stop investing in someone who isn't investing in you.
- **Remind yourself of your worth.** You are not an option. You are the main event. If they can't see that, that's their loss.

DATING IS A GAME OF RESILIENCE

Dating isn't always easy. Some days it feels like everyone is emotionally unavailable, weirdly obsessed with their ex, or incapable of holding a normal conversation. But the key is not letting the bad dates, the rejections, or the weirdos make you give up.

Because at the end of the day, love is still out there. And the only way to find it is to keep going, keep laughing, and never settle for less than you deserve.

Dodging the Dating Villains: Cheaters and Manipulators

Ah, cheaters and manipulators — the human equivalent of that one expired condiment in the back of your fridge that looks fine but will absolutely ruin your night if you trust it. They show up charming, say all the right things, and just when you think you've met your match, *bam*! You're starring in your own personal soap opera where the villain is wearing your favorite hoodie and "borrowing" your Netflix password for their side piece.

Now, I know the internet loves to push the idea that "people are only as good as their options" or that you need to be *so stunning, so irreplaceable* that your partner *would never* cheat. But let's be real — even the most jaw-droppingly beautiful people in the world get cheated on. It has nothing to do with you and everything to do with them.

Manipulators, on the other hand, are basically magicians, but instead of pulling a rabbit out of a hat, they pull emotional trauma out of thin air. They gaslight, twist words, and have you questioning things you *know* happened. You could literally show them a screenshot of their shady text, and they'd convince you that you hacked their phone, joined the CIA, and framed them for no reason.

But don't worry — I'm here to make sure you don't waste a second of your time getting tangled in their web of lies, gaslighting, and nonsense. This section covers the warning signs so you can walk away early, avoid the drama, and keep your self-esteem intact.

Spotting early signs of disrespect

If it takes them two days to reply to "Want to grab dinner?" that's not busy, that's disrespect. If they make a rude comment and follow it with "just kidding," that's not flirting, that's a red flag. If they talk about your body like it's Yelp-reviewed or compare you to their ex? You guessed it: disrespect.

And I don't care how hot they are — we never sacrifice being respected for someone who didn't deserve us in the first place.

Before love comes respect. Always. Here's how to spot the signs of disrespect and walk away with your standards (and sanity) intact:

>> **They're weirdly secretive about their phone.** No, I'm not saying you should be over their shoulder like an FBI agent, but if they clutch their phone like it's the nuclear codes anytime you walk by, that is a sign. If they won't even leave the phone at the table when they go to the bathroom, there's probably something you don't want to but need to see. If you feel the need to snoop, its most likely because they are doing something sketchy to make you feel that way.

>> **They overly love-bomb you.** If someone tells you they're obsessed with you after two days, either you're the most fascinating human alive, or they are setting up a situation where they disappear just as fast. Often, people want the attention of someone being into them but don't care to give mutual affection. Beware of someone who says they want to marry you before they even know what city you're from.

Be wary of giving your personal information out too quickly. You don't want to end up with America's next top stalker.

WARNING

>> **They trash-talk all their exes.** Every ex they ever had was "crazy"? The common denominator is them.

>> **They can't answer simple questions.** If "Where were you last night?" makes them break out in a cold sweat, you already have your answer.

THEY ONLY TEXT AT ODD HOURS? YOU MIGHT BE A SIDE CHARACTER IN THEIR DOUBLE LIFE

If their communication style is giving *mystery novel meets vampire energy* — only texting late at night, responding sporadically, and mysteriously disappearing on weekends — congrats, you may not be the only one they're talking to.

People out here are running full double lives like they're trying to win an Oscar for Best Performance in a Fake Relationship. I once dated a

(continued)

(continued)

> guy who was secretly dating another girl with my exact name. Yes, *another Tiffany*. She found me on Instagram, we put our FBI hats on, compared notes, and realized we had unknowingly been co-starring in the same relationship.
>
> So, naturally, we did what any self-respecting people would do — we teamed up and dumped him on the same day. Lesson here? Cheat on one, lose both. Girl code is undefeated.

Setting boundaries and staying safe

Boundaries are the security system for your love life. If someone doesn't respect them, that is all the information you need. If you say you don't want to move fast and they pressure you, that is a problem. If they push you to do things you are uncomfortable with, that is a problem. If they guilt-trip you for having standards, that is a problem.

There is no such thing as too needy; it is them simply unable to match your needs. The right person will never make you feel bad for protecting your peace. The wrong person will act like respecting boundaries is some unreasonable request. Dating is just like an energy bank — people are either making deposits that build you up or draining you until you're emotionally overdrafted.

Recognizing shady behavior before it escalates

At first they're texting you good morning like you're the love of their life, then they vanish into thin air for 48 hours, only to return with a vague excuse like "Sorry, crazy work week" (on a weekend?). Listen, David Blaine, if you're going to pull a disappearing act, at least make it interesting.

Following are some additional shady behaviors to watch out for:

WARNING

>> **They avoid introducing you to friends or family.** If you've been dating for months and you still haven't met a single person in their life, you're either dating a secret agent or someone who doesn't want to claim you. Either way, it's suspicious. Ideally, you should meet at least one friend in

198 PART 4 **Date or Fade? What Happens after the First Date**

the first month. Bonus points if that friend actually knows you exist

>> **They gaslight you into thinking you're imagining things.** Example: They're openly checking out someone else, you call them out, and suddenly *you're* the problem? If someone makes you question reality (*Was I being dramatic, or was he actually flirting with the waitress for 20 minutes?*), trust me — you're not crazy, they're just disrespectful. Rule of thumb: If someone is calling you crazy for asking them to do something reasonable, like respecting your comfort, they're trying to train you to doubt your own instincts.

>> **They breadcrumb.** They give you just enough attention to keep you interested but never commit to anything real. You are not a pigeon. Stop chasing crumbs.

>> **You're not their first choice — you're their backup plan.** Some people treat dating like a game of musical chairs, and when the music stops and their first pick isn't available, here they come texting you, acting like you're the one they wanted all along. Spoiler alert: You're not.

REMEMBER

At the end of the day, if you're constantly questioning where you stand, it's time to step out of their rotation and put yourself first. You're not here for their convenience.

Spotting manipulative and toxic traits

I once dated a guy who told me, "You'd be nothing without me." Every year since, I've been sending him a bouquet of flowers with a crisp $100 bill — just to remind him that, actually, I'm doing just fine.

Here's the thing: If someone is putting you down, it's not because they don't see your value — it's because they do, and they don't want you to realize it.

There is no such thing as innocent bullying in dating. I've had men tell me:

> "You should stay with me because no one else will love a fat person like you."
>
> "If you hang out with your friends instead of me, I'll just ignore you."
>
> "I don't like you wearing that."

It starts small — a comment about your outfit, checking in on where you are, discouraging you from hanging out with certain people. But before you know it, you haven't seen your friends, you feel like you're always walking on eggshells, and you're at the mercy of their moods.

WARNING

In more serious cases, this kind of emotional manipulation can progress to physical abuse. That's why the small signs matter. If someone tries to shrink you, control you, or make you feel less-than — get out.

We've been conditioned to believe that we want someone to fight for us, but the truth is, some people just like to fight. You are not a remote control. No one should dictate what you do, who you see, or what you wear.

Healthy love doesn't hold you back — it encourages you to go for your craziest dreams and keeps you sparkling, not trying to steal your shine.

TIFF SAYS

I remember when I had a boyfriend who said, "You'll never make it on TikTok. You should just stick to being a server." Fast forward, and now he's still the first person to watch all my stories. Prove them wrong, then move on to someone who sees your value from day one.

Self-respect first: Knowing when to walk away

The hardest part of dealing with a manipulator or a cheater isn't spotting the signs — it's actually leaving.

You might think:

> "But we have so much history."

> "Maybe they will change."

> "I just need to prove that I'm the right person for them."

None of these are reasons to stay. You are not a human rehab center for someone who doesn't know how to love properly. If someone shows you who they are, believe them the first time.

Turning Pain into Power: Finding Confidence After a Breakup

If you got played, remember that it happens to the best of us. Now it's time to move forward:

- **Focus on yourself.** Whether it is a new haircut, a fitness goal, or a major glow-up moment, this is your time.
- **Cut off all contact.** No checking in, no "maybe we can be friends." Keep your energy to yourself.
- **Remind yourself that you didn't lose them — they lost you.** And that is a major loss.
- **Start dating again when you're ready.** There are good people out there, and now, thanks to this guide, you know exactly how to spot the bad ones.

TIFF SAYS

You deserve better, and they know it too. The biggest fear manipulators and cheaters have? That you'll realize you deserve better and walk away. So do it. Do not waste your time on someone who makes you question your worth. Because when the right person comes along, you will not have to investigate their intentions — you will just know. You deserve someone who wants to help you shine brighter, not dim you for their own gain.

> **IN THIS CHAPTER**
> » Money moves: Navigating finances while dating
> » Balancing faith, race, and culture in modern dating
> » Successfully prioritizing your social life, your work, and your dating schedule
> » Aligning future goals without adding pressure

Chapter 17
Beyond Small Talk: Asking the Questions That Really Matter

Getting through the first date is cute, but let's be real — the *real* work starts when you move past the fun surface-level talk. Anyone can bond over their love for trash TV and the fact that they "just *love* a good dive bar," but what happens when you're on date three, four, or (*gasp*) actually considering a future together? This is when you need to start having *real* conversations — before you find yourself two years deep, staring at a partner who thinks "financial planning" means Venmo requesting you for their half of a $2.99 gas station snack.

I call these talks *infrastructure conversations.* You can build the cutest, most aesthetically pleasing relationship on the outside, but if the foundation is cracked (aka one of you wants kids and the other expects to be permanently unemployed in Bali), that whole relationship house is going to collapse.

In this chapter, I explain how to have those important convos *without* scaring someone into thinking you're proposing before the appetizers even hit the table.

TIFF SAYS

Love is about meeting in the middle. Relationships aren't about two people being *exactly* the same. They're about learning to navigate differences, respect each other's lifestyles, and decide what's actually a dealbreaker versus what's just a small compromise. Some differences? Totally workable. Others? *Total nightmare.* The key is knowing which is which before you invest years trying to force something that just isn't meant to fit.

Money Moves: Navigating Finances While Dating

JLo once said, "My love don't cost a thing." And while that's a beautiful sentiment, let's get real — love *might* be priceless, but relationships? They come with a price tag. Between inflation, the cost of eggs reaching luxury car levels, and the internet constantly debating the virtues of "soft life" versus "marrying rich," dating and finances are more intertwined than ever.

The good news? There's no *one* right way to navigate money in relationships. The bad news? If you don't talk about it, your credit score might suffer before your heart does. So before you find yourself awkwardly Venmo requesting your situationship for half the Uber after a night out, here's how to approach the money convo like a pro:

1. Know what you want before you start the conversation.

Before you even *attempt* to bring this up, ask yourself:

- **How do I like to provide?** Are you someone who enjoys covering things for your partner, or do you prefer a more equal split?
- **How do I like to be provided for?** Are you comfortable going 50/50, or do you want someone who takes financial initiative?
- **What financial dynamic makes me feel secure, respected, and comfortable?**

There's no *right* or *wrong* answer, but if you aren't honest with yourself, your bank account will eventually expose the truth. You don't want to wake up two years into a relationship realizing you're *miserable* every time your partner asks you to split the $7.99 bottle of dish soap.

2. **Bring it up without killing the romance.**

    Money convos can get weird fast, but avoiding them is worse. Here are a few non-awkward ways to start the discussion:

    - *"Hey, I know we've been having a great time, and I wanted to get your thoughts on how you usually handle money in relationships. Are you more of a 'split everything' person, or do you prefer something different?"*
    - *"If we planned a trip together, how would you want to split the cost? Just so we're on the same page before I start daydreaming about overpriced beachside cocktails."*
    - *"Do you see finances as a team effort in a relationship, or do you like to keep things separate? No judgment, just curious about how you view it."*
    - *"What's your vibe on money in dating? Some people love the traditional approach, and others are all about the 50/50 split — I want to make sure we're on the same page."*

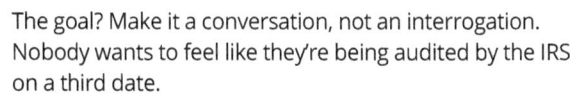

    REMEMBER: The goal? Make it a conversation, not an interrogation. Nobody wants to feel like they're being audited by the IRS on a third date.

3. **Recognize and respect different money styles.**

    Not everyone handles finances the same way. Some people expect the full "traditional provider" treatment — think Uber there *and* back, plus the whole bill, *every time.* Others prefer a fully equal partnership, where rent, vacations, and even who buys the next round of margaritas is balanced. Some people even love financially supporting their partner, while others want to be financially supported. There's no shame in any of it — as long as it's what *you* actually want and not something you're forcing yourself to accept because you're afraid of losing the relationship.

Balancing Lifestyles and Focusing on Shared Values

Another major infrastructure issue in relationships? Lifestyle differences. You're a wellness enthusiast who starts the day with green juice and a 10K run, while they think a vegetable is whatever's on top of their burger. You wake up at 6:30 a.m. to Shakira's "Hips Don't Lie" as your alarm, while they consider anything before noon a war crime. These small differences might seem cute at first — opposites attract, right? — but over time, they can start to feel like you're living in two different time zones.

It's not just about whether one of you is a morning person or a night owl. Think about the bigger picture:

>> Are you a homebody who loves cozy nights in, and they're a social butterfly who wants to host a Super Bowl–level gathering every other weekend?

>> Do you prioritize family traditions while they can barely get through a holiday dinner without breaking into a cold sweat?

>> Are you career-focused with big financial goals, while they still consider paying for Spotify Premium a financial burden?

>> Do you see travel as an exciting adventure, while they think leaving the city limits is unnecessary?

These things matter because compatibility isn't just about chemistry — it's about how you want to live your actual life.

Here are some tips for bringing up lifestyle differences without sounding like a judge on *Shark Tank:*

TIP

>> **Casually drop it in conversation.** If you notice something small (like they never cook at home), use humor: "So, are we looking at a lifetime of takeout or do you have a signature dish hidden up your sleeve?" This keeps the convo light while giving you insight into their habits.

>> **Frame it as "teamwork."** Instead of "I can't deal with how messy you are," try "I feel best in a clean space — what's a system we can both vibe with?" Relationships aren't about

changing the other person, but finding ways to work with each other.

- » **Ask about their future plans.** If they're always talking about living off the grid in a cabin and you need to be within five miles of a Sephora at all times, now's the time to discuss where you see yourselves long-term. A simple "Where do you picture yourself in five years?" can reveal a lot.

- » **See if compromise is possible.** Some lifestyle gaps can be bridged (like agreeing to alternate between nights out and nights in), but if their dream life looks like an episode of *Alone* and yours is a *Sex and the City* reboot, you might need to reconsider long-term compatibility.

WARNING

Don't ignore the red flags in the name of "love." You don't have to be clones of each other, but shared values make life easier. If every dinner with their family feels like an episode of *Jerry Springer*, if they guilt-trip you every time you want a night to yourself, or if their idea of budgeting is "just don't look at the bank account," these are signs to pause. You're not just dating a person, you're also dating their lifestyle. And if that lifestyle feels like a constant battle rather than a balance, it might be time to reconsider whether they fit into the life *you* want.

Navigating Religion in Modern Dating

When it comes to dating, religion can sometimes feel like the unexpected third wheel. Whether it's God, Buddha, astrology, Mother Nature, or the superstition that you'll be single forever if you don't make eye contact before a toast — belief systems run deep.

And just when you think you've got it figured out, you realize there's a *spectrum* of religious types. You've got:

- » **The Holiday Observers:** They only show up for Christmas Eve, Easter brunch, or major cultural holidays when their mom guilt-trips them.

- » **The Sunday Service Crowd:** Church/mosque/temple every week, no exceptions.

> **The "Not That Religious" Until It Comes to Dating Type:** They say they're chill about religion but suddenly need you to convert before meeting their family.

> **The Spiritual-but-Not-Religious:** They meditate, believe in the universe, and *might* judge you for not knowing your full birth chart.

> **The Devout:** Religion is nonnegotiable. Their future partner must align or at least participate.

> **The Religion Skeptic (aka the Atheist Who Finds It All Ridiculous):** They roll their eyes at organized religion, make jokes about the Flying Spaghetti Monster, and would rather discuss philosophy than faith. If you tell them you check your horoscope daily, expect a sarcastic comment.

These differences aren't *just* about where you'll spend Sunday mornings — they can affect everything from wedding traditions to raising kids to what holidays you celebrate (or skip).

Here's how to have "The Talk" about religion without having it feel like an interrogation:

1. Start light; ask about their background casually.

This gives them the space to share naturally without making it feel like you're vetting them for a role in *My Big Fat Religious Wedding*. The following questions can work well:

- *"So, did you grow up with any religious or cultural traditions?"*
- *"Does your family celebrate any specific holidays?"*
- *"Are you someone who has strong faith, or is it more of a personal belief?"*
- *"What's your take on astrology? Because my birth chart says we might be soulmates."*

2. Gauge how important their religion is to them.

If someone brings up religion early, *pay attention*. A person who casually mentions "My faith is super important to me" isn't just saying it for fun — that's a cue that it's a significant part of their life. Follow up with:

- *"How does that show up in your daily life?"*
- *"Would you want your future partner to share your beliefs or just be supportive of them?"*

3. **Ask about their dealbreakers without making it awkward.**

    If you're on different pages but *open* to compromise, ask:

    - "Do you see religion playing a role in your future relationship?"
    - "Would it be a dealbreaker if your partner wasn't part of your faith?"
    - "How do you feel about interfaith relationships?"

4. **If your beliefs are different, don't assume they'll "come around."**

    People don't just *magically* shift beliefs because they love you. If your partner isn't religious and you expect them to *suddenly* become devoted, or vice versa, you're setting yourself up for disappointment. Instead, be upfront about expectations early:

    - "I respect different beliefs, but my faith is a big part of my life. Would that be something you're comfortable with?"
    - "I'm not religious, but I'd be open to learning more about your traditions if that's important to you."

    If you're someone who *does* want a partner to eventually convert or fully embrace your traditions, don't wait until the wedding invites are being printed to bring it up.

REMEMBER

Dating across different faiths or beliefs *can* work, but only if both people are clear on their expectations and willing to compromise where it matters. Love alone won't erase cultural misunderstandings, fix major lifestyle differences, or make someone suddenly embrace your traditions. Talk early, talk honestly, and don't ignore the red flags. If you can find common ground, great. If not? Better to know now than five years in when your mother-in-law is sending you passive-aggressive Bible verses because you won't baptize the kids.

When Dating Gets Political

Dating in today's world without discussing politics is like trying to eat soup with a fork — messy and ultimately frustrating. With the political divide feeling more like the Grand Canyon than a friendly disagreement, it's no surprise that figuring out where someone stands has become a major part of modern dating. Sure, there *are* couples out there who make it work despite voting for opposing candidates, but let's be real: If your fundamental rights, identity, or ethics are on the line, you probably don't want to find out three months in that your new partner thinks *The Handmaid's Tale* is an instruction manual, not a dystopian warning.

REMEMBER

Now, this isn't about slapping a giant "good" or "bad" label on someone based on their beliefs. Instead, it's about figuring out if your values align and whether you'd be comfortable building a life with someone who may see the world through an entirely different lens. If you're someone who fights for social justice, reproductive rights, or marginalized communities, it might be difficult to date someone who actively votes against those causes. On the flip side, if you're a staunch conservative, dating someone who gets their news solely from *The Daily Show* might make for some *very* tense Sunday brunches.

So how do you *actually* bring up politics without turning the date into a live presidential debate? Here are some ways to casually bring up politics without killing the vibe:

- » **Test the waters with a lighthearted comment.** Try something neutral but revealing, like "So, do you pay attention to politics, or are you one of those 'I just can't' people?" Their response will give you an idea of whether they engage with politics at all or avoid it like an ex at a party.

- » **Use a pop culture reference.** Mention a politically charged show, book, or event, like "Did you see how crazy the reactions were to the new voting laws?" or "The Barbie movie broke the internet. Some people said it was too 'woke' — thoughts?" This can help you gauge their perspective without immediately diving into policy debates.

- » **Ask about their involvement without assuming their stance.** Instead of "Who did you vote for?" try "Do you keep up with politics, or do you mostly focus on other things?" If they say, "Oh, I don't really follow politics," that might be a red flag for you. If they say, "I stay informed, but I hate discussing it," that's something to note as well.

- » **Find out what they're passionate about.** Ask, "Are there any causes or issues you care a lot about?" This gives them space to express what matters to them without forcing the conversation into party lines.

» **Use humor to keep it light.** "If we were a political scandal, what do you think it would be called?" "If you had to run for office, what would be your campaign slogan?" This keeps things playful while still showing you whether they have any interest in the topic.

What if you find out you're politically opposed?

Let's say you're deep into the conversation, and it turns out they think climate change is a hoax or that voting doesn't matter. Now what?

» **Decide if it's a dealbreaker.** Some political disagreements can be managed; others are foundational. If their beliefs impact core values that are important to you (like human rights, equality, or bodily autonomy), it's okay to say, "This won't work."

» **Ask yourself if you'd be comfortable long-term.** Could you see yourself at Thanksgiving dinner explaining why your partner believes conspiracy theories about the moon landing? If the idea makes your skin crawl, it might be best to exit now.

» **Don't waste time trying to change them.** If you're looking at them like a *fixer-upper house* that just needs a little "reeducation," step away. People don't change unless they *want* to.

Aligning your ethics before you hear wedding bells

Look, politics *do* matter in relationships. If you're passionate about certain issues, don't be afraid to bring them up. Love isn't just about chemistry — it's about compatibility in the way you see the world. And if they expect you to compromise on your core beliefs just to keep things "peaceful," remind yourself that peace at the expense of your values isn't peace at all. It's just pretending.

So before you fall head over heels, take a moment to ask: *Do we align where it truly counts?* Because you don't want to be three years in, engaged, and *then* realize you're about to marry someone who thinks "both sides are the same."

Dating Within or Outside Your Culture

Dating within or outside your culture is kind of like deciding whether to watch a movie with subtitles. Some people are totally into it, willing to learn, and excited to embrace something new, while others immediately panic and ask, "Wait, do I have to read the whole time?" Cultural compatibility in relationships isn't just about language or traditions — it's about shared values, respect, and whether your future in-laws are about to become your biggest fans or your biggest stressors.

The "but my family will lose it" dilemma

For some, dating outside their culture feels like announcing at Thanksgiving dinner that you're moving to Mars — shock, confusion, and at least one dramatic "But what will the neighbors say?" If your family is traditional, they might expect you to marry within your background to preserve customs, faith, or just to keep things "easy." You might get hit with questions like:

- *"But will they understand our traditions?"*
- *"What about raising the kids?"*
- *"How will we communicate with their family?"*

THE LOVE ACROSS CULTURES SUCCESS STORY

I once had a client who grew up in a strict Indian household where matchmaking was the norm. She, however, had other plans — she moved to New York, and fell in love with a Brooklyn hipster who thought chai tea was just a fancy latte. Her parents were *not* impressed. But with honest conversations and a willingness to learn, her boyfriend slowly earned their trust (and built a respectable spice tolerance). They ended up having a wedding in India, proving that love doesn't have to fit inside cultural borders — it just needs mutual respect and good communication.

And then there's the classic "But they won't understand our inside jokes!" — which, fair, but that's what Google Translate and years of patient explaining are for.

How to talk about culture on early dates

If you want to bring up cultural values without making it sound like a final exam, try approaches like these:

- **Traditions and holidays:** "Does your family have any specific traditions that mean a lot to you?"
- **Expectations and future:** "Would you be open to learning about a partner's culture, or do you see yourself only dating within your background?"
- **Family dynamics:** "On a scale of 'super chill' to 'they have my wedding colors picked out,' how involved is your family in your dating life?"
- **Shared values:** "What's something from your background that's really important for you to pass down?"

This keeps it casual but opens the door for deeper discussions if things progress.

When family just won't get on board

If your family isn't supportive, ask yourself:

- Are they just uncomfortable with change, or do they have valid concerns?
- Are they open to getting to know your partner, or is their mind made up?
- Will you regret making a decision based on their opinions instead of your own?

At the end of the day, *your* love is *your* love. If someone is mistreating you, of course, listen to your family's warnings. But if their only complaint is "This isn't how we do things," then it's up to you to decide what makes *you* happy.

TIFF SAYS: Dating within or outside your culture is about balance. If both people are willing to learn, respect, and meet halfway, cultural differences become *assets* instead of dealbreakers. Just don't expect your partner to instantly master all your traditions — there's a learning curve, and sometimes it starts with them butchering the pronunciation of your last name.

Aligning Sexual Values Without the Awkwardness

Sex in dating can be a huge factor — but what happens when the *lack* of it becomes the bigger topic? For some, sex before marriage is an absolute no-go due to religious beliefs, personal values, or the fact that they were once told at church camp that so much as *thinking* about it would send them straight to eternal damnation. Others are out here treating dating like an open bar — sampling everything before deciding what they like best. Then, somewhere in the middle, you have the "I just want to be sure I actually like you before we do anything crazy" crowd.

REMEMBER: No matter where you stand, one thing is for sure: Sexual compatibility (or lack thereof) needs to be talked about early to avoid a lot of confusion and frustration later. Nothing is worse than realizing someone's waiting for marriage *after* you've sent your most fire "Come over" text — only to get hit with "Actually, I don't do that" like a brick wall to the face.

Waiting until marriage versus waiting until . . . Thursday

There are plenty of reasons people practice celibacy. Maybe it's faith. Maybe it's personal growth. Maybe they just saw one too many TikToks about hookup culture destroying modern relationships and decided they're retiring from the game. Whatever the reason, it's totally valid — as long as it's what *they* actually want.

On the flip side, some people see sex as a vital part of compatibility. Like, *would you buy a car without test-driving it first?* If you wouldn't commit to a lease without checking the apartment's plumbing, maybe you're also the type who wants to make sure the *connection* is functional before signing the long-term contract.

No judgment — both perspectives are fair, but it's crucial to make sure you and your partner are on the same page.

So how do you even bring this up?

Look, you don't have to sit across from your date with a clipboard like you're conducting a *60 Minutes* interview. But you also don't want to just *assume* someone's expectations match yours, only to find out later that they were playing a completely different game.

Here are a few ways to ease into the conversation without making it weird:

>> *"What's your take on hookup culture? Are you more of a 'wait until it's meaningful' type or a 'go with the vibe' kind of person?"*

>> *"I know everyone has different views on intimacy — where do you stand on that when it comes to relationships?"*

>> *"What's something you think is important to build a strong relationship before getting physical?"*

This keeps things open-ended and lets them express *their* stance rather than putting them on the spot with "Soooo, are we doing this or nah?"

WARNING

One of the biggest dating disasters happens when people pretend to be okay with something they're *definitely not* okay with. If you're holding out for marriage but are too afraid to bring it up, *you're going to run into issues.* If you're someone who values physical intimacy early on but pretend to be fine waiting, *you're setting yourself up for resentment.* Worst-case scenarios include

>> Waiting for someone to "come around" only to realize they never will.

>> Agreeing to something you're uncomfortable with just to keep them around.

>> Ending up in a situation where neither of you is happy because you both lied about what you actually wanted.

Moral of the story? Just say what you actually want. The right person will respect it. The wrong person will expose themselves — and you'll save yourself a lot of wasted time.

Tackling Other Big Topics: Family, Your Future, and More

Getting into serious conversations about family, marriage, and the future can feel like stepping on a landmine. You don't want to be out here saying, "So how many kids are we having?" before the appetizers arrive, but you also don't want to wake up two years later realizing you've been dating someone who *thinks marriage is a scam* and *wants to live on a commune off the grid*.

TIP Here's how to bring up these *big topics* in a way that won't make them run for the hills:

- **Family views:** "What was your parents' relationship like growing up? Do you think it shaped how you see dating now?"
- **Marriage goals:** "Do you see marriage as a goal for yourself, or are you more go-with-the-flow about it?"
- **Kids or no kids?** "Some people have a clear 'yes' or 'no' on kids, others are open — where do you stand?"
- **Lifestyle expectations:** "If you had the perfect relationship, what would it look like day to day?"

Because the worst thing you can do? Fake compatibility just to keep someone around. Love is about respect — whether that means respecting someone's decision to wait or respecting that you need a partner who aligns with your needs. So talk about it early, talk about it openly, and most importantly, talk about it in a way that doesn't make the waiter at your dinner date wish they had noise-canceling headphones.

THE TRUTH ABOUT ULTIMATUMS: DO THEY REALLY WORK?

Ultimatums in relationships are like sending a "We need to talk" text — you *think* it's going to make the other person step up, but more often than not, it just sends them into a spiral of panic and bad decision-making. If you have to threaten someone into proposing,

> moving in, or *finally* deleting their dating apps, are they really doing it because they want to — or just to avoid losing you? Spoiler alert: Relationships built on pressure don't last.
>
> Instead of dropping a "marry me or else" bomb, try communicating why this milestone is important to you. If they still won't budge, maybe it's not an ultimatum you need to give them, but an *exit strategy*.

Handling different family goals when you're not aligned

One of you wants three kids, a golden retriever, and a house in the suburbs. The other thinks kids are sticky, dogs shed too much, and the city is the only place worth living. Welcome to the *what are we doing?* conversation.

If you're serious about someone, these differences can't be ignored. Here's what to do:

- » **Be honest with yourself first.** If your dream is a big family, don't downplay it just to keep someone around.
- » **Ask them where they stand.** Are they a "never kids" or a "not sure yet" person? Because there's a difference.
- » **See if there's room for compromise.** Maybe they don't want *four* kids, but they're open to one. Maybe they hate suburbs but would consider a quieter part of the city. *Is there a middle ground, or are you just delaying an inevitable breakup?*

REMEMBER

The earlier you figure this out, the less time you'll spend trying to turn a "no" into a "maybe" that will never happen.

Successfully prioritizing your social life, work, and dating schedule

Your career is thriving, your friends miss you, and your dating life is . . . a disaster. Balancing all three is basically an Olympic sport, and most of us are out here with a participation trophy. The key? Intentional scheduling.

- **Don't let work take over your life.** Yes, the grind is important, but if you don't have time to text someone back, you're not "busy," you're just *unavailable*.
- **Make dating a priority.** If you're free every night but somehow "too busy" for a date, you're just avoiding putting yourself out there.
- **Block off time for friends.** Relationships fade when neglected, whether they're romantic or platonic.

If you have a particularly demanding career, trying to juggle your job and dating is a full-time job in itself. You want love, but you also want to *secure the bag*. How do you balance both without burning out?

- **Be upfront about your schedule.** If you're in a crazy work season, say that.
- **Make the time you *do* have count.** Even if it's just a coffee date or a late-night FaceTime, effort matters.
- **Don't date someone who sees ambition as a problem.** If they're constantly guilt-tripping you for being busy, that's a *red flag*.
- **But also . . . don't let work be your excuse.** If you *always* prioritize emails over dates, the real issue might not be time — it might be avoidance.

REMEMBER

Finding balance means making space for *all* the things that matter — not just the ones that scream the loudest.

What to do when their family isn't a fan of you

Ah, the nightmare scenario: You're madly in love, but their family sees you as nothing more than a *temporary inconvenience*. Maybe it's cultural, maybe it's personal, maybe their mom just decided *no one is good enough for their baby*. Whatever the reason, here's how to handle it:

- **Be respectful, but don't beg for approval.** If they don't like you, kissing up won't change it.
- **Ask your partner for support.** If they aren't standing up for you, *that's the real problem*.

> **Know when to walk away.** If their family's opinion is causing major strain and they refuse to set boundaries, *do you really want in-laws who treat you like a villain?*

At the end of the day, you're dating them — not their parents. But if their family dynamic is *ruining* the relationship, it might be time to rethink things.

Winning over the friends: How to make a good impression

Meeting *the friends* is a relationship milestone right up there with "sharing a streaming password" and "surviving a weekend trip together." If their friends like you? You're golden. If they don't? You'll be fighting an uphill battle every time your name comes up in the group chat.

Here's how to make a solid first impression:

> **Be friendly, but not *too* try-hard.** No one likes someone who's trying *too* much to be liked.

> **Find common ground.** Sports? Reality TV? A mutual hatred of slow walkers?

> **Avoid controversial topics.** This is *not* the time to go on a rant about why your favorite reality star deserved better (or politics).

> **Don't monopolize their time.** They still need space for their friendships — *you're the new addition, not the replacement.*

TIP

If their friends see that you're good for them, they'll *want* to like you. If they don't? Well, you might want to ask yourself why.

How to share mental health struggles with your partner

Dating while dealing with mental health struggles is no easy feat. The big question: *How much do you share, and when?*

> **Early on, keep it light.** First dates aren't therapy sessions. No one needs your entire trauma résumé over appetizers.

- **As things progress, open up gradually.** "Hey, just so you know, I deal with anxiety" is *a lot* different from dumping *every* deep insecurity on them all at once.
- **Gauge their response.** Do they listen and support, or do they make you feel like you're "too much"? *Their reaction tells you everything.*
- **Prioritize your healing.** A partner can support you, but they *can't* fix you. That's your job.

The right person will make space for your struggles — without making you feel like a burden.

5

Romance, Rewritten: Loving and Dating on Your Own Terms

IN THIS PART...

Figure out if/when to have sex.

Learn to date after divorce.

Find out about LGBTQIA+ dating and how to thrive.

IN THIS CHAPTER

» Setting and holding to your boundaries

» Being realistic about what sex can and can't do for a relationship

» Banishing shame

» Making sure your relationship with sex is serving you

» Telling your partner what you want without feeling awkward

Chapter **18**
No Pressure, Just Pleasure: Navigating Sex in the City

Sex is one of those topics that everyone seems to have an opinion on — when to do it, when *not* to do it, if you're moving too fast or too slow. Whether it's dissecting details over brunch or spiraling to your best friend about how you're in a rut and haven't had any in a while, it can feel like everyone is having the best sex of their lives *except you*. Movies and social media make it look effortless — sweaty but cinematic, casual yet emotionally profound. Meanwhile, in reality, half the time you're just hoping your hair doesn't get stuck under their arm or that they don't suddenly bring up their ex mid-hookup (it happens, unfortunately).

But here's the thing: Good sex isn't just about the timing — it's about *your* timing. It's not about what your friends are doing, what some random person from a dating app expects, or even what you used to believe was "right." It's about what *feels right for you.*

Because at the end of the day, sex should bring pleasure both in the moment and in the long run. Otherwise, what's the point?

Let's be real, your sex life is nobody's business but yours (and maybe your group chat). This chapter is here to help you figure out what *you* want between the sheets (or on the couch, or wherever your heart desires) without shame or pressure and explore your sexual desires from a place of power and confidence.

Staying True to Your Boundaries Without Feeling Pressured

Sex should be fun, personal, and, most importantly, an empowering experience. It's about feeling confident in your choices, not worrying if someone is going to judge you for them. Whether you're in college, in a long-term relationship, or just living your best single life, the golden rule is this: Consent is key, and pressure is a no-go.

WARNING

If someone is trying to convince you to do something you're not ready for — whether it's moving too fast, trying something you're uncomfortable with, or acting like they deserve access to your body because they bought you dinner — *run, don't walk.* Your body is not a Groupon deal that comes with a "spent enough time, now redeem for sex" clause. No matter the situation — whether it's a casual fling or a committed relationship — you always have the right to decide what feels good for *you* without shame, guilt, or manipulation.

So how do you set those boundaries early? Here are some ways to make sure you're in control of your own comfort while also fostering open communication:

>> **Decide your boundaries before you're in the moment.**
You don't want to be figuring out what you're okay with *while* someone's whispering in your ear asking if you're into some very questionable Google search results. Before you even get to that point, take some time to decide:
   - What are your hard *no's*?

224   PART 5 Romance, Rewritten: Loving and Dating on Your Own Terms

- What are things you might be open to *eventually*, but not right now?
- What are your expectations around intimacy in relationships versus casual dating?

>> **Say it early; say it often.** Setting sexual boundaries isn't a *one-time* conversation — it's an *ongoing* one. Some ways to bring it up without making it awkward:

- "I'm into taking things slow. I like to get to know someone before getting physical."
- "I really value comfort and trust when it comes to sex, so I like to communicate a lot beforehand."
- "I have some personal boundaries that are really important to me. I'd love to talk about what we're both comfortable with."

>> **Watch for red flags.** Unfortunately, not everyone will respect boundaries the way they should. Here are a few signs someone might try to push yours:

- They act like setting boundaries "kills the mood." (Newsflash: The real mood killer is making someone uncomfortable.)
- They guilt-trip you, saying things like "But I thought we really had a connection...."
- They ignore your no and try again later. (If they don't hear you the first time, they won't listen the second or third, either.)
- They make jokes about your boundaries as if they're optional (spoiler: they're not).

>> **Boundaries apply to every type of relationship.** It doesn't matter if it's a one-night stand or a long-term relationship — your comfort should always be a priority. You deserve mutual respect, clear communication, and a connection that makes you feel good about yourself. No one should ever make you feel like sex is an obligation, a favor, or some kind of "milestone" they're entitled to cash in on. If someone makes intimacy feel like a *transaction* instead of a shared experience, they are not the right person for you.

> **SHAME? WE DON'T KNOW HER**
>
> **TIFF SAYS**
>
> If you want to wait for the *right* time, person, or situation, that's great. If you want to have sex when it feels good for you, that's great too. The only opinion that matters is *yours*. The whole point of setting boundaries is to make sure your sex life — whether it's with a committed partner or a casual connection — is one that leaves you feeling comfortable, respected, and fully in control of your own choices.

The Truth about Sex: It Won't Make Someone Love You More

Let's set the record straight — sex is *not* a love potion. It won't turn a bad texter into a devoted boyfriend. It won't make someone who barely acknowledges your existence suddenly see wedding bells. And it *definitely* won't fix a broken situationship (in fact, it might just extend the free trial of disappointment).

Yet so many people believe that intimacy equals investment. When I was in college, I had a friend who thought that if someone wanted her physically, it meant they cared. If someone *didn't* want her every night, she assumed she wasn't attractive enough, lovable enough, or just *enough* in general. She was searching for a long-term relationship but didn't think she was worthy of one, so she settled for being "the fun girl" instead. And because she put all her value into sex, she attracted people who *only* valued that part of her.

It wasn't until she had a major realization — that *she* should be enjoying sex too, that *she* should be in control of who had access to her — that everything changed. She stopped chasing validation and started choosing partners who met *her* standards, not the other way around. And the wild part? The moment she flipped the script, she finally found the love she had always wanted. Now she's been in a relationship for five years with someone who loves her *fully* — both in the sheets and in the streets.

REMEMBER

The biggest lie society tells us is that sex is some magical relationship glue. Spoiler alert: If they weren't serious about you before, they won't be serious about you after either. That doesn't mean sex isn't important — it just means that it should be happening on *your* terms, with *your* comfort, and with people who see you as a whole person, not just a convenient late-night option.

It's about mutual enjoyment, not obligation. It's about connection, not coercion. It's about respect, not reward. And whether it's a one-night stand or a long-term relationship, you deserve for sex to be something that benefits you too — not just a way to make someone else stay interested.

TIFF SAYS

My friend's story proves one major thing — your self-worth should never be tied to whether or not someone desires you. Because the right person won't just want you for a night. They'll want you in their life.

Owning Your Choices Without the Guilt Trip

People seem to love to make judgments about other people's choices about sex. Got multiple partners? "You're wild!" Don't have any partners? "You're a prude!" Stay celibate? "You're repressed." Love casual sex? "You have no self-respect." At this point, the only winning move is to stop playing society's game and start doing what works best for you.

Here's the reality: You get to decide how you experience sex, and nobody else's opinion gets a vote. If casual sex feels right for you, amazing. If you prefer to wait until you're in love, that's great too. The key is making sure that whatever you're doing is *your* choice, not something you're doing out of pressure, guilt, or because you think it's the only way to keep someone interested.

Casual sex without the emotional hangover

At the end of the day, sex isn't a moral issue — it's a personal one. If you want to have casual sex, have it on your terms, safely, and with partners who respect you. Following are some of my suggestions for navigating casual sex:

- **Know your own boundaries.** Just because sex is casual doesn't mean respect is optional. Be clear with yourself about what you're comfortable with and what's off-limits.
- **Communicate like an adult.** No, "wyd" at 2 a.m. is not communication. Be honest about your expectations, whether it's a one-time thing or a recurring friends-with-benefits situation.
- **Ignore society's opinion.** If someone tries to shame you for having a healthy sex life, remind them that their outdated views are not your problem.
- **Safety first, always.** Protection, consent, and emotional well-being should never be compromised — whether it's a hookup or a long-term relationship.
- **Make sure you're enjoying it too.** If you're having sex just to please someone else and not because you actually *want* to, it's time to reevaluate. You deserve pleasure, excitement, and a great time — this is not a charity event.

TIFF SAYS

Sex is yours to define. Make sure your choices align with what makes you feel empowered, not ashamed. Because the only person who gets to define your worth? You.

Virginity and embracing your journey

Let's be honest — if you haven't had sex yet, it can sometimes feel like you're starring in a remake of *The 40-Year-Old Virgin* (minus the questionable chest-waxing scene). Everywhere you turn, movies, TV shows, and your overly nosy friends make it seem like you should have had some grand sexual awakening by now. But here's the truth: There's no timeline for sex.

TIFF SAYS

One of my clients used to struggle with this exact insecurity. She was in college, still a virgin, and felt like she was some rare species in a world where everyone was seemingly swiping right for casual flings. Coming from a strict Mormon background, she saw her virginity as a sacred part of her beliefs and didn't want to have casual sex just because "everyone else was doing it." But then she got into a serious relationship and made the choice to have sex before marriage. At first she struggled with guilt, feeling like she had betrayed the values she was raised with. But over time, she realized something crucial: Her worth wasn't tied to her virginity, and she was allowed to evolve in her beliefs.

Society loves to make it seem like virginity is either something to get rid of as soon as possible or something that defines your entire worth. Spoiler alert: It's neither. Whether you're waiting for marriage, waiting for the right person, or just haven't found the right moment, you are not "behind" in life. Your experiences — or lack thereof — don't make you any less desirable, mature, or lovable.

Here are some ways to handle any pressure you may be feeling like a pro:

>> **Stop letting other people's experiences define yours.** Just because your best friend lost their virginity at prom doesn't mean you have to. This isn't a group project.

>> **Know that virginity is a social construct.** News flash: The whole concept of virginity was literally made up. There's no "sex fairy" who grants you wisdom after your first time. It's just another experience — not a magical transformation.

>> **Set your own boundaries.** If you're waiting, make sure it's because *you* want to, not because of guilt, fear, or pressure from anyone else. Your body, your choice.

>> **Don't let anyone shame you — either way.** Whether you're waiting or not, some people will have opinions. Ignore them. If someone makes you feel bad about your choices, that's *their* problem, not yours.

TIFF SAYS Your worth has nothing to do with sex. At the end of the day, virginity doesn't define you. What matters is that you're making choices that align with who you are and what makes you feel empowered. And if your beliefs change along the way? That's okay too. Growth is part of life, and the best relationships — whether sexual or not — are built on respect, mutual understanding, and the freedom to be your authentic self.

Reclaiming Your Confidence in Sex

Sex is not a reward or something you "owe" anyone. It's a choice that should make you feel safe, happy, and respected. And if at any point you feel like your relationship with sex isn't serving you? You have every right to hit the reset button and redefine it on your own terms. Here's how:

- **Forgive yourself for the past.** Whatever choices you've made (or didn't make), they don't define you. You are allowed to change, grow, and redefine your relationship with intimacy at any time.
- **Recognize that sex is not a performance.** You're not auditioning for *Euphoria*. You don't have to be perfect, wild, or do something you're uncomfortable with just to "prove" you're good at sex.
- **Focus on what feels good for you.** Instead of worrying about whether you're meeting someone else's expectations, think about what genuinely brings you joy, pleasure, and connection.
- **Detox from shame.** Society loves to tell us that we're either too prudish or too promiscuous. Block out the noise. What works for you is what matters.
- **Make choices that align with your values.** If casual sex makes you feel good and empowered, great! If waiting until a deep emotional connection is what you prefer, also great! Just make sure you're making choices based on your own wants and needs — not fear, pressure, or insecurity.

Knowing How to Tell Your Partner Your Specific Needs

One of the biggest misconceptions about sex is that your partner should just "know" what you want. Like, what is this? Telepathy? A rom-com with perfectly choreographed intimacy? No. Great sex requires communication.

And yet so many people hesitate to actually say what they want out of fear of making things awkward or "ruining the moment." But here's the reality: If you're too afraid to talk about it, how are you supposed to enjoy it?

Here are some tips for bringing up your needs in an open and conversational way:

- » **Ease into it with casual conversation.** Instead of making it a big "we need to talk" moment, bring it up naturally. For example:
  - "You know what I really like? When you do X. . . ."
  - "I've always been curious about trying Y. What do you think?"
  - "Is there anything you've been wanting to try?" (This keeps the convo open-ended and fun.)
- » **Use humor to lighten the mood.** Sex talks don't have to be intense. Something as simple as "Okay, we need to discuss how good you are at Z — because I need that to happen more often" can make the conversation feel exciting instead of awkward.
- » **Be clear about boundaries.** If something makes you uncomfortable, *say it*. Don't wait until you're in the moment and trying to wiggle out of a situation you didn't want in the first place. Boundaries are *sexy* because they show confidence and self-awareness.
- » **Talk about what turns you on.** Instead of just saying what you *don't* like, focus on what you *do*. Positive reinforcement works wonders. "When you do X, I love it." Boom. Easy.
- » **Normalize the conversation.** The more you talk about what you like, the less awkward it becomes. Don't save these convos for when you're already in bed — bring them up in casual settings so that they feel natural, not forced.

REMEMBER

At the end of the day, sex is best when both people feel seen, heard, and satisfied. The only way to make that happen is to speak up. And if someone makes you feel bad for expressing what you need? They're not mature enough to be in your bed, let alone your life.

> **IN THIS CHAPTER**
>
> » Keeping the past in its place when dating post-divorce
>
> » Figuring out what you even want out of this whole dating thing
>
> » Fully letting go of your ex
>
> » Knowing how the game has changed since you last dated

Chapter 19
Second Chances: Thriving in the Dating World Post-Divorce

Dating after divorce can feel like stepping into a nightclub at 2 a.m. when you just wanted a quiet glass of wine. The lights are too bright, the music is too loud, and everyone seems a little too young. You survived the emotional equivalent of a roller coaster, a legal battle, and a really bad reality TV show all at once, and now you're expected to just . . . date again? When you were last single, people actually called each other on the phone. Now, a text that just says "wyd?" at midnight is considered effort.

But take a deep breath — this isn't starting over; it's starting fresh. Dating apps might feel like the Wild West, but approach them with an open mind (and a strong Wi-Fi connection). Worried about what to wear? Ask your kids — if they laugh, you're wearing the wrong thing; if they roll their eyes, you nailed it. Debating whether to date younger or older? Who cares — date whoever makes you feel good. Nervous about putting yourself out there? You survived a divorce; you can survive a bad date. The hardest part — leaving what wasn't serving you — is already behind you. Now it's time to step into this new era of dating feeling hot, confident, and ready for whatever comes next.

Whether you're looking for a fun fling, a serious relationship, or just someone who actually replies to texts in a timely manner, the dating world is yours for the taking. Welcome back to the single world — we missed you!

How to Move on Without Bringing the Past to Dinner

So you're back in the dating world. Maybe it's been a few years. Maybe it's been a few *decades*. Either way, it's a whole new ball game, and you're suddenly realizing that the last time you flirted, texting wasn't even a thing. Now people are falling in love through memes, and the idea of "calling someone" is basically the equivalent of sending a carrier pigeon. It's easy to look back at the past and think, *Why am I even doing this again?* But hold up — dating after divorce isn't about rehashing old wounds. It's about getting out there with a fresh perspective, a little more wisdom, and hopefully a lot more fun. So let's break it down into a few easy guidelines:

- » **Leave the baggage at the door (seriously, drop it).** Look, everyone who's been married has some kind of emotional baggage. But your new dates aren't your ex, so let's not treat them like they're about to drain your bank account and "forget" to take out the trash for the next ten years. Walk into new connections with a *clean slate mentality*. If you catch yourself saying, "Well, my ex always . . ." just stop. The past is a reference, not a roadblock. Instead, focus on what *you* want now, not what went wrong before.

- » **Update your dating playbook (because it's not 2005 anymore).** Things have changed. Dating apps exist, ghosting is a thing, and people will literally communicate their interest with a *fire emoji reaction* instead of using words. If you haven't flirted since Myspace was popular, you might need to brush up on the *modern* dating game. That means setting up a profile (yes, you need photos that aren't from your cousin's wedding in 2011), learning that "wyd" at midnight isn't a love letter, and realizing that "exclusive" is no longer assumed — it's a *conversation*.

» **Define what you actually want (and own it).** Before you start panic-matching with every person on a dating app, ask yourself — what do you *really* want this time? Do you want something casual? Are you looking for a new long-term partner? Or do you just want someone to text you good morning so your coffee tastes better? There's no wrong answer, but the key is being honest about it. Saying, "I'm just seeing what's out there" when you actually want a serious relationship is a fast track to Frustration City.

» **Don't compare new people to your ex (even if your friends do).** It's easy to get caught in the trap of *Wow, this person is so different from my ex!* Or worse, *Ugh, why does this remind me of them?* News flash: No one is your ex. That's kind of the point. Instead of using past relationships as a measuring stick, appreciate each new connection for what it is. Sure, your ex might have hated road trips, but this new person? They might love them. Just because one person made you swear off love forever doesn't mean the next will.

» **Flirt like you own the room (even if you haven't flirted in a while).** You've been off the market for a while, so it's normal to feel *rusty*. But here's the thing — confidence is attractive at any age, no matter how long it's been. Start small. Make eye contact. Compliment someone's outfit. Laugh at their dumb joke. You don't have to perform a full rom-com makeover to get back in the game. Just ease into it, and remind yourself that dating is supposed to be *fun*, not a performance review.

» **Remember, love is not a speed race.** There's no timeline for finding someone new. You don't need to get engaged within a year to "prove" that you're still desirable. You also don't need to swear off relationships forever just because your last one didn't go as planned. Take your time. Date for the experience, not just the outcome.

REMEMBER

Dating after divorce is about more than just finding love again — it's about rediscovering *you*. The new, wiser, more self-assured version of yourself that knows what they want, what they *won't* tolerate, and how to have a good time along the way. So go ahead, get back out there. The dating world is waiting.

Dating for Fun After Losing "the One": Deciding What You Want

After a marriage ends — whether it was a happy ending or a dramatic, "this belongs in a Netflix series" type of ending — one of the hardest things to figure out is *what you even want now*. Do you want marriage again? Are you just trying to enjoy yourself? Should you be dating at all, or would it be better to disappear into a remote cabin and only reemerge when you have it all figured out? (Spoiler: You'll probably never *fully* have it figured out, and that's okay.)

If you've been in a long-term marriage, the dating world can feel like stepping into a time machine — except instead of landing back in the past, you've been transported to a world where texting counts as effort and people refer to relationships as "situationships." It's a lot. But the key to not feeling overwhelmed is knowing exactly what you want this time around — and most importantly, *why* you want it. The following suggestions help to break it down.

Deciding whether you even want to get married again

There's no rule that says just because you were married before, you have to do it again. Maybe marriage felt like a dream. Maybe it felt like jury duty. Maybe you loved it, but now you just want to date for fun with no long-term pressure. Whatever it is, get clear on *your* desires before letting other people (or society) tell you what's next.

Ask yourself:

>> Do I miss marriage, or do I just miss companionship?
>> Was I truly happy in my past marriage, or did I just like the *idea* of it?
>> Would I feel fulfilled in a long-term relationship without the legal paperwork?
>> Am I dating for *me*, or am I trying to prove something to my ex?

There's no wrong answer here — just make sure you're being *honest* with yourself.

Letting go of thinking you need to have it all figured out now

It's okay not to know exactly what you want immediately. Some people jump straight into dating thinking they need a brand-new *forever person* ASAP, while others feel paralyzed by the idea of starting over. The good news? You don't have to decide everything overnight. Dating isn't a test — you can explore, figure things out along the way, and change your mind as you go.

TIP: Instead of overthinking, start asking yourself, *What feels good to me right now?* Do you want to try casual dating for the first time? Are you looking for something exclusive but not marriage-level serious? Are you just testing the waters? No pressure — just clarity.

Taking a crack at dating without an end goal

If your entire dating history has revolved around commitment and "where is this going?" conversations, it might be time to try dating for the *experience* instead of the *expectation*. Go on dates with people who make you laugh, challenge your perspectives, or introduce you to new experiences — without the pressure of thinking it will lead to marriage, moving in together, or even a second date.

TIP: Sometimes, the best way to know what you *don't* want is by experiencing different types of connections.

Avoiding letting your past relationship define your future

Just because your last relationship ended doesn't mean every new one will. One of the biggest mistakes people make post-divorce is carrying all their past fears, baggage, and "never again" rules into a fresh relationship before it even has a chance.

If you keep waiting for the next person to mess up the way your ex did, you'll never let anyone in. Instead, give yourself permission to experience new relationships without assuming they'll follow the same pattern. Not everyone is your ex — don't make them pay for the ex's mistakes.

Remembering that love doesn't have to be the same every time

Maybe you were married for 20 years and the thought of another "forever" commitment makes you break out in a sweat. That's fine. Maybe you actually loved being married and can't wait to find someone who wants the same. That's fine too. Love and relationships come in all forms, and what worked for you before doesn't have to be *the* template for what you do now.

REMEMBER You get to decide what your next chapter looks like. Whether it's marriage, casual dating, or something in between, the most important thing is that it's what *you* want — not what others expect from you. And if you change your mind along the way? That's part of the journey too.

How to Fully Let Go of Your Ex

So your ex has moved on — to a new city, a new partner, or someone who wasn't even *born yet* when you had your first heartbreak. Maybe you're still catching yourself checking their Instagram, asking mutual friends if they seem happy, or wondering what went wrong.

The truth? Holding on to an ex is like carrying a bag of bricks everywhere you go. It's heavy, exhausting, and honestly, it's ruining your posture. It's time to drop the weight and move forward. Here's how to actually, *fully* let go:

» **Accept that closure isn't a grand finale moment.** You might be waiting for a final conversation where they apologize, admit they were wrong, and give you that magical "closure" you think you need to move on. But in reality? Most exes don't come back with a poetic monologue straight out of a rom-com. Closure isn't something you *get* from them — it's something you *give* yourself. Accept that you may never get a satisfying ending, and that's okay.

» **Stop asking about them (yes, even casually).** You don't need a "friendly check-in" from your mutual friends about what they're up to. You *definitely* don't need to know if they're "so happy" with their new partner. Curiosity is normal, but constantly keeping tabs keeps you stuck. Set a rule: No asking. No stalking. No casual "oops, my finger slipped" social media searches. Every time you go looking for them, you reopen a wound that's trying to heal.

» **Remember why it ended (and romanticize reality, not the past).** Breakups have a funny way of making us forget why things *didn't* work. Suddenly, all you remember is how they used to bring you coffee in bed and how you "just got each other." But what about the constant miscommunication? The nights you cried yourself to sleep? The fact that they never put in the effort you deserved? Every time you find yourself putting them on a pedestal, remind yourself of the full picture.

» **Break the emotional habit.** If you talked to your ex every day for years, it's normal to feel like something is missing. But instead of texting them when you're sad or lonely, build new habits. Call a friend. Journal. Pick up a hobby. The goal is to *retrain your brain* so they're no longer your go-to source of comfort.

» **Get rid of the little reminders.** Still wearing their hoodie? Still have the playlist they made you? Still rereading old texts? Let. It. Go. Donate, delete, and detox your space from their lingering presence. You don't need to set their stuff on fire (unless that helps), but holding onto these small things keeps them emotionally tethered to you.

» **Stop telling yourself the "what if" story.** "What if we just tried one more time?" "What if they changed?" "What if they come back?" Here's the thing: *What if they don't?* The longer you cling to the idea of a reunion, the more you block yourself from new love. Instead of fantasizing about a comeback, start imagining a future where you are completely free — and *actually happy*.

» **Remind yourself that moving on doesn't mean they win.** Sometimes we hold on because we feel like moving on means admitting defeat. But letting go isn't losing — it's *winning your life back*. You're not giving up on them; you're choosing yourself. And that's the best decision you'll ever make.

> **MAKE PEACE WITH THE FACT THAT THEIR NEW LIFE ISN'T YOUR BUSINESS**
>
> **TIFF SAYS** Maybe they're with someone new. Maybe they're posting "soft launch" photos with their new partner. Maybe they got engaged in what feels like record-breaking time. None of this is *your* business anymore. Focus on your own life, your own joy, and your own next steps. Because the truth is that your best days aren't behind you — they're waiting ahead.

How to Reenter the Scene Without Looking Like a Lost Tourist

So you're divorced and thinking about dating again. First of all, congratulations! Not on the divorce itself (unless, of course, you threw a party for it, in which case, *double congrats*), but on deciding to put yourself back out there. Whether your marriage lasted two years or 20, stepping back into the dating world after being off the market can feel like waking up from a coma and realizing people are out here *dating on apps, ghosting like it's an Olympic sport, and referring to "talking stages" like it's an actual relationship status*. Breathe. Dating hasn't *really* changed — it just got a few more confusing features. And you? You've got experience, wisdom, and (hopefully) a better idea of what you *don't* want this time around. Let's make your dating comeback *fun* instead of *chaotic*.

>> **Reframe dating as an adventure, not an obligation.**
Dating after divorce doesn't mean "finding someone ASAP so I can fill the void." It means approaching dating with curiosity, fun, and *absolutely zero desperation*. Ask yourself: *Why am I dating again?* Are you looking for love? Something casual? Validation that you *still got it*? (Spoiler alert: You do.) There's no wrong answer, but knowing what you want will save you from situationships with people who text you "wyd" at 11 p.m. and disappear for a week.

>> **Your dating skills might be rusty — and that's okay.** If your last relationship started before emojis were a full-on

language, you might feel a little out of practice. But flirting, like riding a bike, comes back — just with a few wobbly moments at first. The good news? You already know how to be in a relationship, so you've got an advantage. Start small:

- **Rebuild your social confidence.** Say hi to strangers at coffee shops. Compliment someone in a way that *isn't* about their looks. ("That's a great book choice," rather than "You have nice arms.")
- **Master the modern text game.** If you're unsure how to start, keep it simple and flirty: "This might be the best coffee I've ever had — unless you can recommend something better?"
- **Remember that you're the prize.** You don't need to convince anyone to like you. *Do you even like them?*

» **Pick your dating strategy wisely (or go old-school, if you dare).** Dating apps are now a thing, and if you're terrified of them, you're not alone. But think of them like grocery stores — each one attracts a different kind of shopper. Some apps are more geared toward long-term relationships (*think of these as the Whole Foods of dating*). Others are more casual (*the 24-hour convenience store experience — you get what you get*). Want to meet someone organically? Well, you might have to leave your house. If the idea of meeting people in real life makes you break into a cold sweat, start small:

- Say yes to social events (even the awkward ones — there's always wine).
- Go to places where people actually talk — bookstores, hiking groups, networking events (bonus: you'll look confident and mysterious).
- Tell your friends you're open to setups (they've been waiting for this moment).

» **Let go of the "divorced" label and just date.** News flash: Divorce is *not* a red flag. It just means you've lived and learned. Don't go into dates feeling like you have to explain yourself or prove anything. You don't need to bring up your ex in the first five minutes (*or ever, if you don't want to*). You also don't need to rush into anything just to prove you're "back in the game." Take your time, date at your own pace, and remember: *Your past does not define your future.*

» **Accept that dating will be weird (but fun).** Look, dating is awkward for *everyone* — not just people who are divorced. There will be bad dates. There will be people who talk about their ex way too much. There will be moments where you think, *Wait . . . why am I doing this again?* But there will also be moments where you laugh until your stomach hurts, meet people who surprise you, and realize that love (or whatever you're looking for) is absolutely still out there for you.

OWN YOUR COMEBACK STORY

TIFF SAYS

Dating after divorce isn't about "finding someone to replace your ex." It's about stepping into this new chapter of your life feeling empowered, confident, and *totally in control of what you want.* If you want love, go find it. If you just want to flirt and have fun, do it. The point is, you've already done the "forever" thing once — now, you get to date *on your own terms.* And that, my friend, is pretty damn exciting.

IN THIS CHAPTER

» Being proud of who you are

» Dating while you're still figuring out your identity and sexuality

» Perusing the queer dating cheat sheet

» Getting familiar with LGBTQIA+ dating apps

» Flexing your flirting muscles

» Finding queer-friendly dating spaces and events

Chapter 20
Out and About: Navigating the LGBTQIA+ Dating Scene

Dating is complicated enough when you know someone is into your gender, but in the LGBTQIA+ world, we've got an extra step: figuring out if they actually like you, or if they just want to borrow your eyeliner and trauma-dump about their ex.

Unlike straight dating, where the assumed default is attraction, queer dating comes with a few extra layers of mystery. Maybe they're just being friendly. Maybe they think you'd make a great brunch buddy. Maybe they're flirting, but you won't find out for sure until you're three drinks in and they mention their "super-supportive boyfriend." It's a guessing game, and there's no answer key.

On top of that, queer love stories are still underrepresented, meaning a lot of us are out here winging it without a clear roadmap.

Hollywood loves giving us two extremes — the hypersexualized party machine or the token GBFF — without much nuance in between. But real queer dating? It's messy, beautiful, confusing, and just as full of ghosting, situationships, and "what are we?" conversations as any other dating scene.

Whether you're fresh out and testing the waters or a seasoned pro tired of running into your ex at every event, the key to thriving in LGBTQIA+ dating is defining your own path — free from labels, expectations, and outdated stereotypes. In this chapter, I show you how to navigate it all while keeping your confidence intact.

Figuring Out Your Identity: Embrace Self-Discovery and Be Proud of Who You Are

Figuring out your identity can feel like trying to assemble a mystery puzzle — except no one gave you the picture on the box, and some of the pieces don't seem to fit (or maybe they belong to a completely different puzzle). The good news? There's no rush to complete it, and you get to decide what the final picture looks like.

REMEMBER

First, let's clear up a common confusion: Gender and sexuality are not the same thing. *Gender* is who you *are*. It's your identity — whether you're a man, woman, nonbinary, genderfluid, or somewhere else on the spectrum. *Sexuality* is who you *like*. Men, women, everyone, no one? However you identify, it's valid.

Now that we've got that sorted, here's how to actually figure things out without spiraling into an existential crisis:

» **Drop the pressure to have a label immediately.**

Some people wake up one day and just *know*. Others take time to explore. Both are completely okay. You don't have to declare your identity on a billboard today — just focus on what feels right for you.

» **Observe without overthinking.**

Who do you find yourself drawn to in movies, books, or real life? Do certain gender expressions or pronouns feel more natural or comfortable? Are there moments in media,

244 PART 5 Romance, Rewritten: Loving and Dating on Your Own Terms

conversations, or even TikToks where something clicks in a way you didn't expect?

» **Try things out (no, this doesn't have to be physical).**

If a label feels good, use it. If it doesn't, that's fine too. Experiment with different pronouns or expressions in a safe space and see what feels like *you*. If dating apps are your thing, adjust your preferences and notice what feels right.

» **Understand that identity can evolve.**

You are not a phone contract — you are allowed to upgrade, change, and grow at any time. Who you are today might be different from who you are five years from now, and that's not being "indecisive." That's being human.

» **Be proud — even if you're still figuring it out.**

The biggest lesson? You don't need to have every answer right away. Being proud isn't about having a neat little box to check — it's about embracing who you are in this moment and letting yourself evolve at your own pace.

TIP: And if anyone tries to tell you who you should be? Politely remind them that *this is your life, and you're the only one who gets to decide who you are.*

Putting Yourself Out There When You're Still Figuring It Out

Dating while you're still exploring your identity is like trying a new coffee order — you might love it, you might hate it, but the point is you're allowing yourself to try. Here's how to navigate dating with confidence, even if you're not 100 percent sure where you land yet.

Tips for dating while still figuring things out:

» **You don't owe anyone certainty.** It's okay to say, "I'm still figuring things out." Your identity is yours to explore on your own timeline, not on someone else's deadline.

» **Curiosity is allowed, but honesty is key.** If you're experimenting with dating different genders or exploring new aspects of yourself, just be transparent. Something as simple as "I'm still learning about myself, but I'd love to see where this goes" keeps things real.

>> **Date for experience, not validation.** You're not here to "prove" anything to yourself or anyone else. Don't date someone just to check a box — date because you genuinely want to connect.

>> **Find spaces that feel safe and supportive.** Whether it's LGBTQIA+ friendly events, online communities, or dating apps that cater to exploration, put yourself in environments where you feel seen, not judged.

>> **Give yourself permission to change.** Maybe today you identify one way, and a year from now, it shifts. That's okay. Sexuality and gender can be fluid, and you don't need to lock yourself into anything permanently.

>> **Trust your gut (and have fun with it).** If someone makes you feel pressured or confused in a way that doesn't sit right, trust that feeling. The right people will respect your journey, not rush it.

>> **It's okay to take breaks.** Dating is a learning process, not a race. If it ever feels overwhelming, take a step back and focus on self-discovery before jumping into something new.

TIFF SAYS

At the end of the day, dating is about connection — not about having all the answers. So put yourself out there, enjoy the ride, and remember: You're allowed to figure things out as you go.

Queer Dating Cheat Sheet: How to Navigate Love in Every Category

Dating is already like trying to solve a mystery while blindfolded, but in the queer space, the rules can feel even more confusing. Don't worry — I got you. Here's your funny (but useful) guide to dating as a **gay man, lesbian, bisexual, or trans person.**

TIFF SAYS

Date who makes you happy. Queer dating is messy, fun, chaotic, and beautiful all at once. Whether you're looking for love, casual fun, or just figuring it out — *enjoy the ride, stay safe, and never settle for less than you deserve.*

Gay men dating (man x man)

Dating as a gay man comes with its own set of challenges, expectations, and sometimes, unspoken rules. From navigating hookup culture to finding real connection, you can slay through all the chaos:

- **The U-Haul effect (but for men?):** The lesbian stereotype gets all the attention, but let's be real: Some gay couples go from first date to discussing joint skincare routines and co-signing an apartment lease in record time. *Pace yourself, king.*

- **Masc versus femme versus whatever:** Some guys will treat Grindr like it's *The Hunger Games* of masculinity, but love who you are, whether you're into lifting weights or lifting iced coffees.

- **Top, bottom, verse — talk about it:** The silent battle of "who's doing what" will haunt you if you don't communicate. Save yourself the awkward "soooo . . . what are we?" moment.

- **Avoid the Peter Pan syndrome guys:** Some men will treat their 30s like a never-ending circuit party. If you want a relationship, don't chase the guy who only texts at 2 a.m.

Lesbian dating (woman x woman)

Welcome to lesbian dating — where eye contact can spark a situationship, and moving in by date three is just part of the lore. Whether you're new to the scene or a seasoned gay gal navigating the apps, exes, and flirty baristas, I want to help you find connection that will last longer than just reading each other's astrology charts:

- **The U-Haul is real.** I don't make the rules, but yes, many lesbians fall hard and fast. Just because you *vibed* doesn't mean you should share a pet after a week.

- **Exes everywhere.** The lesbian dating pool is more like a *puddle.* You will run into exes, date your best friend's ex, or end up in a friend group where *everyone* has kissed. It's fine; just laugh through it.

> **Communication is key.** You will likely have deep conversations about emotions before you've even figured out your coffee orders. Be ready to talk about your *feelings* (a lot).

> **Protect your heart, birth chart (and playlists).** Lesbians bond over music, and when you break up, suddenly Phoebe Bridgers is illegal in your playlist. *Plan accordingly and, most importantly, take your time, because even if your rising signs align there may be other signs that it's the wrong fit.*

Bisexual or pansexual dating (men and women and/or all genders)

Dating while bi or pan means your options are wide open — and so are the misunderstandings. Keep the following in mind as you navigate love, attraction, and dating with confidence — without ever shrinking yourself to fit someone else's idea of who you should be:

> **You are not "confused."** Some people will assume you're in a *dating crisis*. You're not. You just have options, and options are fabulous.

> **People will ask annoying questions.** "So do you prefer men or women more?" "Are you going to cheat?" Smile, nod, and redirect the conversation to their terrible taste in movies.

> **Navigating different dating spaces.** Sometimes you'll feel too gay for straight spaces and too straight for queer spaces. *Go where you feel good, not where you feel judged.*

> **Own your bisexuality.** You don't have to prove anything. Date who you want, love who you want, and don't let anyone tell you what you *should* be doing.

Trans dating (trans and nonbinary love)

Dating as a trans person can be beautiful, empowering, and, yes, complicated. From navigating safety and disclosure to finding partners who see and respect you fully, you want to be sure to date on *your* terms. You don't just deserve love — you deserve love that's real, safe, and rooted in respect:

- **Your body, your business:** Whether you're pre-op, post-op, no-op, or just existing, you do not owe anyone an explanation about your body. Set your own boundaries.
- **Filtering out the chasers:** If someone's treating you like their secret fantasy instead of a person, *run*. You deserve someone who sees *you*, not just their idea of you.
- **Navigating disclosure:** Tell people about your trans identity *when you feel comfortable*. There's no perfect time, just what feels right for you.
- **Affirming relationships only:** You deserve someone who celebrates your identity, not just tolerates it. If they "don't date trans people" but "make an exception" for you? That's a red flag, babe.

Using LGBTQIA+ Dating Apps Like a Pro

In today's world, dating apps are the modern-day matchmakers — except instead of a well-meaning aunt setting you up with a "nice" person, you're sifting through an endless scroll of mirror selfies, bios filled with astrology signs, and cryptic "here for a good time, not a long time" disclaimers. But while dating apps can feel chaotic, they can also be an incredibly effective way to find exactly what you're looking for — whether that's love, a situationship, or just someone to watch *RuPaul's Drag Race* with. The key? Using them *intentionally*. Because if you treat dating apps like a clearance rack, you're going to end up with a lot of mismatched energy and regret.

The Grindr grind: The Wild West of dating apps

Grindr is not for the faint of heart. It's fast, it's hyper-direct, and sometimes it feels like a chaotic Thunderdome of headless torso pics and unsolicited invitations to "come over." If you're looking for something casual, this app is basically Amazon Prime for hookups — except there's no return policy. But if you're hoping for something deeper, you'll need to do some filtering.

How to use Grindr with intentionality:

- **Be clear in your bio.** If you're looking for more than just a one-night adventure, say it upfront. Otherwise, you're going to get a lot of "wyd" texts at 2 a.m.
- **Don't fall for the headless torso trap.** If someone can't even show their face in a profile pic, they probably aren't going to be super open about anything else either.
- **Use the block button liberally.** If someone is making you uncomfortable, sending unsolicited pictures, or just being generally unhinged, don't hesitate to block and move on.
- **Ask the right questions.** Before meeting up, make sure you're actually aligned — unless you enjoy walking into situations where one person thinks it's dinner and the other thinks it's ten minutes of "chill time" before they go back to playing video games.

Field: The playground for exploration

If Grindr is the Thunderdome, then Field is the *choose-your-own-adventure* book of dating apps. Whether you're exploring non-monogamy, kink, or alternative relationship structures, Field is where people go when they want to have honest and intentional experiences. But like any app, it requires some finesse.

How to use Field the right way:

- **Know what you want before you download it.** If you're curious about nonmonogamy but have never even Googled what it entails, maybe start there first.
- **Be transparent about boundaries.** Field is full of people who know exactly what they want, and you should too. Communicate what you're comfortable with.
- **Don't feel pressured to try everything.** Just because someone says they're into something doesn't mean you have to be. Stay true to yourself.
- **Read profiles carefully.** Unlike some apps where people barely write bios, Field users often spell out exactly what they're looking for. Take the time to read before you swipe.

Hinge, Tinder, and the more mainstream apps: Where the bios matter

Not everyone in the LGBTQIA+ community sticks to queer-specific apps, and that's totally valid. Some apps are great for longer-term connections, but only if you *use them that way*. If your entire bio is just "6'2, masc, don't be weird," what exactly are people supposed to work with?

How to make these apps work for you:

- **» Actually fill out your bio.** People can't match with your personality if you don't give them anything to work with. A blank profile just screams, "I'm only here to lurk."
- **» Be honest about what you want.** If you're looking for something serious, don't play it cool and pretend you're just going with the flow.
- **» Be selective with your matches.** Just because someone is hot doesn't mean they're compatible with you. If they can't hold a conversation past "what's up," it's okay to move on.
- **» Message like a human being.** No one is excited to respond to "hey." We're better than that.

Archer: A New Era of LGBTQIA+ Dating

If you've been waiting for a queer dating app that isn't just about hookups but also isn't trying to push you into marriage by the third date, **Archer** might be worth a shot. It's built for LGBTQIA+ folks who want to connect beyond the usual "DTF?" conversations.

How to approach Archer:

- **» Use the features.** Archer offers a more curated dating experience, so take advantage of prompts and profile customization.
- **» Be open to genuine connections.** Not every match has to turn into a relationship — some might turn into friendships or great networking opportunities.

- **Don't be afraid to make the first move.** It's a newer app, so users might be feeling things out. Lead the way.

The IG DM slide: A classic that still works

Look, sometimes the best dating app isn't an app at all — it's Instagram. If you're too nervous to approach someone in person, the art of the IG DM slide is undefeated.

How to successfully slide into DMs without being creepy:

- **Engage first.** Like a few stories, comment on something relatable. Don't just pop up out of nowhere with "wyd."
- **Find a natural opening.** Reply to a story in a way that actually starts a conversation. "This meme is hilarious" is better than "Hi."
- **Don't be too thirsty too fast.** If you're coming in hot with fire emojis and heart eyes before they even know you exist, you might as well be waving a red flag.
- **Accept the outcome gracefully.** If they don't reply, take the L and move on. No need to double-text yourself into embarrassment.

At the end of the day, dating apps are what you make them. They are planes to your love destination, not the destination themselves. If you use them with *intention,* you can actually find what you're looking for. If you're just swiping mindlessly, you're probably going to end up on an accidental date with someone who thinks Mercury in retrograde is a valid excuse for being emotionally unavailable.

Whether you're on Grindr, Field, Archer, or sliding into DMs, just remember: Be clear about what you want, have fun with it, and never let a bad app experience convince you that love (or a good hookup) isn't out there.

Flirting and Putting Yourself Out There in LGBTQIA+ Spaces

Flirting in LGBTQIA+ spaces is an art form — one that relies less on tired pickup lines and more on *vibes, confidence, and the ability to make solid eye contact without looking like a deer in headlights*. Whether you're at a queer bar, a pride event, or just making eyes at someone across the room at a coffee shop, here's how to turn subtle chemistry into a conversation (and maybe something more).

Eye contact: The ultimate queer love language

If you're making eye contact across a crowded room and holding it for just a *little* longer than necessary, congratulations — you're flirting. The trick is to find the balance between "I think you're cute" and "I might be a serial killer."

How to master eye contact:

1. **Lock eyes for a second or two, then look away casually (not in a panic).**
2. **Repeat this once or twice — if they keep looking back, they're interested.**
3. **Add a small smile (not a full Joker grin, just enough to be inviting).**
4. **If they respond with a smile or move closer, that's your cue to go say hi.**

What not to do:

>> Stare them down like you're a detective solving a crime.
>> Panic and immediately look at your phone like you were *never* looking.
>> Assume they're straight and that you've made a terrible mistake: Queer eye contact is a secret handshake — you'll know it when you see it.

The art of the compliment

Everyone loves a good compliment, but make it specific and authentic. Instead of "You're hot" (which is fine, but boring) try "That jacket is amazing, where'd you get it?" (which opens the door for conversation). Or "I love your energy — you look like you have great taste in music" (intriguing *and* flirty).

TIP: Compliment their style, tattoos, or even their drink choice at a bar. If they respond enthusiastically, keep the conversation going.

Flirt like you're already friends

The best flirting feels effortless, like you already know each other. Here are a few tips:

- **Use playful teasing.** "You look like the kind of person who gives great concert recommendations — prove me right."
- **Throw in a little accidental touch.** Try brushing their hand when reaching for a drink or lightly tapping their shoulder when laughing.
- **Joke about something happening in the space around you.** "I swear that DJ just read my Spotify Wrapped because every song is from my top five."

Body language: Open, relaxed, and facing them

Your body will flirt for you before your words do. Here's how:

- **Face them directly** instead of angling away like you're halfway to an exit.
- **Keep your arms uncrossed.** Crossed arms scream, "I'd rather be anywhere else."
- **Mirror their movements subtly.** If they lean in, you lean in slightly too.
- **Take up space confidently.** Walk into a room like you belong there, because you do.

Make the first move without overthinking it

Queer spaces are full of people trying to figure out *who's interested in who*. If you wait for someone else to make the first move, you might be standing there all night. Try the following instead:

- **Just say hi.** A simple, confident "Hey, I'm [your name]. I had to come talk to you" works wonders.
- **If they're dancing, join in nearby.** If they start vibing with you, you're in.
- **Use your surroundings.** If it's a trivia night, a drag show, or a concert, comment on what's happening to start a convo.

The power of walking away at the right moment

One of the most underrated flirting techniques? Knowing when to exit before the conversation gets stale:

- If things are going well, leave them wanting more. Say, "I have to get back to my friends, but I'd love to continue this conversation later," then exchange numbers.
- If they seem unsure but intrigued, *don't linger too long* — mystery is attractive.
- If they're clearly not into it, *gracefully bow out* — no harm, no foul.

Confidence is key — even if you have to fake it

Confidence isn't about being the loudest person in the room — it's about knowing that *you're worth talking to*. If you struggle with confidence, act *as if* you're the most interesting person in the bar.

Remind yourself that rejection isn't personal — it just means they weren't the right fit. Even if a conversation doesn't lead to anything romantic, you're still practicing putting yourself out there — which is a win.

Where to Go and Meet People: Your Queer Social Playground

So you've got your flirting skills ready, your eye contact game is strong, and now you're wondering — where exactly do you meet people in the LGBTQIA+ dating scene? Contrary to popular belief, you don't have to wait until Pride Month to find a date.

Here's where you can put yourself out there and meet potential matches IRL and online:

- **Your local gay bar or LGBTQIA+ club:** These spaces exist for a reason — to connect and celebrate the community. If you're unsure where to start, do a quick Google search for LGBTQIA+ bars in your city or search on TikTok (because let's be real, it knows your interests better than you do).

- **Queer meetup groups and events:** Sites like Meetup, Eventbrite, and Facebook Events list LGBTQIA+ gatherings, from poetry nights to drag brunches to game nights. If you're more of a low-key mingler, this is a great way to meet people without screaming over club music.

- **LGBTQIA+ cruises and travel groups:** Ever wanted to sip a cocktail on a cruise ship surrounded by fabulous queer people? Gay cruises like Atlantis Events and Olivia Travel (for queer women) offer incredible experiences where you can meet people in an adventurous, relaxed setting.

- **Community centers and LGBTQIA+ bookstores:** If you love intellectual conversations and cultural experiences, check out LGBTQIA+ bookstores, community centers, or art galleries. These places attract like-minded people who share your values.

- **TikTok and Instagram queer recommendations:** TikTok is basically a personal concierge for gay culture — search for "LGBTQ bars in [your city]" or "best queer-friendly hangouts" and let the algorithm bless you with ideas.

» **Queer sports leagues and hobby groups:** Into dodgeball? Rock climbing? Join an LGBTQIA+ sports league or a book club — it's a natural way to meet people with shared interests without the pressure of dating right away.

REMEMBER: At the end of the day, putting yourself out there means trying new places, saying yes to invites, and stepping outside your comfort zone. Whether it's dancing at a gay bar, attending a queer hiking event, or flirting on a gay cruise while sipping a pina colada, just remember — the more spaces you explore, the more chances you have to meet someone amazing!

The Part of Tens

IN THIS PART . . .

Ten affirmations for before and after the big date

Avoiding ten red flags — no exceptions!

> **IN THIS CHAPTER**
>
> » Confidence boosters: Hyping yourself up like your own hype squad
>
> » Reality checks: Keeping your expectations in check
>
> » Post-date pep talk: No matter what happens, you win

Chapter 21
Ten Things to Tell Yourself Before and After a Date

So, you've got a date. Exciting, right? Or maybe terrifying. Either way, it's happening. Whether you're about to meet the love of your life, a temporary fling, or someone who will make you regret ever downloading a dating app, you need a game plan. And more importantly, you need the right mindset.

Here are ten things to tell yourself before and after your next date, divided into three key areas: Confidence Boosters, Reality Checks, and Post-Date Pep Talks.

TIFF SAYS

The best dates are the ones where you feel like yourself. No matter what happens, the best thing you can do before a date is remind yourself who you are. You're fun, attractive, and deserving of good energy. If the date goes great? Amazing. If not? At least you have a funny story for the group chat. Now go out there and own your date like the main character you are!

Confidence Boosters: Being Your Own Hype Squad

Before others are going to hype you up, you need to be your own bestie and hype team! If you need a little help, try the confidence-boosting statements in this section.

"I am the prize."

No matter what happens tonight, remind yourself that *you* are the main event. You are not auditioning for a role in someone's else's life — they are auditioning for yours. Act accordingly.

"I look amazing, and if they don't notice, they are blind."

You put in the effort. Maybe you're rocking that outfit that makes you feel invincible. Maybe your hair is serving, or your skin is glowing. Either way, you're walking in like Beyoncé at an award show.

"The goal is to have fun, not to find 'the one.'"

The moment you stop treating dates like life-or-death interviews, you actually start enjoying them. Not every date has to be a soulmate screening — sometimes it's just a chance to flirt, eat good food, and enjoy human interaction.

"I will not let my overthinking ruin this."

You don't need to rehearse every possible conversation in the mirror before leaving. *They like pineapple on pizza? Great. They don't? Not a dealbreaker.* Take a deep breath and roll with it.

"My ex is not a reference point."

If they order the same drink as your ex, laugh the same way, or have a similar cologne, *do not panic*! This is not your ex. You are dating new people because your past relationship is *in the past*. Act like it.

Reality Checks: Managing Your Expectations

Sometimes on a date, the vibes are vibing — and sometimes, you're just ignoring red flags because the person across from you has good bone structure. This section offers a few quick reminders to keep you grounded, clear-headed, and not planning a wedding after one spicy marg.

"If it's bad, I can leave."

Let's be honest, some dates are *horrific*. If they show up talking about their crypto portfolio or refer to their ex as "crazy" five minutes in, *you are allowed to exit*. No, you do not have to suffer through three courses just to be polite.

"I do not owe them anything, no matter how nice they are."

Kindness is a basic human requirement, not a VIP pass to your time, energy, or body. If they're nice, great. That doesn't mean you owe them a second date, a kiss, or anything beyond common courtesy.

"I will not take it personally if they don't like me."

Sometimes, people just don't click, and that's okay. You are not everyone's cup of tea, just like not everyone is yours. If they're not feeling it, they are simply making room for someone who will.

Post-Date Pep Talk: No Matter What Happens, You Win

Whether it was sparks, silence, or straight-up weird, the date is done — and you showed up. That's a win. Here's your post-date pep talk to remind you that your worth isn't tied to how someone else feels about you.

"I survived, and that's a win."

Whether it was a romantic success, an awkward disaster, or a neutral "meh," you did it. *You put yourself out there.* You deserve a gold star (or at least a post-date snack).

"I will not spiral if they don't text first."

If they like you, they will text. *If they don't, it's not your problem.* Your worth is not defined by a goodnight text, a follow-back, or how long it takes them to respond. *You have a life — live it.*

IN THIS CHAPTER

» Watching out for manipulative behavior

» Never putting up with lack of care of your feelings

» Putting your safety first

Chapter **22**
Ten Red Flags to Avoid at All Costs

What might seem like a tiny, harmless quirk on a first date could actually be the opening act for a full-blown circus of red flags later on. And trust me, those flags never show up alone — they bring their whole marching band by the time you're in a serious relationship.

No red flag is too small to ignore because those seemingly minor issues can snowball into "What was I thinking?" moments down the line. Remember, love without respect is like a taco without the shell — messy, unsatisfying, and probably not worth it.

If you spot any of these patterns, don't convince yourself to turn those red flags into green lights. You deserve someone who doesn't have a behavior list straight out of "How to Lose a Partner in 10 Days." Trust me, you're way too awesome to settle for a walking, talking caution sign.

The Love Bomber

We've all been on that date with someone who's basically a love salesperson — promising you a future filled with romance, trips to Paris, and undying devotion . . . all before they even know your middle name or where you grew up. Spoiler alert: These grand promises usually lead to a future of ghosting.

Sometimes we want the fantasy of love so badly that we cling to their sweet nothings like it's the last lifeboat on the *Titanic*. They'll talk about apartment hunting or having kids by date two, and *bam* — just when you think you're starring in your own rom-com, you sleep with them, and suddenly they're Houdini. Gone. Poof. Or worse, they become "too busy to hang" while still mysteriously active on social media.

Here's the thing: If someone is throwing around big promises early on, chances are they've done this before. Don't get blinded by their wordy fireworks; actions speak louder. The faster the spark, the quicker the burnout. Sure, it's fine to get excited about someone and daydream about what could be, but if they're telling you things like "You're the best thing to ever happen to me," and you still don't know whether they're a lefty or a righty, it's probably time to cancel your love-bombing subscription.

> **REMEMBER** Real love isn't built on empty promises. It's built on mutual respect and a solid foundation, not a whirlwind sales pitch.

The "You Up" 4 a.m. Texter

Ah, the infamous late-night texter — the one who couldn't make a solid dinner plan if their life depended on it but somehow always remembers your number after a few drinks. They're the master of the "Netflix and Chill" invite (minus the Netflix, let's be real).

If you're just looking for a casual hookup, this could be your MVP. But if you're searching for someone who wants to actually *date* you, this person is about as reliable as an umbrella in a hurricane. No matter how ridiculously attractive they are or how much you want them to be "the one," remember this: Someone who's genuinely interested in you will make an effort to take you out and make you feel special — not just hit you up when the bars close.

> **TIP** Here's a rule to live by: No OpenTable reservation = No open hearts from you.

Trying to turn an emotionally unavailable texter into your soulmate is like trying to turn a flip phone into a smartphone — it's just not built for that. If someone only reaches out after 10 p.m., chances are they're either

>> A little tipsy (or a lot tipsy) when you're trying to be tipsy in love

>> Already committed to someone else and treating you like their backup plan

>> Just looking for a "situationship" that never involves daylight or dinner tables

So, if their interest only sparks when the moon is high and their inhibitions are low, save yourself the trouble and swipe left on their late-night nonsense. You deserve someone who makes you feel like a priority — not just an option.

The Jealous Type

Jealousy is like a bad cold — it's contagious, exhausting, and can wreak havoc on your relationship. Sure, we've been told that jealousy is a sign someone cares, but if Lifetime movies have taught us anything, it's that the jealous spouse usually ends up flipping tables or worse. Bottom line: There's no such thing as *innocent jealousy.*

Beware of the partner who

>> Doesn't want you to talk to anyone but them

>> Gets agitated when you chat with the waiter for two seconds too long

>> Throws a fit when you make plans with your bestie

>> Accuses you of cheating just because you didn't text back within five minutes

WARNING: These are *massive* red flags that could spiral into toxic, controlling, or even abusive behavior in the future. A secure person won't feel the need to micromanage your life or monopolize your attention. They'll trust you — and trust is the bedrock of any healthy relationship.

The jealous type? Oh, they'll make sure *everything* ends in a fight. Have plans with friends? Fight. Didn't "like" their Instagram post fast enough? Fight. Said hello to a neighbor? You guessed it — fight.

If someone can't feel secure in your affection without turning into a private investigator, it's time to cut your losses. You deserve someone who doesn't just trust you but encourages your independence. After all, relationships are about building each other up — not trapping each other in jealousy-fueled drama.

The Gaslighter

If you've ever sat across from someone on a date who spent 45 minutes mansplaining macroeconomics (like it's their personal TED Talk) and acted like you couldn't possibly understand, you know what I'm talking about. It's not just boring and rude — it's an early warning sign of professional gaslighting.

So, what is *gaslighting,* you ask? It's when someone tries to convince you the sky is pink when you know darn well it's blue — or worse, makes you doubt your worth, your decisions, or your entire sense of reality. It starts small: "If you wear that outfit, everyone will think you look trashy." Then it snowballs: "No one will ever love you like I do," as they try to lock you into a relationship where happiness is not on the menu.

Gaslighters are experts at making you question yourself, your beliefs, and your confidence — all while inflating their own egos to godlike proportions. They'll spin lies so well they could get a job at NASA — launching insecurities straight into orbit.

The only gas you need is for your car. Drop the gaslighter and find someone who truly believes in you and fuels your confidence.

The Freeloader in Disguise

Once, I went on a date with a ridiculously attractive musician. We had a whirlwind romance — shows, late-night conversations, and everything felt like a fairy tale. But then my friends came over one day and pointed out something I had been blissfully ignoring: My entire apartment was covered in *his stuff*.

At first, it was romantic. He'd take me out, charm me with his guitar, and whisper sweet nothings. But before I knew it, he was "forgetting" his wallet at dinner, casually asking me to cover things, and eventually . . . he was basically *living with me*. I thought it was just the fast pace of true love, but after a much-needed girl-talk therapy session, my friends staged an intervention. Reality hit: This guy wasn't my soulmate — he was a freeloader.

WARNING

Here's the scary part about dating: You don't always know someone's motives. Sure, they say it's love, but toxic types might just need a free place to crash — or in some cases, avoid paying NYC's outrageous hotel rates. (Yes, that's a thing people do!)

Beware of anyone who bulldozes through your boundaries. If you say you want to take things slow or prioritize your career and they guilt you into changing your plans for *their* benefit, that's not a partner — that's a scammer.

REMEMBER

Love is about mutual respect, not manipulation. If someone's treating your life like a timeshare opportunity, it's time to hand them a one-way ticket out the door.

The Zero Boundaries Person

When you first get excited about someone, it's natural to want to make them happy. But what's *not* natural — or healthy — is when their happiness comes at the expense of your own. Boundaries aren't just optional accessories in a relationship; they're the foundation of mutual respect.

If you don't want to have sex on the second date, that's your choice — and it's something that should never be questioned. Beware of the Zero Boundaries Person: They're the type to bulldoze over your wishes to create a false sense of attachment. Whether it's pressuring you to open up about a traumatic past when you're not ready, insisting you call out of work to stay in bed all day, or disregarding your comfort zone entirely, they're experts at putting their needs above yours.

A healthy relationship is about mutual support and growth. You want someone who encourages you to reach your goals, not someone who's pushing you to do things you're uncomfortable with.

> **REMEMBER:** Boundaries aren't walls — they're guardrails. And if someone keeps veering off the road, it's time to take the wheel and drive far, far away.

The Secret Keeper

No matter who you are or what you look like, you never deserve to be someone's secret. You want to date someone who's proud to show off the amazing person they're lucky enough to be with. Sure, the first few dates might be too soon for a big friend or family introduction, but if it's been a few months and you still haven't met *anyone* from their life? That's a clear red flag — they're keeping you a secret.

Once, I dated a guy who adored me in private. But when we went out, it was always to low-key spots, far from prying eyes. I never met his friends, and eventually, during a heated breakup, he admitted the truth: He personally liked my body but was embarrassed about what his friends would think of him dating someone bigger. Ouch, right? That stung — but here's the silver lining: After him, I met people who *couldn't wait* to show me off.

The truth is, the problem isn't you — it's *them*. If someone keeps you hidden, it'll only hurt more as time goes on. There are plenty of reasons someone might want to keep you a secret: Maybe they're already with someone (or worse, married), or they don't see a future with you and aren't willing to build a life together. Whatever the reason, it's not your job to wait around and wonder.

You're a Lamborghini — not some car to keep hidden in the garage collecting dust. You deserve someone who proudly puts you in the spotlight, not someone who makes excuses to keep you in the shadows.

A Little Too Close to Their Ex

Not all breakups end in disaster, and sure, some people stay friendly with their exes. That's fine ... to a point. But the real question is: *How close are they?* If someone actively prioritizes their ex — sometimes even more than you — that's a glaring red flag.

If they constantly bring up their ex on your dates, it's time to stop and consider: Are you the rebound? Let's face it, dating someone fresh out of a breakup is like trying to build a house on quicksand. Breakups are messy, and the last thing you want is to be the one cleaning up their emotional baggage, only for them to run back to their ex and leave you holding nothing but tears and a metaphorical mop.

Your best bet? Let them marinate in singledom for at least six months. That gives them enough time to check their emotional baggage at baggage claim and start fresh — with you.

WARNING
If they're constantly calling their ex "crazy," pay attention. More often than not, it says more about them than their ex. Respectful people don't trash talk their past relationships — they've moved on in a healthy way.

Bottom line? Don't play second fiddle to their unresolved feelings. You deserve to be someone's priority, not their emotional Band-Aid.

The "Joke" Insulter

Someone who's truly interested in you will never say things to hurt your feelings — period. But then there's the "Joke" Insulter, the person who throws out hurtful comments and hides behind a flimsy excuse: "I'm just kidding!" Spoiler alert: They're not kidding, and it's a giant red flag.

Examples? Oh, they're experts at backhanded digs like

>> "Wow, you're really going for seconds? Haven't eaten all year, huh?"

>> "That pink sweater is so cute — very Peppa Pig chic!"

>> "When you laugh, you sound like a . . . uh, never mind."

Insults aren't jokes, and they're definitely not funny. In the early stages of dating, these comments are often tests — they're gauging how much you'll let them get away with. And if you let it slide, these "jokes" tend to evolve into full-blown critiques that chip away at your self-worth and confidence.

The bottom line? Words matter. If their idea of flirting is tearing you down, then the only thing you should be laughing at is the thought of wasting another minute on them. Remember: Love builds you up; it doesn't come with a punchline at your expense.

The Control Freak

Saving the worst red flag for last, let's talk about the controlling partner. At first it might show up as tiny red flags on a first date — like them ordering for you without asking (cue *White Chicks*: "perhaps a salad, perhaps *not*"). It might seem charming or confident at first, but trust me, it's not.

Other ways control can sneak in early:

>> They dismiss your thoughts or laugh at your ideas, making you feel like your opinions don't matter.

>> They push their preferences on you, like insisting on where to go or what to do, without considering your input.

>> They show "concern" that feels more like micromanagement, asking for constant updates on your whereabouts "just to make sure you're safe."

WARNING

While these behaviors may seem minor at first, they're often a preview of bigger problems down the line. Controlling tendencies can escalate to dictating how you dress, who you see, and even what life choices you make. It's about power — not love or respect — and it's the opposite of a healthy relationship.

A good partner builds you up and celebrates your individuality. If someone is dismissing your voice or pushing you into a supporting role in *The Story of Their Life*, it's time to rewrite the script. You're the star, not the puppet.

Index

A

abusive behavior
  aggression and bullying, 82–83, 267, 272
  disrespectful conduct, 196–197
  manipulation and toxic traits, 199–200
accidental touching, 254
activities, 87, 155
adventurous text messages, 59
advice, 12–14
  from family, 46
  from friends, 46, 144
  harmful rules, 13–14
  from social media gurus, 13
affirmations, 148–149
aggression
  bullying, 82–83
  control freaks, 272
  disrespectful conduct, 196–197
  jealousy and, 267
  manipulation and toxic traits, 199–200
AI bot, 26, 89
alcohol, 147, 267
ambitions, 218
anxiety, 11. *See also* insecurities
apps. *See* dating apps
Archer queer dating apps, 251–252
arms, crossing, 254
asking out
  digitally, 85–91

friends or colleagues, 83–85
paying check and, 112
in person, 81–83
someone who likes you, 91
what to say, 82, 83
who should ask first, 78
assumptions, 2, 121
attractiveness, 48
authenticity, 60, 135–136
availability, emotional, 43
awkwardness
  about finances, 126
  because of income level, 124
  laughing at, 146
  locations leading to, 102–104
  post-divorce dating and, 241
  when talking about sex, 231

B

background in photos, 24
backup plans, 90, 199. *See also* emergency exit plans
baggage
  emotional, 91–93, 271
  ex-partners and, 156–157
  post-divorce dating and, 234
Baira, Tiff, 1–2
banter, 63, 87
bars, 63, 256
best-case scenario, 142

bills. *See* check etiquette
bios, 24. *See also* dating apps
  brevity of, 24
  clarity in, 25
  confidence in, 25
  fun facts in, 25
  generic, 25
  humility in, 25
  humor in, 25
  intentions of, 25
  lightheartedness in, 24
  positiveness in, 24, 26
  quirky, 25–26
  samples, 26
  upfront, 24–25
bisexual dating, 248
bitterness, 189
blind dates, 74
blocking text messages, 189, 201, 250
blueprint. *See* dating blueprint
body language, 254
boosting statements, 262
boredom, 33
boundaries
  about sex, 224–226, 231
  bulldozing through, 268
  casual sex and, 228
  communicating on Field dating app, 250
  person without, 269–270
  respecting, 43
  setting, 198
  virginity and, 229
bowing out, 65, 67, 162, 255

Index   273

bragging photos, 24
breadcrumbing, 8, 199
breaking up. *See also* post-divorce dating
  cheaters and manipulators, 196–200
  confidence after, 201
  dating chaos, 192–195
  lesbian dating and, 248
  nicely, 94
  rejection to redirection, 190–192
  silent treatment, 186–187
  situationships, 187–189
breathing deeply, 143
budgets, 99–102, 122–125
bullying
  aggression and, 82–83
  control freaks, 272
  jealousy and, 267
  manipulation and toxic traits, 199–200
Bumble app, 20
burnout, 193
butterflies. *See* nervousness
BYOB (Bring Your Own Bottle) restaurants, 101

C

call to action, 26
Captain Too Much, Too Soon, 110
careers, 174
casual dating, 11–12, 19, 109
casual feelings, 10
casual sex, 10, 214
  boundaries for, 228
  dating apps and, 19
  emotions and, 227–228
  on first date, 11
  Grindr dating app, 249–250
  protection for, 21–22, 228
  self-worth and, 226
  shaming because of, 228
catfishing, 10–11, 89, 106
celibacy, 214
cheat sheets, 246–249
cheating, 182–183
  being accused of, 267
  LGBTQIA+ dating and, 249
  manipulators and, 196–200
check etiquette, 111–126
  being prepared to pay, 113
  cultural or personal expectations, 122
  debates on, 114–116
  different income level, 122–125
  grabbing first, 115
  itemizing bills, 118
  for LGBTQIA+ dates, 116–117
  making affordable, 122–125
  overly generous offers, 122
  paying for self, 48–49
  payment options, 114–116
  payment preferences, 117–118
  red flags for, 118–120
  silent bill stare-off, 121
  splitting bills, 114–115, 120–121
  standards on, 112–113
  survival guide for, 120–122
chemistry
  first date and, 164
  IRL (in real life) dating and, 15
  red flags and, 44
  sex and, 180
children, 216
clarity, deserving, 9, 49
classy photos, 23
closure, 188, 238
comfort zone, 269–270
commitment
  to first date, 107, 109–110
  lack of, 9
  sex and, 164
  to someone else, 267
  "What are we?" phase, 181–184
communication
  about budgeting dates, 123
  about casual sex, 228
  about cultural differences, 212–214
  about finances, 113, 204–205
  about interests, 154
  about lifestyle, 206–207
  about sexual values, 214–215
  about travel, 155
  about where going, 177
  after first date, 165
  contextuality in, 81
  conversation starters, 24–25
  cultural differences, 212–214
  ending, 65–67, 95
  family views, 216–220
  on Field dating app, 250
  future plans, 216–220

heavy topics, 158
ice breakers, 66
  on IG DM slide, 252
  infrastructure conversations, 203
  of intentions, 20–21
  on key topics, 174
  lack of, 43
  lesbian dating and, 248
  listening to, 145
  making relaxing and engaging, 154
  politics views, 209–212
  positivity in, 156
  religion views, 207–209
  sexual talk, 158, 224–225, 230–231
  shared values, 206–207
  spicy talk, 158
  starting at random encounters, 61
  starting in coffee shops, 61
  starting with stories, 57
  style of, 174
  talking about ex-partners, 156–157
  walking away, 255
comparing to others, 35
compatibility, 93, 180, 190–191
complainers, 119
"complicated situations," 92
compliments, 56, 57, 60
  on dating apps, 27–28
  for LGBTQIA+ dating, 253
  lighthearted, 153
  overdoing, 110
  when asking someone out, 84
compromising, 207, 217
condoms, 21–22

confidence, 139–149
  affirmations for, 148–149
  after breakup, 201
  in bios, 25
  boosting statements for, 262
  changing "what ifs" to "what could be," 141–142
  courage and, 80–81
  drinking before dates, 147
  for first date, 130
  from friends, 144
  getting back, 189
  kit for, 135
  nerves turning into excitement, 142–144
  not overthinking, 145–146
  on personal appearance, 48
  post-divorce dating and, 241
  practicing and projecting, 33
  self-worth and, 31, 255
  in sex, 229–230
  turning insecurities into, 131
  when entering rooms, 254
  when nervous, 140–141, 146
  when rejected, 146–147
confusion, 16, 195
connections, 59, 179, 251–252. See also matches
consistent efforts, 43
contact info, exchanging, 66
control, 124, 199–200, 272
conversations. See communication
cool text messages, 59
courage. See confidence

coworkers, dating, 93–94
creepiness, 55
cultural differences, 212–214
cultural expectations, 122
cultural norm, 115
current photos, 23

D

date invitations, 77–95
  asking out digitally, 85–91
  asking out friends or colleagues, 83–85
  asking out in person, 81–83
  declining, 94–95
  making first move, 78–80
  nervousness and, 80–81
  using caution, 91–94
date me hints, 66
dating anxiety, 11
dating apps, 17–28. See also bios
  Archer queer apps, 251–252
  asking someone out on, 85
  casual sex and, 19
  choosing, 20
  compliments on, 27–28
  dating profile on, 22–26
  deleting, 183–184
  Field dating app, 250
  getting matches, 27
  ghosting on, 186–187
  Grindr dating app, 249–250
  how changed dating, 18–19
  IRL (in real life) dating and, 19, 27–28

Index   275

dating apps *(continued)*
 for LGBTQIA+ dating, 249–252
 messaging on, 27
 moving to text messaging, 87–88
 one-night stand protection, 21–22
 queer dating app, 249–250, 251
 relationship goals and, 19–21
 securing, 28
 swiping on, 11–12, 18, 19
dating blueprint, 42–46
 building own rules for, 48
 checklist for what is important, 45
 chemistry or red flags, 44
 dating patterns, 43–44
 dealbreakers, 43
 ideal partner checklist, 42–43
 learning from ex-partners, 44–45
 not settling, 45
 opinions of others, 46
 sexual comfort zone, 46
 sticking to standards made, 45–46
dating history, 93
dating paralysis, 18
dating patterns, 43–44
dating playbook, 234–235
dating traps, 8
dating value, 32–34
day dates, 173
dealbreakers, 43, 159, 210
deep thinker text messages, 59
desperation, 31, 110
digital relationships, 86–87. *See also* dating apps
directness, 14, 84–85

disrespectful conduct, 196–197, 271–272
divorce. *See* post-divorce dating
DM slide, 252
"Don't talk to a man first" rule, 48
doom-and-gloom scenarios, 141–142
double-bookers, 109
drinking, 147, 267

E

embarrassment, 54, 140, 177, 270. *See also* insecurities
emergency exit plans, 90, 161, 194. *See also* backup plans
emojis, 56
emotional baggage, 91–93, 271
emotional connections, 179
emotional manipulation, 199–200
emotional maturity, 43
emotional suffocation, 110
emotionally available, 43
emotionally unavailable texters, 267
empty promises, 266
entertainment dating, 11–12
enthusiasm, 110, 142–144
exclusivity, 9–10, 174. *See also* cheating
excuse machine, 109
exercising, 131, 142–143
exiting
 communication and, 65–67
 emergency exit plans, 90, 161, 194
 flirting technique and, 255
 graceful exits, 161–162

ex-partners
 close relationship with, 271
 comparing to others, 235
 following on social media, 183
 learning from, 44–45
 lesbian dating, 247
 new life and, 239
 post-divorce dating and, 238–240
 reminders of, 239
 talking about, 92, 156–157, 197
expectations, 106, 179, 213, 263
eye contact, 11, 60, 81, 253

F

FaceTime, 88–89
fake emergency text messages, 90
fake romance, 157–158
family
 children and, 216
 dinner with, 103
 dynamics, 213
 introducing to, 198–199
 questions about, 216–220
 values, 174
 views of, 216
 who don't like you, 218–219
fatigue swiping, 19
features, focusing on, 131
feelings, casual, 10
Field dating app, 250
fighting, 268
filters, photos, 23
finances, 113, 124–126, 204–205. *See also* check etiquette
Find My Friends, 90

first date, 151–167
  acting like friends, 152–153
  avoiding awkward moments, 102–104
  being stood up, 106
  budgets for, 99–102
  ending on high note, 162–165
  graceful exits, 161–162
  greetings, 152–154
  kissing after, 162–163
  locations for, 97–99
  making second date, 166–167
  nervousness before, 140–141
  paying for self on, 48–49
  personal touches for, 98
  post-date check-ins, 166
  protection on, 88–90
  at public place, 90
  red flags for, 105–110
  relaxing and engaging during, 154–155
  research on, 98
  sex on, 48, 163–164
  topics and actions to avoid on, 155–160
  transportation for, 90, 165
  using video calls, 11
first impression, 129–138
  being self, 135–136
  dressing for first date, 130–133
  hygiene checklist, 134–135
  posture and presence, 138
  smelling good, 136–137
first moves, 78–80
flashiness, 24, 100

flirting, 53–68
  commitment and, 11
  by eye contact, 253
  "flirting purgatory," 109
  for LGBTQIA+ dating, 253
  in LGBTQIA+ spaces, 252–256
  online, 15
  online vs. real life dating, 14–15
  in person, 60–68
  post-divorce dating and, 235
  post-pandemic dating anxiety and, 11
  rejection and, 54
  on social media, 57
  tailored texting and, 58–60
  texting playbook for, 54–58
"Flirty Fridays," 54
forgiveness, for sexual past, 230
"forgot my wallet" move, 118, 120
freeloaders, 268–269
fresh start, 233
friends
  advice from, 144
  good energy from, 194
  hyping up dates, 145
  introducing to, 198–199
  jealousy over, 267
  post-divorce dating and, 239
  for protection on first date, 90
  support system, 132
  when to meet, 175–178
  winning over, 219
fun observations, 56
fun-but-uncertain stage, 177

funny bios, 25
future plans, 207
  deserving clarity for, 9
  expectations, 213
  goal alignments, 92–93
  potential of "perfect person," 41
  questions about, 216–220

G

games, 8
gaslighting, 196, 199, 268
gay bars, 256
generic bios, 25
generosity, 122, 124–125, 126
genuine interest, 63
ghosting, 8
  after sex, 179
  on dating apps, 186–187
  on first date, 106
  reasons for not doing, 95
  red flags, 266
glow-up strategies, 130–131
goals, 92–93, 174, 269–270
good impressions, 219
Good Morning Texters, 109
go-to plans, 143
graceful exits, 161–162
gray zone, 187–188
greetings, 152–154
Grindr dating app, 249–250
grooming, 130–133
group photos, 23
group settings, 62
guilt feeling, 124
guilt trips, 119, 225, 227–229. *See also* manipulators
gurus, social media, 13
gut feelings, 88, 90, 92, 181

Index   **277**

H

"haha," in text messages, 57
happy hour, 100
harmful rules, 13–14
headless torso photos, 250
health, protecting, 21–22, 228
heartbreaks, surviving, 185–201
   cheaters and manipulators, 196–200
   dating chaos, 192–195
   finding confidence after, 201
   post-divorce dating and, 238
   rejection to redirection, 190–192
   silent treatment, 186–187
   situationships, 187–189
heartless romantics, 11–12
"help me out" approach, 84
heterosexual relationships, 112
high note, ending on, 162–165
hints, 66, 88
history, dating, 93
hobbies, 56, 85, 155, 257
holiday observers, 207, 213
honesty, 94, 126, 161, 217
hooking up. *See* casual sex
Houdini act, 118. *See also* ghosting
hugs, 152
humble bios, 25
humor. *See* playfulness; sense of humor
hurting feelings, 271–272
hygiene checklist, 134–135

I

ideal partner checklist, 40–41, 42–43
identity, LGBTQIA+, 244–246
"if they wanted to, they would," 79
IG DM slide, 252
"impress me" clause, 115
income levels, 122–125
income-based theory, 115
incompatibility, 124
independence, encouraging, 268
infrastructure conversations. *See* communication
initiating contact, 195
inner circle, 175
innocent jealousy, 267
insecurities, 29–37
   about sexual past, 230
   comparing to others, 35
   confidence and, 130, 131
   from gaslighting, 268
   judgements, 36
   knowing dating value, 32–34
   looking in wrong places, 30–32
   from opinions of others, 36
   rejection, 34–37
   self-care and, 132
   in solo dating, 76
   virginity and, 229
inside jokes, 57
Instagram, 183, 252, 256
instincts, 88, 90, 92, 181
insulters, 271–272
intentions
   being honest with self, 49
   in bios, 25
   communicating, 20–21
   for dating, 15
   silly, 145
interest questions, 56
interviewing, 63
invitations, date. *See* date invitations
"Irish exits," 162
IRL (in real life) dating, 14. *See also* first date
   chemistry, 15
   dating apps and, 19, 27–28
   protection for, 88–90
   in safe place, 28, 90
   texting and flirting, 14–15
itemizing bills, 118

J

jealousy, 267–268
joking, 57, 254, 271–272
judgements, 36, 76

K

kissing, 162–163

L

last-minute plans, 195
late-night texter, 266
lavish dates, 99
League app, 20
LGBTQIA+ bookstores, 256
LGBTQIA+ clubs, 256
LGBTQIA+ dating, 243–257
   Archer queer dating apps, 251–252
   check etiquette and, 116–117
   complimenting, 253
   dating apps for, 249–252

dating cheat sheets, 246–249
eye contact, 253
flirting, 252–256
meeting people, 256–257
self-discovery, 244–245
while figuring out yourself, 245–246
LGBTQIA+ spaces, 252–256
Life360, 90
lifestyles, 124, 206–207, 216
lighthearted bios, 24
lighting, photos, 23
listening, 145
locations for dates, 97–104, 153
  avoiding awkward moments, 102–104
  for bisexual and pansexual dating, 248
  for first date, 97–99
  making affordable, 99–102
  safe, 28, 90
loneliness, 33, 91
losing interest, 175. *See also* ghosting
love
  finding in new places, 75–76
  post-divorce dating and, 234
  sex and, 226–227
love bombers, 110, 157–158, 197, 265–266
love language, 174

M

manipulators, 196–200, 269
mansplaining, 268
marketing self, 22–23
marriage, 214, 216, 236. *See also* post-divorce dating

"marry me or else" bomb, 217
matches, 27, 251–252
matchmakers, 72–75
maturity, emotional, 43
meaningful gestures, 100
meeting people, 69–76
  choosing matchmaker, 72–75
  LGBTQIA+ dating, 256–257
  solo dates, 76
  in Tinder Passport, 75–76
  where and how, 70–72
"men should pay" rule, 114
mental compatibility, 180
mental health issues, 219–220
messaging. *See* texting
micromanagers, 267
mindsets, optimism, 141–142
mirroring movements, 254
mixed signals, 43, 49
Modern Dating For Dummies Cheat Sheet, 3
"money fishing," 99
moving forward, 239
multiple dating, 9–10, 174. *See also* cheating
muting text messages, 189
"my family will lose it" dilemma, 212
mysterious text messages, 59

N

narratives about self, 54
navigating dating, 8–12, 15–16
negative bios, 26
nerdy charmer, 59

nervousness. *See also* insecurities
  advice from friends, 144
  affirmations to overcome, 148–149
  of being rejected, 146–147
  courage and, 80–81
  before dates, 140–141
  drinking before dates, 147
  not overthinking, 145–146
  red flags and, 44
  turning into excitement, 142–144
nonbinary love, 248–249
non-heteronormative relationships, 78
nonmonogamy, 250
nostalgia trick, 84

O

old rules, 7–8, 48–49
one-liners, 64–65
online dating. *See* dating apps
online flirting, 15
open-ended questions, 91–92
opinions of others, 13, 36, 46. *See also* family; friends
optimism, 16, 141–142
outdated dating rules. *See* old rules
outfits, 24, 130–133
overanalyzing yourself, 36
overthinking, 143
  about LGBTQIA+ identity, 244–245
  confidence and, 145–146
  post-divorce dating, 237

Index 279

P

pandemic, anxiety, 11
pansexual dating, 248
paralysis, from dating, 18
parties, 61
"pay your own way" plan, 116
payment options, 114–116. *See also* check etiquette
"perfect person," 40–42, 192
performance, sexual, 230
The Perks of Being a Wallflower (film), 29
personal expectations, 122
personal hype person, 91
personal touches, text messages, 60
pet photos, 24
Peter Pan syndrome, 247
photos
  changing, 27
  commenting on, 57
  on dating apps, 23–24
  headless torsos, 250
  liking, 57
players, 9–10, 174. *See also* cheating
playfulness, 55, 153
  in challenges, 57
  for creative dates, 126
  on free dates, 123
  in questions, 56
  in roasting, 63–64, 84
  teasing and, 254
  touching and, 158–159
  when asking someone out, 82
"Playing hard to get," 49
playlists, 248
pleasure, sexual, 228
politics, 209–212
pop culture, 155, 210
positive anchors, 143
positive bios, 24
positive reinforcements, 231
post-date
  check-ins, 164, 166
  pep talk, 263–264
  silence, 186–187
post-divorce dating, 233–242. *See also* heartbreaks, surviving
  dating again, 240–242
  letting go of ex-partner, 238–240
  moving forward, 234–235
  wants, determining, 236–238
post-pandemic dating anxiety, 11
power dynamics, 124
power trips, 272
pre-date
  emergency kit, 137
  mindsets, 141–142
  preparation for, 88–89, 144, 145
pressure
  on Field dating app, 250
  guilt trips and, 119, 225
  releasing, 154
  sex and, 227–229
procrastinators, 109
profiles, 22–26
  on Field dating app, 250
  post-divorce dating and, 234–235
  red flags on, 26
  reviews, 11–12
protection
  casual sex and, 228
  feeling safe, 41
  on first date, 88–90, 107–108, 164
  in meeting up, 28
  for one-night stand, 21–22
  for transportation after first date, 165

Q

Q&C (Questions and Compliments) method, 70
queer dating. *See* LGBTQIA+ dating
queer eye contact, 253
queer meeting up groups, 256
questions
  about family and future plans, 216–220
  about politics, 209–212
  about religion, 207–209
  answering simply, 197
  asking, 15, 173, 250
  for bisexual and pansexual daters, 248
  cultural differences and, 212–214
  finances and, 204–205
  gaslighters and, 268
  interesting, 56
  lifestyle and shared values, 206–207
  open-ended, 91–92
  playful, 56
  sexual values and, 214–215
  simple, 197
  of values, 41–42, 174
  "What are we?" question, 9, 181–184
  "What could be?" question, 141–142
  "What ifs?" question, 141–142, 239
  "Who cares?" method, 116
  "Will we ever?" question, 9
quirky bios, 25–26

R

random encounters, 61
rapid-fire romance, 73–74
rebounding, 271
red flags, 8, 265–272
 auditioning for approval, 147
 for check etiquette, 118–120
 chemistry and, 44
 constantly performing, 41
 control freaks, 272
 dating patterns and, 43–44
 desperation, 110
 emotional baggage, 92–93
 ex-partners and, 271
 freeloaders, 118, 120, 268–269
 friends view point, 178
 gaslighting, 268
 guilt-trips and, 207
 jealousy, 267–268
 "Joke" Insulters, 271–272
 love bombers, 265–266
 on profiles, 26
 reality checks, 263
 secret keepers, 270
 for setting up dates, 105–110
 sexual pressure, 224, 225
 shady behavior, 198
 "too soon" zone, 176
 treatment of servers, 160
 use of condoms, 21–22
 using heart eyes, 252
 "you up" texter, 266–267
 zero boundaries person, 269–270
rejection, 80
 because of timing, 95
 confidence and, 146–147
 flirting with, 54

 nice ways of rejecting, 94
 not end of world, 81
 part of dating, 190
 to redirect, 37, 190–192
 reframing, 80
 self-worth and, 34–37
relationships
 close relationship with ex-partners, 271
 goals on dating apps, 19–21
 material for, 10
 milestone checklist, 183
 situationships and, 9, 188
 success in, 49
 when serious, 19, 182
relaxing, 154–155
religion, 207–209
respectfulness, 271
ride-share apps, 91
roast method, 63–64, 84
romantic text messages, 58
romantics, heartless, 11
rosters, 8, 9–10, 181–182
rude behavior, 160
rules
 building own, 47–50
 harmful, 13–14
 "men should pay" rule, 114
 third date rules, 180
 using old rules, 7–8
 "you asked, you pay" rule, 114

S

schedules, 217–218
second dates, 166–167, 172–175
secret keepers, 270
secretive conduct, 197. *See also* cheating; players

securing dates, 28
self narratives, 54
self-care, 130, 132, 146, 194, 201
self-discovery, 244–245
selfies, 23
self-love
 knowing dating value, 32–34
 looking in wrong places, 30–32
 rejection, 34–37
self-respect, 30, 200
self-worth. *See also* insecurities
 confidence and, 54, 149, 255
 reminding self of, 195
self-esteem, 190
sex and, 226
situationships and, 189
sense of humor, 16, 143, 153–154, 231. *See also* playfulness
serial daters, 109
serious relationships, 19, 182
servers, treatment of, 160
set ups, 74–75
settling, 32–34, 45
sex, 223–231. *See also* casual sex
 boundaries for, 224–226, 231
 chemistry, 164, 180
 comfort zone, 46
 commitment and, 164
 communicating about, 158, 224–225, 230–231
 compatibility, 180
 consent for, 224
 explaining needs for, 230–231
 feeling comfortable doing, 179

Index   281

on first date, 48, 163–164
forgiveness for past, 230
ghosting after, 179
guilt trips and, 225, 227–229
having confidence in, 229–230
losing interest after, 179
love and, 226–227
marriage and, 214
performance, 230
pleasure, 228
red flags, 224, 225
self-worth and, 226
sense of humor and, 231
sexual comfort zone, 46
values, 214–215
when to have, 178–181
sexuality, 244
shady behavior, 198
shaming, 228, 229
sharing locations, 90
short bios, 24
silent bill stare-off, 121
silent splitters, 119
silent treatment. *See* ghosting
silly intentions, 145
simple questions, 197
simultaneous dating, 9–10
single status, 93, 174
situationships, 8, 9, 187–189, 267
smiling, 60, 132, 134
social hangouts, 63
social life, 217–218
social media. *See also* dating apps
  asking for, 89
  detoxing from, 193
  exchanging info on, 66
  gurus, 13
  relationship milestone checklist and, 183
  to see if really single, 93
  unfollowing accounts on, 132
solo dates, 31, 76
speed dating, 73–74
spicy talk, 158
stalking, 88
standards
  finding "perfect person," 40–42
  making dating blueprint, 42–46
  setting, 30
  sticking to, 45–46
STI testing, 21
stories, 23, 57
straightforward connectors, 59
strategies, 191, 241
strengths, showing in text messages, 59
suffocation, 110
Sunday service crowd, 207
sunglasses in photos, 24
survival guide, 120–122
swiping, 11–12, 18, 19

T

teamwork, 206–207
teasing, 56
"test the waters" approach, 83
texting, 197–198
  after first date, 165
  blocking, 189, 201
  from boredom, 33
  fake emergency text messages, 90
  Good Morning Texters, 109
  late at night, 197–198
  mirroring energy, 60
  online vs. real life dating, 14–15
  overload, 110
  pitfalls, 57
  playbook for, 54–58
  post-divorce dating and, 241
  right away, 85
  silence and, 186–187
  tailoring for flirting, 58–60
  timing for, 56
  unavailable texters, 267
  "you up" texter, 266–267
third date rules, 180
TikTok, 11–12, 256
timelines, 49
time-wasters, 109–110
Tinder app, 20, 75–76
tolerance, dealbreakers, 43
"too soon" zone, 176
touching, 158–159, 254
toxic behavior. *See* abusive behavior
Toxic Bingo, 43–44
traditions, 213
trans dating, 248–249
transparency, 113
transportation, 90, 165
traps, dating, 8
trash talk, 197
trauma dumping, 156
traveling, 155
triple-texting, 58
trust, 13, 60. *See also* cheating; confidence; insecurities; jealousy

U

U-Haul effect, 247
ultimatums, 216–217
unavailable texters, 267
unfiltered self, 41
unfollowing accounts, 189
upfront bios, 24–25
"up-the-nose" photos, 23

V

vague bios, 25
validation and sex, 226
values
   dating value, 32–34
   questioning, 41–42, 174
   sexual, 214–215
   shared, 43, 206–207, 213
Venmo, 119

video calls, 11, 88–89
virginity, 228–229
"volleyball method," 63
vulnerability, 78. *See also* insecurities

W

walking away, 83, 195, 200, 219, 255. *See also* bowing out; breaking up
weddings, 103
weight, confidence with, 48
"What are we?" question, 9, 181–184
"What could be?" question, 141–142
"What ifs?" question, 141–142, 239
"Who cares?" method, 116

"Will we ever?" question, 9
witty texter, 58
work schedules, 217–218
worst-case scenario, 141–142

Y

"you asked, you pay" rule, 114
"you up" texter, 266–267

Z

zero boundaries person, 269–270
zero commitment, 9
zero tolerance, 43
Zoom, 88–89

About the Author

Dubbed New York City's official Gen Z Cupid, **Tiff Baira** is a dynamic host, dating and relationships expert, confidence coach, model, singer, and newly minted author.

Having garnered millions of likes across social platforms, Tiff successfully infuses her unique blend of humor, honesty, and heart into her rapid-fire content, diving deep into the highs and lows of navigating love, dating, and self-discovery in today's world.

This August 19, 2025, Tiff's relationship expertise and devotion to instilling confidence into hopeful singles everywhere have culminated into the release of her debut book, *Modern Dating for Dummies* (Wiley). Billed as a must-have guide to real-world dating, the book shows readers how to bring out the fun and exciting parts of the journey to find love as Tiff dispenses smart, practical advice on how to spot red and green flags, navigate popular apps, find useful flirting tips, end (or start) a situationship, get back on the scene after a breakup or divorce, and so much more. Tiff is also widely regarded for her work as a standout host — she has starred in the Roku original series *Match Me in Miami* and currently hosts and executive produces her latest weekly shortform series, *Take Me Out,* where she invites complete strangers (as well as celebrity guests such as Florence Pugh, Andrew Garfield, and Ilana Glazer) to embark on spontaneous first dates with her.

She also continues to star as the face of the incredibly viral woman-on-the-street series *Street Hearts* (Fallen Media), as well as its spin-off woman-on-the-train series, *Love Train.* Both titles are set in the heart of NYC's chaos, as the matchmaking host pairs up two strangers straight from the busy streets (or subways) of Manhattan to dive into a journey of potential connection. Tiff's on-screen work playing Cupid in the city that never sleeps has attracted notable guests and co-hosts, including Camila Cabello, Lil Nas X, Jonathan Van Ness, Nick and Vanessa Lachey, Jason Derulo, Michael Bublé, and many more.

Tiff's transparency and nuanced, refreshing takes have captured the attention of national media, including *The Drew Barrymore Show, The Jennifer Hudson Show,* the *Tamron Hall Show,* the *Today* show, *The New York Times, Time Out* magazine, *People* magazine, and *New York* magazine, to name just a few. Her undeniable ability to uplift and inspire viewers has attracted opportunities to partner with renowned brands to create one-of-a-kind, sponsored content that feels organic, such as Tinder, Meta, Kate Spade, Bumble & Bumble, Dyson, Tubi, Kay Jewelers, La Colombe Coffee Roasters, and many more.

TikTok: @tiffbaira

IG: @tiffbaira

Dedication

To my parents and grandmother — thank you for your unwavering love and belief in me; your fierce faith taught me resilience, self-worth, and how to lead with my heart.

Dad, your eternal optimism and quiet strength have been my compass. You've always told me that *nothing* is ever out of my league — and you meant more than just dates. You taught me to walk into every room knowing my worth. Even after the heartbreaks, the ghosting, the chaos — you'd remind me, "Love happens when you love yourself first." And you were right.

Mom, you are pure light. The way you walk through the world — with grace, joy, and zero apologies — is a masterclass in self-love. You showed me that believing in love is never foolish; it's brave. Your unwavering belief in me, and in the magic of life itself, has pulled me out of the darkest moments. Everything I am is stitched together with the warmth of your love.

Bobby, my ride-or-die since we were ten. From our car rides through New Orleans to late-night heart-to-hearts now, you've never left my side. You've seen every version of me — and loved them all. You're the first person I call after a date, the one who keeps it real, and the only one who knows how to make me laugh through the tears. You are my home. My truest bestie for life.

And finally — to **all my online baddies,** my day-ones, my lovers of love: This is for you. Thank you for showing up, for staying, for building this world of love with me. I hope these pages whisper to your soul that you *were always the prize*. You are the dream. And the love you're searching for? It's already within you.

Author's Acknowledgments

To my dream team — Caroline, Alyssa, Samantha, Mark, Julia, Kelly, John, and Jade — thank you for being the brilliance behind the scenes. You've been my anchors, my sounding boards, and the force that turned vision into reality. Your dedication, creativity, and faith in me made every step of this journey feel possible.

Tracy Boggier, Chrissy Guthrie, and the incredible team at Wiley — thank you for taking a chance on me and guiding me through my very first book with such grace, patience, and passion. Your support has been a gift, and it is truly an honor to walk this journey with you.

To New York City — The place I moved to ten years ago in pursuit of love, only to discover the greatest love story was the one I built with *you*. You challenged me, changed me, and held me through every chapter. This city made my dreams come true, broke me open, and taught me how to choose myself — again and again. You were never just a backdrop. You were the co-star. This one's for us.

Publisher's Acknowledgments

Senior Acquisitions Editor: Tracy Boggier

Development Editor: Christina Guthrie

Copy Editor: Amy Handy

Senior Managing Editor: Kristie Pyles

Production Editor: Tamilmani Varadharaj

Cover Image: © BlackJack3D/Getty Images; Author Photos: © Julianna McGuirl Photography